# CRITICS AT WORK

## CULTURAL FRONT

General Editor: Michael Bérubé

**Manifesto of a Tenured Radical**
Cary Nelson

**Bad Subjects**
**Political Education for Everyday Life**
Edited by the Bad Subjects Production Team

**Claiming Disability**
**Knowledge and Identity**
Simi Linton

**The Employment of English**
**Theory, Jobs, and the Future of Literary Studies**
Michael Bérubé

**Feeling Global**
**Internationalism in Distress**
Bruce Robbins

**Doing Time**
**Feminist Theory and Postmodern Culture**
Rita Felski

**Modernism, Inc.**
**Body, Memory, Capital**
Edited by Jani Scandura and Michael Thurston

**Bending Over Backwards**
**Disability, Dismodernism, and Other Difficult Positions**
Lennard J. Davis

**After Whiteness**
**Unmaking an American Majority**
Mike Hill

**Critics at Work**
**Interviews 1993–2003**
Edited by Jeffrey J. Williams

EDITED BY JEFFREY J. WILLIAMS

# CRITICS AT WORK

*Interviews 1993–2003*

**New York University Press** • *New York and London*

**NEW YORK UNIVERSITY PRESS**
New York and London
www.nyupress.org



Library of Congress Cataloging-in-Publication Data
Critics at work : interviews 1993–2003 /
edited by Jeffrey J. Williams.
p. cm. — (Cultural front)
Includes bibliographical references.
ISBN 0–8147–9389–4 (alk. paper) —
ISBN 0–8147–9390–8 (pbk : alk. paper)
1. Critics—United States—Interviews.
2. Criticism—United States—History—20th century.
3. Criticism—United States—History—21st century.
4. American literature—History and criticism—Theory, etc.
I. Williams, Jeffrey (Jeffry J.) II. Cultural front (Series)
PS78.C75 2003
801'95'0904—dc22 2003017730

New York University Press books are printed on acid-free paper,
and their binding materials are chosen for strength and durability.

Manufactured in the United States of America

c 10 9 8 7 6 5 4 3 2 1
p 10 9 8 7 6 5 4 3 2 1

*To the memory of Michael Spinker—*

*critic,*

*editor,*

*teacher,*

*and conversationalist extraordinaire.*

# Contents

# Acknowledgments

The first people to thank are obviously all those interviewed in this volume. Some might have been wary at first sight of a tape recorder in front of them, but, speaking from my side of the microphone, the interviews were not only worthwhile but invigorating, filled with real talk, fascinating detail, and good humor. I would also like to thank the other interviewers who took up their recorders, particularly Rob Boynton, a top-flight cultural critic in his own right and, luckily for me, a practiced and punctual editor. A *merci bien*—and a good bottle of Bourdeaux—goes out to Vince Leitch, who offered consistent encouragement, even after my lengthy disquisitions about the state of criticism. A warm thanks goes to Eric Zinner, Editorial Director at NYU Press, who offered his characteristic editorial acumen. Eric, then a fledgling assistant editor at Routledge, did my first book, a collection called *PC Wars*, and I know of no better hands to put a manuscript in.

A fat thanks goes to Laura Rotunno and Eric Leuschner, who have worked on the *minnesota review* for several years while finishing graduate work at the University of Missouri, and who prepared the manuscript, gathered the photos, and stayed on top of things throughout, particularly while I was on leave. Laura, who is not nicknamed "Bulldog" for nothing, was precisely the person you'd want in charge, and Eric, who is an ace researcher and who offered me a tour of the library fearing that I didn't know my way around it, was precisely the person you'd want to make sure you got your facts right. Thanks also to the many people who have worked on the review over the years and who helped. Finally, on the more personal side of ivy-covered walls, thanks to my daughter, Virginia Williams, who has had to bear many meals with loud and garrulous critics. She now works in film production, and my only request is that when she owns the company, I get to run the publishing division.

# Preface

If you are interested in modern literature, you have probably come across a few volumes of the series *Writers at Work*. Each volume gathers interviews with poets, novelists, and dramatists that originally appeared in the *Paris Review*, which regularly features two or three interviews. The series, which runs to seven or eight entries, covers a panorama of figures, from Faulkner and William Carlos Williams to Joan Didion and Allen Ginsberg.

My title obviously alludes to *Writers at Work*. *Critics at Work* gathers interviews with cultural critics from literary studies, philosophy, and history that have regularly appeared (with one exception) in the *minnesota review*, a journal that I edit, over the past ten years. Although the interviews at first were more makeshift additions to special issues than a concerted project, after conducting a few I realized that they gave some larger sense of where criticism has been and where it is going. I also realized that interviews had certain virtues not usually found in the standard academic article: they offer an overview of a critic's work that one rarely finds in one place; they sketch some of the institutional contexts of criticism as well as some uniquely personal moments; they provide an occasion to comment on pressing issues of the moment; and they are readily accessible but intellectually on point. We don't usually pay the kind of attention to critics that we do to writers, but we should. Whether you think of contemporary criticism as a great good or a scourge of literature, or simply want to figure out what it's about, I think it useful to hear how critics, in their own voices, conceive of what they do. After all, like any writer, critics have something to say about their craft, as well as their ideas, experiences, and politics.

Like any volume of *Writers at Work*, this volume is an aggregate, formed by its occasions; it does not purport to offer a comprehensive view of all contemporary criticism, though it does encompass a diverse and telling range of critics. The original interviews were conducted over a decade, beginning with Eve Sedgwick's in 1993 and concluding with Robin D. G. Kelley's in 2003. With a couple of exceptions, they were conducted in person, on tape, and edited thereafter. Editing primarily entailed trimming lengthier passages, as well as excising some false starts and phrases like "you know." They are thus not exact transcripts (as a folklorist or anthropological method might specify), but they do largely retain each person's words as spoken, albeit boiled down. Like a remixed CD, they are reprinted here with some minor clarifications or cuts of obviously dated material.

Each interview is prefaced with a capsule summary of that critic's work and where it might fit in the map of criticism (which I elaborate in the introduction), a biographical précis, and a discursive bibliography. Overall, rather than holding to a strict chronological order by date of birth that one might find in a text like *The Norton Anthology of Theory and Criticism*, the volume is arranged in pairs to emphasize some of the explicit dialogue between critics. Though not a hard-and-fast rule, the first half generally deals with theory and the influence of previous critical movements such as the New Criticism and the New York Intellectuals, and the second half addresses the turn to cultural studies and politics.

The first pair, with Stanley Fish and with Cathy Davidson, Alice Kaplan, Jane Tompkins, and Marianna Torgovnick, who were members of a writing group at Duke, tells something of the rise of theory and the prospects for critical writing. The third and fourth interviews, with Gerald Graff and Richard Ohmann, focus on the institution of criticism. The next two, with Morris Dickstein and Louis Menand, recount the views of present-day New York Intellectuals. Seven and eight, with Paul Lauter and E. Ann Kaplan, report on the struggles to change the canon and to look at popular culture.

Barbara Foley and Alan Wald, in the ninth and tenth interviews, recount parallel stories of coming of political age in the sixties and their pursuant efforts to revise American literature. The next pair, Nancy Fraser and K. Anthony Appiah, come out of philosophy to engage cultural politics. In thirteen and fourteen, Eve Kosofsky Sedgwick and Lauren Berlant interrogate sexual politics. And the closing pair, with Andrew Ross and Robin D. G. Kelley, speak to the current possibilities of cultural politics and the public intellectual.

One might decipher other pairings, overlaps, and threads along the way. Most of the interviews deal with theory. Many explicitly talk about academic life and the current state of the university. A good number deal with cultural studies (from Kaplan to Ross). Many recount their training in British literature, but others talk about the growing centrality of American studies. A couple report on the state of African American studies (Appiah, Kelley). Several address feminism (Tompkins, Fraser, Sedgwick, Berlant). Some record the revival of pragmatism (Dickstein, Menand, and Fraser). Many take up the question of the public intellectual, sometimes positively, sometimes not (Fish, Graff, Menand, Appiah, Ross, Kelley). And a number attest to the surprise of and commitment to teaching.

Altogether, the interviews herein flesh out the *work* of criticism, in its various senses—the texts we read, the ideas we think through, the experience of working in the institutions that house criticism, and the sometimes heady, oftentimes hard process of putting words on the page.

# Introduction

## *The Talk of Criticism*

Jeffrey J. Williams

*Critics at Work* offers a guided tour through the central, sometimes confusing, and frequently controversial developments in contemporary literary and cultural criticism. The tour guides, however, are not distant observers but have been primary participants in those developments, and they report on theory, cultural studies, the literary canon, the recent focus on race, sexuality, and other identities, the state of the university, and the role of the intellectual. Throughout, they consider the not always easy negotiation of politics and culture.

But they don't offer up the smooth gloss of the museum tour guide. It often seems that criticism is a series of set statements occurring in a rarefied thought chamber, as one might infer from the monumental texts in an anthology or names in a history. *Critics at Work* takes criticism out of that vacuum and underscores the personal, institutional, and worldly trajectories that critics traverse. It shows how criticism is indelibly marked by history large and small, as the critics here variously report on the formative influence of the sixties, the "Culture Wars," the job crisis and the looming corporatized university, or simply where they grew up and what career paths they experienced.

One lesson of *Critics at Work* is that criticism is always *in answer* to its situation. Sometimes that situation is the state of professional critical practice, sometimes more broadly political, sometimes idiosyncratic, and most of the time all those together. For instance, Stanley Fish explains his invention of reader response criticism as a reaction to the New Critical caveat against "the affective fallacy," embodied by his towering graduate school teachers at Yale, and an adaptation of theories of interpretation from French structuralism that he happened upon during a trip to Paris. Or Richard Ohmann and Paul Lauter recount, after their traditional training as literary scholars, being politicized through the crucible of the sixties, which spurred their efforts to radicalize critical practice thereafter. Alternatively, Nancy Fraser, Barbara Foley, and Alan Wald tell of their work with Students for a Democratic Society and other groups in the sixties and how their scholarly work started precisely with politics. Overall, *Critics at Work* gives a glimpse of what it was like to be there, at that time, in that place, for people to come to think, talk, and write the way they do.

By their very mode, the interviews herein show some of the push and pull of intellectual life and thought. They exemplify, as Wittgenstein declared of philosophy, that criticism is not a set body of doctrine but an activity, replete with qualifications, disagreements, and sometimes even changes of heart. Critics are a garrulous lot, whether making sense of the past, arguing over the present, or imagining the future.

While *Critics at Work* encompasses many different voices, positions, and experiences, along the tour one can trace the outline of a history of the present in criticism. One prominent signpost reappearing throughout is "theory," whether going under the name of poststructuralism or postmodernism, deconstruction or hermeneutics, Marxism or feminism, pragmatism or public sphere theory, antiessentialism or antifoundationalism. *Critics at Work* lends some definition to what theory has meant, recounting its heady rise and prevalence, for some its failures, and for most its residual influence.

In the standard account, theory changed the face of criticism during the late 1960s and the 1970s. Although critics in its various camps often fought fierce polemical battles, they generally shared several predispositions. They drew on contemporary philosophy, especially Continental philosophy, lending a high speculative tenor to criticism. Rather than being a handmaiden to literature or other writing, it seemed criticism had big conceptual fish to fry; the goal of criticism was not just to provide new interpretations of Milton but to understand how interpretation itself works. Or gender. Or society. They reconfigured criticism less as a traditional humanistic pursuit and more as a "human science," on the model of linguistics. Departing from the "common language" of criticism, they adopted technical languages and concepts befitting such a science. But it was not a dry language; if you read any criticism of that era (or any of the attacks on it), one striking sense you glean is that criticism was an exciting pursuit laden with high stakes. Critics no longer conceived of themselves as guardians of the museum of high culture, polishing the monuments, but as primary participants in the realm of ideas.

One way to characterize this moment is that theory, and particularly literary studies, which provided the home for much theory, took the mantle of philosophy (asserted from Aristotle through Kant's *Conflict of Faculties* up to the mid–twentieth century) as the disciplinary pursuit that arched over all others. In a famous passage in a 1976 essay, the philosopher Richard Rorty dethroned philosophy and announced the new dispensation of speculative criticism, in turn defending it by placing it in this prodigious genealogy:

> Beginning in the days of Goethe and Macaulay and Carlyle and Emerson, a new kind of writing has developed which is neither the evaluation of the relative merits of literary productions, nor intellectual history, nor moral philosophy, nor epistemology, nor social prophecy, but all these things mingled together into a new genre. This genre is often still *called* "literary criticism," however, for an excellent reason. The reason is that in the course of the nineteenth century imaginative literature took the place of both religion and philosophy in forming and solacing the agonized conscience of the young. (66)

*Critics at Work* gives a wide-angle picture of this "genre," as well as the experience of doing it, and also tells how it has changed since.

The most auspicious change has been the emergence of cultural studies, which is another signpost recurring throughout this volume. Through the 1980s and 1990s criticism shifted, as a book by Anthony Easthope succinctly put it, from "literary into cultural studies," and indeed now it seems that most critics, especially younger critics, would assign their various pursuits to that name. The standard account has it that critics desisted from the abstract realm of theory and its focus on language (in the oft-cited phrase of the philosopher Jacques Derrida, "there is no outside the text") to take up the more concrete domain of culture and its instantiation of history and politics. Terry Eagleton, a former harbinger of the theory boom, encapsulates the turn from high theory in a 1990 interview:

> I think that back in the seventies we used to suffer from a certain fetishism of method; we used to think that we have to get a certain kind of systematic method right, and this would be *the* way of proceeding. . . . I would now want to say that, at the level of method, pluralism should reign, because what truly defeats eclecticism is not a consistency of method but a consistency of political goal. (76)

Cultural studies is hard to pin down because of that pluralism, but it aligns along several coordinates. One is a redefinition of the object of study, broadly construed as culture rather than high literary or philosophical texts. It is no longer solely imaginative literature—as Rorty defines it, novels and poems—but also films, TV, pop music, videos, and so on that fuel the imaginations of young critics. Culture, however, encompasses not just specific products but what one of the progenitors of cultural studies, Raymond Williams, called the "whole way of life." A key dimension of this holistic sense of culture is identity, and much of the criticism gathered under the name of cultural studies focuses on the vectors of gender, sexuality, race, ethnicity, nationality, and class that inflect our identities.

It would be overstating the case to see this shift as a wholesale departure from theory, and in fact cultural studies consistently draws on theory, but its use, as Eagleton remarks, is less exclusionary and more plural if not eclectic—for instance, one might employ a poststructural understanding of signification alongside a Marxist focus on ideology to discern the cultural significance of punk fashion. Rather than being a handmaid to literature or a philosophical pursuit, cultural studies looks to decipher the web of interactions that embed cultural products and practices; the goal of criticism is not to provide new interpretations of Milton, nor to make large claims for how interpretation works, but to understand his poetry as part of the context of Reformation politics, or of white, British masculinity, or of the nascent colonial venture. Accordingly, the style of cultural studies tends toward "thick description," elaborating its contexts. Somewhat ironically, in one sense cultural studies represents the assimilation of the theoretical critique of foundationalism, which undercuts the impulse of theory for an overarching method. In another sense, cultural studies represents a shift from modeling criticism on philosophy and linguistics to the more synthetic, humanistic pursuits of history and cultural anthropology.

Probably the most consequential—and controversial—coordinate of cultural studies is politics. For contemporary critics, whether arguing to expand the canon to include women or people of color, or against the limitations of heterosexuality, the task has explicit, if diverse, political stakes. Cultural studies sees culture not as a set of self-contained artifacts judged on their own terms (the traditional, formalist view), nor as an ancillary part of a "superstructure" (the traditional Marxist view), but as a primary terrain of social struggle over representation. (As Gerald Graff observes in his interview, representation is perhaps the dominant concern of contemporary criticism.) Critics thus conceive of themselves, rather than as guardians of tradition or key players in the realm of ideas, as primary participants in "cultural politics."

While *Critics at Work* connects some of the pieces of the puzzle of the official history of criticism, it also suggests alternative histories. The history of criticism is typically construed as a branch of the history of philosophy—theory superseded the New Criticism, and cultural studies superseded theory, just as the empiricists superseded the rationalists, or deconstruction superseded phenomenology, whereby critics pass their batons to the next in line in an orderly relay. Like most received narratives, such stories hold a certain validity, or more pragmatically they are useful in helping us make sense of the disparate texts we have in front of us, but *Critics at Work* also makes clear that criticism travels a number of different paths and moves in fits and starts, leaps and reversals. For instance, many of the critics herein have been doing cultural studies, as the saying goes, all along, and have persistently foregrounded the politics of culture. Some, like Jane Tompkins, have left theory behind; some, like Stanley Fish, have been "vending the same wares" over a long career of theory; and others, like Eve Sedgwick and Lauren Berlant, see theory *as* cultural politics.

Another way that *Critics at Work* provides an alternative history is through its very mode. Though admittedly only partial, it presents pieces of an oral history of criticism over the past thirty or more years. Those interviewed, alongside their comments on critical practice, offer some sense of the lived experience of conducting that practice. Some of that experience is specific to the academic institution—for instance, Morris Dickstein's telling of attending Lionel Trilling's courses, or Cathy Davidson and Jane Tompkins's of their tenuous job paths, or Andrew Ross's of the vagaries of academic celebrity. Some of it is more broadly historical, such as Alan Wald's recounting his work in SDS. Some of it is of race and class origin, as Robin Kelley tells of growing up in Harlem during a time of radical political hope. And some of it is idiosyncratic and deeply personal, as Nancy Fraser reminisces about selling her philosophy books while expecting social revolution. These experiences are of course contingent, but they are nonetheless tangible and formative. *Critics at Work* weaves some of the threads of the social and institutional formations that generate criticism.

This dimension—the material experience of critics—is usually left out of our accounts of criticism. When we talk about criticism, it often seems as if ideas come fully formed and have a life of their own. We typically summarize essays or books as a person's "body" of work. These interviews dispel that sense, showing how critics' ideas embody their personal, institutional, and historical positions. Despite the current commonplace that a critic is always "positioned," such positions usually take the form of a pronouncement of a single conceptual coordinate or identity—"as a Marxist, I would argue . . ." or "as a feminist, I advocate . . ."—as if our criticism stems directly from that base, and through a single, definable path. These interviews give a fuller sense of the positions that critics inhabit and how they inflect criticism. Put another way, we don't issue our positions, but in a sense they are issued to us by the circumstances we encounter and the trajectories we traverse.

One term I have used (in an essay, "The Posttheory Generation," and in the introductions to the interviews here) to describe changes in criticism as well as the experience of working in our critical institutions is "generations." The concept of "generations" provides a way to talk about critical change not just as an innovation in thought but as a response to social and institutional formations. It emphasizes that criticism is the activity of a cohort, formed by its contexts, rather than a unique product of discrete individuals. Further, it provides a way to talk about change not just as a shift of wind in the zeitgeist or fashion, but as rooted in its specific historical and institutional moments.

The predominant sense of a generation, of course, is the colloquial one of decades of birth. While this sense might lead to some reductiveness, it foregrounds the cultural and historical currents that embed a generation. To this colloquial sense, I would graft a more specific sense, similar to what the sociologist Pierre Bourdieu called the "habitus." Bourdieu employed this term to explain how institutions work over time; though they are "objective structures," they only endure through their flexibility in incorporating "agents" at particular moments, by producing a common set of "dispositions" (57). A critical generation, in my use, indicates not simply age but placement in an institutional habitus; criticism is shaped by the socioinstitutional matrix of a time, inculcated particularly in graduate training, as well as in other professional channels and protocols. A generation is formed and held together by a common set of "dispositions"—such as theory, or valuing the practices of what is called theory. In short, to speak in terms of generations places individuals in their historical and institutional formations, and critical views as part of their professional habitus.

The critics associated with the initial foment of theory—Fish, Graff, Ohmann, Tompkins, and others here, as well as Jacques Derrida, Sandra Gilbert, Fredric Jameson, J. Hillis Miller, and Edward W. Said, to name a few—are almost all of what is called the "silent generation," pinioned between the World War II and baby boomer generations, and born roughly in the 1930s (generations usually encompass an extended decade, so more precisely the late 1920s through the early 1940s). They were almost universally trained during the 1950s or early 1960s as traditional scholars in standard literary fields (or, in the case of Derrida, history of philosophy), and in fact most of their cohort continued that traditional work. I would call them, in part borrowing from feminism, which has a keen sense of generational bearing (see, for instance, *Generations: Academic Feminists in Dialogue*), the first wave or harbingers of "the theory generation." In this light, it is not hard to see both the prevalence and wane of theory as that of a generation, as that generation came to and cedes institutional positions of authority.

They were followed by, and the teachers of, a second wave largely composed of those in the boomer generation—those generally born in the extended decade from the 1940s through the mid 1950s, attending graduate school in the late 1960s through the 1970s and early 1980s. If the first wave propounded manifestos for theory, this generation was its army, storming the institutional ramparts and making common the practice of theory. In a sense, the imperative of the first wave was only realized in its embrace by the second wave. Though at any given time there is a gamut of critical practices—many of this cohort continued other kinds of criticism, from bibliography to myth criticism, and some critics took to theory belatedly, or left it precipitously—the theory generation became what Bourdieu calls the "legitimating bodies" of the institution, and theory the dominant professional disposition.

I would call the next generation to enter the scene, those born largely after the boomer generation, from the mid 1950s through the early 1970s, and trained in graduate school in the 1980s and 1990s, the "posttheory generation." "Post" indicates their belated encounter with theory, after the heady debates over its establishment and after it had become normal practice. The posttheory generation indicates a revisionary posture toward theory, and the turn to cultural studies as the current professional disposition represents the assertion of this generation and its interests. As I mentioned earlier, in some ways cultural studies represents the assimilation of theory (Louis Menand exemplifies this when he remarks, "I'm a postmodernist as much as anyone," while he writes a revivified cultural journalism), although in some cases it avers an explicit departure from theory.

The chief institutional condition that has formed these generations and thus influenced contemporary criticism, I believe, is the transformation of the research university. The burgeoning research university of the 1960s provided the leisure and resources for extrapedagogical pursuits such as theory. It granted reduced course loads, funding for conferences and travel, and training in foreign languages that spurred the importation of things like Continental theory. It also mandated—based on the model of the sciences promulgated by Cold War imperatives and abetted with Cold War funds, which supplanted the more traditional humanistic model—a research agenda. In turn, theory gave the humanities, particularly literary studies, that research agenda. (The university is not a necessary cause of the thing called theory, but its success was a contingent result, I would hold, of the conditions of the university.) The agenda was shaped in response to a competition for prestige within the university (this is usually called the "two cultures" argument, between science and humanities), but it was also formed through what I call "disciplinary emulation." As the biologist R. C. Lewontin observes in "The Cold War and the Transformation of the Academy," the humanities operated more in cohabitation than conflict with the sciences, in essence piggybacking on the massive expansion of the sciences through administrative "overhead" (30). One of the central protocols was a drive for scientific innovation, and theory, in one sense, represents an emulation of this drive, over the more traditional use of criticism as sustaining a tradition—through scholarship or commentary.

Another important institutional condition is ideological. A common view is that the theory generation arose because of the absorption into the university of the radical sixties generation, who brought their politics there, doing "politics by other means." While some theorists did and do espouse a radical politics, this view has been disputed by critics such as Aijaz Ahmad, who argues that theory instead represents the domestication of political dissent, "displac[ing] an activist culture with a textual culture" (1), and the quelling of intellectuals, absorbed by specialized academic pursuits. Whether this is true is an open question, which might be contested by many of the critics interviewed in this volume.

One inescapable condition of the current generation in literary and cultural studies is the downsized university, and more generally the larger changes in the public institutions of the welfare state of which the university is part. An ideological component of this shows itself in the "culture wars" and attacks on political correctness usually projected on the faces of academics. In some sense, posttheory is another name for criticism in the postresearch university. One way to see the embrace of cultural politics is as a more direct engagement of critics with the conditions in front of them, as it were. Another way to see it, in professionalist terms, is as an effort to relegitimate academic pursuits such as literary studies by claiming a cultural efficacy.

I would add one further consideration to my concept of generations: it is also a mode of affiliation. If we consider professional entry in terms of a game, we do not freely make up the rules as autonomous individuals; we are "regulated," in Bourdieu's phrase, by the professional habitus, and the rules of the game are definable, even if diverse or contradictory. But we do have choices in how to move around the board. One does not just become a theorist because one was born in 1952, went to grad school in the late seventies, and so on. One chooses a generational affiliation, and one of the more intriguing facets of criticism is how critics have adopted or departed from certain generational affiliations. Many of the critics here deliberately turned away from the training of their generational habitus. For instance, Richard Ohmann, Paul

Lauter, and Ann Kaplan were trained in the 1950s, but they clearly affiliated themselves with later generations.

When thinking about generations, an inevitable question is what the next generation will bring us. My conjecture is that it will be marked by a return to literature, in part to justify literary studies, in the face of calls for accountability and jeopardized funding, by calling forth its traditional bearing. In diverse ways, these interviews speak to the resurgence of public intellectual work, which, whatever its politics, reconfigures criticism in a more traditional literary sense—as letters for the common reader. I would also speculate that there will be a renewed emphasis on pedagogy—which is already occurring in the growth of the field of rhetoric and composition—in part to rediscover literature, and also that will accommodate the pressures, in the downsized university, to get back in the classroom.

Other than what it tells of the history of contemporary criticism and its institutional vectors, *Critics at Work* raises questions about the mode of critical writing itself. Interviews, as I have argued, have distinctive virtues—they are synthetic, engaging a critic's range of work; they give a sense of historical and institutional context inflecting that work; and they show criticism as an active process. But interviews are not usually considered part of criticism proper—they are usually considered ancillary to a critics' real work; they are seen as less serious if not ephemeral; and sometimes they are even deemed to be a degraded form, reflecting the influence of pop culture.

But, if we turn this around, what constitutes criticism proper? What shape does criticism normally take, and how does its shape inform our understanding of it? Most contemporary criticism—and I have been assuming throughout that criticism has primarily been housed in the academy over the past thirty or more years—comes in a standard shape and size: the twenty-page or so article or book chapter, replete with references and notes. And we expect—in the sense that reception theorist Hans Robert Jauss uses, of our "horizon of expectation"—that it addresses a registered academic topic, that it "argues" for a particular view correcting, modifying, or expanding previous views of that topic, and that it does so in a fairly specified, technical manner. The standard critical article is strictly regulated, both conceptually and stylistically; it does not range far afield, nor does it adopt an informal or personal style, except in an occasional anecdotal flourish. This form is entirely naturalized; it would seem strange, and in fact be deemed unpublishable by academic protocols, if an article did not meet these expectations. But it is really a somewhat rarefied form of critical writing—nothing like a *New Yorker* article, or a Hazlitt, Orwell, Ozick, or Hitchens essay—that came to predominance only in the post–World War II university.

This is not just a question of style. The mode of the article governs how we usually construe the history of criticism—as a series of "key statements," "central arguments," or "positions," each delivered in the discrete unit of an article or book chapter. We often intone the heuristic of "conversation" to describe this history. But its dialogue occurs within fairly limited parameters, the response of discrete statement to discrete statements. In this construal the history of criticism records a sequence of points and counterpoints, connected in a self-contained lineage. The points are depersonalized, and for the most part detached from time, place, and most other kinds of context, other than their position in the lineage. In a manner of speaking, the model of the history of criticism this construal assumes is Euclidean: one can graph it, as most anthologies of criticism do, in a straight chronological line, or in a more variable equation yielding derivation trees of schools or issues.

Perhaps this is a necessity of telling a story, whether of one's genealogy or of history. Any narrative construal makes its choices of plot line and exemplary instances for the sake of coherence, and one can more readily hold in mind the straight plot of *Tom Jones* than the twists and turns of *Tristram Shandy*. But there is a gravitational pull of such forms, to the exclusion of alternative representations, and one could say that such narratives are generated as much by their tacit form as by the events they presumably represent. Although we have investigated how representation works culturally with a great deal of finesse, we barely think about the way that the default form of the article represents thinking. And although much criticism on writing, particularly on composition pedagogy, stresses process, the standard article represents critical thought as a finished product, with process invisible, the ladder pushed away. An article becomes a kind of timeless statement, if not for the ages, for the shelf life of a database. As Richard Ohmann remarks in his interview, we typically cite someone's work in the present tense rather than one of its moment.

Although there is a theoretical danger in claiming that interviews are a more immediate representation of thought, closer to the originary presence of the speaking subject in Derridean terms, they do present one alternative representation that I think worth heeding. The deconstructive theorist Paul de Man famously criticized the way in which we assign a voice to linguistic structures, in effect personifying them (18). But I would reverse the order of this: Do we not then reify people, by taking their products, their acts, their speaking, as impersonal? Put another way, if we are attuned to the rhetorical dynamics that inflect our speaking and see the interview as a kind of fictional construction, like dialogue in a novel or in Plato's philosophy, that dialogue presents an alternative representation of thinking, one that is distinctly non-Euclidean, in forays and loose ends, in stories as well as logical arguments, and in interests as well as truths. It is one that dramatizes the processes of thinking and thus affirms the value of a thoughtful life. This, I believe, is a useful heuristic that suggests other ways for doing criticism and for representing how we think.

One reason for the preponderance of the article is that it is quantifiable, readily measurable in academic evaluations—and hence its prevalence in the post–World War II university. But one of the tasks of criticism, it seems to me, is precisely to question the preponderance of such forms. This volume suggests, explicitly in some of the interviews as well as implicitly in its general form, that we should open criticism, and our valuations of work in criticism, to other forms.

## WORKS CITED

Ahmad, Aijaz. *In Theory: Classes, Nations, Literatures*. New York: Verso, 1992.

Bourdieu, Pierre. *The Logic of Practice*. Trans. Richard Nice. Stanford, Calif.: Stanford UP, 1990.

de Man, Paul. *Allegories of Reading: Figural Language in Rousseau, Nietzsche, Rilke, and Proust*. New Haven: Yale UP, 1979.

Eagleton, Terry. *The Significance of Theory*. Oxford: Blackwell, 1990.

Easthope, Anthony. *Literary into Cultural Studies*. London: Routledge, 1991.

Lewontin, R. C. "The Cold War and the Transformation of the Academy." *The Cold War and the University: Toward an Intellectual History*. Ed. Noam Chomsky et al. New York: New P, 1997. 1–34.

Looser, Devoney, and E. Ann Kaplan, eds. *Generations: Academic Feminists in Dialogue*. Minneapolis: U of Minnesota P, 1997.

Rorty, Richard. "Professionalized Philosophy and Transcendentalist Culture." *Consequences of Philosophy (Essays: 1972–1980)*. Minneapolis: U of Minnesota P, 1982. 60–71.

Tompkins, Jane. "Me and My Shadow." *Gender and Theory: Dialogues on Feminist Criticism*. Ed. Linda Kauffman. Oxford: Blackwell, 1989. 121–39.

Williams, Jeffrey J. "The Posttheory Generation." *Day Late, Dollar Short: The Next Generation and the New Academy*. Ed. Peter C. Herman. Albany: SUNY P, 2000. 25–44.

# 1

# Stanley Agonistes

## *An Interview with Stanley Fish*

Most anyone who has spent any time reading contemporary criticism, and a good number of people besides, will know the name Stanley Fish. Indeed, his reputation seems larger than life; by legend, he is even said to be the model of the unforgettable Morris Zapp in David Lodge's academic novels. As a scholar, he is variously known as the leading critic of Milton of his generation; a pioneer of reader-response criticism; a progenitor of antifoundationalism and advocate of the "no consequences" argument in theory; and the key humanities player in critical legal studies. As an administrator, he is known for spearheading the famous (and infamous) Duke English department of the 1980s, taken to represent all that was right (or wrong) with theory, and for pumping up the visibility of the University of Illinois–Chicago, where he now serves as dean. As a public figure, he has been a spirited defender of the humanities in the "culture wars," occasionally appearing in the pages of the *New York Times* and on television programs like *The O'Reilly Factor*.

Fish is a prime figure in what might be called the "theory generation" in literary studies. As he tells here, he was trained under the New Criticism at Yale but came to more radical views of interpretation after his encounter with French structuralism. Ever a contrarian, he turned around the New Critical prohibition against considering audience response, terming it the "affective fallacy fallacy" in perhaps his most influential theoretical work, *Is There a Text in This Class? The Authority of Interpretive Communities*, where he proposed that meaning resides not in texts but in "interpretive communities." Thereafter, Fish turned the tables on theory itself, arguing for "antifoundationalism" and, along with Walter Benn Michaels and Steven Knapp, inciting the "against theory" movement of the late 1980s and 1990s. Challenging the assumption that we generate our interpretations from the principles or theories we hold, Fish argues that theory stems from our practices, occurs only after the fact, and has no consequences.

Fish was born in 1938 in Providence, Rhode Island, where his father was a plumbing contractor. The first in his family to go to college, he attended the University of Pennsylvania, receiving his B.A. in 1959, and Yale, in a few short years completing an M.A. (1960) and Ph.D. (1962). He taught at University of California–Berkeley from 1962 to 1974, publishing two books before he was thirty, most notably a touchstone of Milton criticism, *Surprised by Sin: The Reader in "Paradise Lost."* From 1974 to 1985 he was Kenan Professor of English at Johns Hopkins and published two works of reader-response criticism, *Self-Consuming Artifacts: The Experience of Seventeenth-Century Literature*, nominated for a National Book Award, and *Is There a Text in This Class?* Extending his concern with interpretation and its consequences, he also began to teach in the law school at Hopkins. In 1985 Fish moved to Duke as Arts and Sciences Distinguished Professor of English and Law, and as chair of the English department. After stepping down as chair in 1993, he became executive director of the Duke University Press through 1998, when he took a position as dean of arts and sciences at the University of Illinois at Chicago.

Fish's early books, on Renaissance literature and reader response, include *John Skelton's Poetry* (Yale UP, 1965); *Surprised by Sin* (St. Martin's, 1967; rev. ed., Harvard UP, 1999); *Self-Consuming Artifacts* (U of California P, 1972); and *The Living Temple: George Herbert and Catechizing* (U of California P, 1978). After *Is There a Text in This Class?* (Harvard UP, 1980) he widened his sights to consider law, pragmatism, and professionalism, as well as literature and theory, in three collections of his essays: *Doing What Comes Naturally: Change, Rhetoric, and the Practice of Theory in Literary and Legal Studies* (Duke UP, 1989); *There's No Such Thing as Free Speech . . . and It's a Good Thing, Too* (Oxford UP, 1994), which concludes with "The Unbearable Ugliness of Volvos," mentioned here; and *The Trouble with Principle* (Harvard UP, 1999). His Clarendon lectures, *Professional Correctness: Literary Studies and Political Change* (Oxford UP, 1995), take on the political claims of much contemporary academic criticism. The anthology *The Stanley Fish Reader* (ed. H. Aram Veeser; Blackwell, 1999) offers a diverse selection of his work. His *How Milton Works* (Harvard UP, 2001) culminates his long engagement with that poet, begun, as he tells here, when he had to teach Milton as an assistant professor. Some of the more prominent journalistic coverage includes a *New York Times Magazine* profile, "Souped-Up Scholar," by Adam Begley (3 May 1992), and a *New Yorker* profile, "The Dean's List," by Larissa MacFarquhar (11 June 2001).

This interview took place on 3 March 2000 en route—going about eighty miles per hour, passing a microcassette back and forth—between the St. Louis airport and Columbia, Missouri, where Fish gave a lecture. It was conducted by Jeffrey Williams and transcribed by Jacqueline Chambers, then a Ph.D. student at Missouri and an assistant for the *minnesota review*. It originally appeared in an issue on "Academostars."

**Williams:** I first want to ask you about the star system. It seems such a fraught thing, which everybody is conscious of but also bemoans. What do you think of it?

**Fish:** Well, I think the star system is inevitable given that the coin or currency in our profession is in part prestige, so what you expect stars to do is to attract graduate students and to make a program more visible. If it's more visible, you'll get the kind of attention that will appeal to upper administrators, to boards of trustees, and to legislators if you're in a state university. The knock against the star system is that paying high salaries to so-called stars works at the expense of long-time members of programs, departments, and colleges, who then enter into a relationship of second-tier citizens to those brought in from the outside and given privileges and perks they never had. To some extent, there will be moments when that tension is experienced and lived by a community, but it's not necessary, and I think it will pass.

First of all, in most cases money spent to hire a star is not money taken away from those who have been in an institution for a long time; rather, if you didn't hire stars, the money that you saved is money that a department will never see. University members don't understand this because they believe that the finances in a university operate according to the old diagrammatic pie, but this isn't the case. Universities' finances exist in pots of money, and at every level of the university there are cash reserves and funds which are, in effect, slush funds, although they usually have other names—soft money, opportunity funds, and so forth. They are not funds available for the kinds of things about which long-term faculty members complain. Ironically, if you succeed in hiring people who are considered stars, the material conditions of your own working life will eventually, if not immediately, improve, because when people come in with large reputations and with perks and equipment as a part of a package, there's immediately a pressure to provide at least some of those benefits to others. Another way of putting this is to say that the entire tone of a unit will be enhanced if someone arrives who is being treated exceptionally well. The spirit changes.

Now it's true, of course, that some who have been longtime inhabitants of a place and who have spent many years being disappointed, being underpaid, being undernoticed, will have entered into a strange relationship with that unhappy situation. To put it simply, they've learned not only to tolerate it but to love it. They love it, in part, because they regard it as their badge of virtue. If we are being treated so badly, the reasoning goes, we must be superior persons.

**Williams:** This is what you talk about in "The Unbearable Ugliness of Volvos," about the constitutive tendency of academics toward self-abnegation.

**Fish:** Yes, and that means that you must be very careful when you attempt to improve the conditions in the academic workplace either by bringing in stars or by other means, because there will be people who, although they seem to be the beneficiaries of your efforts, will resent them.

**Williams:** What kind of change does the star system represent? It seems to me that the profession has shifted from a patrilineal model, by which a master teacher conferred his prestige upon a student, to the star model, which represents individuals largely without a history or lineage.

**Fish:** I think a lot of the changes have come about because of structural changes in the way business is done. When I was a graduate student in the late fifties and early sixties at Yale, there were no outside speakers coming in, there was no lecture circuit, there were many fewer journals than there are today, and they were fairly tightly controlled by editors and boards of editors who had been in place for a while. You tended more to be involved with your colleagues and to regard their work as the work to which you should pay attention.

**Williams:** I can see how that might have fostered more "community" in a department—now it seems that we are independent contractors operating out of our departmental sites—but the downside of that is it relied upon a rigid distinction among the academic hierarchy, between junior and senior faculty.

**Fish:** Yes, I think that was true in my first position at Berkeley. The distinction between junior and senior faculty is, of course, still real and still strong in many ways, but it isn't as strong as it was when I first entered the profession, where it was more or less a relationship of apprentice to master. I remember I was offered a job the year I went out on the market at the University of Wisconsin, and one of the things I was going to be doing if I went there was be a section leader in a course taught by Helen White. This was presented to me as if it would be a great honor. I don't think that you could hire a bright young Ph.D. from a first-rate graduate school today and woo him or her by saying "You can be a section leader in so-and-so's large and famous course."

It's also the case that, because of revolutions in communications—first Xerox, then fax, and now various forms of e-mail—the community you can be a member of is not bounded by geographical spaces. It is certainly not bounded by the geography of your own campus. This has created a world in which you know people better who actually teach five hundred or a thousand miles away than you might know a colleague down the hall, whose work is in an area entirely different from yours. This has produced an interesting culture where a bunch of people are known to many academics across the nation, and indeed internationally, by their first names, and in fact that's a test of the star system.

**Williams:** Who do you know by first name?

**Fish:** The first-name test only works within the limits of, say, literary studies, or philosophy, or other disciplines. It's very rare when you can get a first name that will be instantly recognized across the disciplines. I can think of one: Noam. If you're going to speak knowingly of Noam, a lot of people in different disciplines are going to know that it's Noam Chomsky. Now, in the literary discipline, if you speak of Jacques, that of course means Jacques Derrida. Or if you say Edward, it's probably going to be Edward Said. Some people have had the benefit of having names that are unusual—take Hillis as an example. Some names are easily available to pass the first-name test—Gayatri or Homi. Again, all the people who refer knowingly and familiarly to

Edward are not going to be his colleagues in the old sense, so I think this is the big change that's occurred, along with the advent of the lecture circuit. All of this is entirely different from what it was in 1960.

**Williams:** I have an essay about "name recognition," which takes a point from you about self-abnegation; contrary to the usual complaints about the star system, it is in fact one of the significant and tangible rewards we have. If you write a paper or book, even if you live in mid-Kansas, somebody might recognize your name when you go to MLA, or someone from Harvard might cite you. Aside from the star system, what other changes have you seen in the profession over the past thirty-five years, especially in criticism? I'm struck by the fact that you and a number of other figures associated with theory, like Greenblatt and Harold Bloom, were trained at Yale. It would be hard not to see what you do as a response to the kind of graduate school formation you had.

**Fish:** Well, I can only think in terms of my own trajectories, which do not include all of the changes that have occurred in criticism. Actually, someone who might be better as an example for answering this question is my wife, Jane Tompkins, who's always changing and abandons fields as soon as she's conquered them, whereas I have pretty much done the same kinds of things and asked the same kinds of questions for forty years now, although the materials have changed. For me, the important part of graduate school was my colleagues, especially three: Richard Lanham, a very good friend of mine, a great student of rhetoric, of composition, and now of the Internet and computers; Michael O'Loughlin, an eighteenth-century scholar who wrote *The Garlands of Repose* and who was and is one of these people who has read everything in every language that you can think of; and Bart Giamatti, who was the commissioner of baseball and before that the president of Yale, and before that a very funny and witty Renaissance scholar. The courses that we all took were basically courses in rhetoric—not in the way in which we define the rhetoric taught now in composition and rhetoric programs, but the history of rhetoric—the pre-Socratics, Aristotle, Quintilian, Cicero, Demosthenes, etcetera. We all learned and memorized the figures of speech, which is a thing that stayed with me. I still teach courses in rhetoric.

The emphasis on rhetoric, or rather the training in rhetorical theory and practice, led me directly to concerns with the reader and reader-response theory. When I got to Berkeley in my first job I found two other people with the same interest, although they were trained at Harvard: Stephen Booth, whose edition of Shakespeare's sonnets and book on Shakespeare's sonnets are classics, and Paul Alpers, a great critic of Spenser's *The Faerie Queene*. It turned out that all three of us, with suitable differences, were doing the same kind of work—beginning to think about readers and the reading experience in a structural way, therefore ignoring, or in my case polemically repudiating, "the affective fallacy," which was very much in vogue then.

But the important thing that happened, not only to me but to many others, was the sudden importation into our circles of French and German literary theory in the middle to late sixties, which is about as early as most Americans began to be aware of it. In my case, it was an accident; in the summer of 1968 or 1969 I went to Paris because I had seen, on a bulletin board, an offer of an exchange of a penthouse apartment in Paris for a house in Berkeley. I had a house in Berkeley. And so my wife and I and our then less-than-two-year-old daughter packed up for the summer in Paris, and it's there that I fell in with a bunch of people who were then forming all of the theories that were soon to be so discussed.

The reason I got into this circle is because one of my undergraduate teachers at the University of Pennsylvania, Seymour Chatman, a structuralist scholar of narrative and metrics, who was in Paris and spoke French very well, knew that we were coming. He very graciously met us at the airport, and then introduced me to all kinds of people and to seminars with people like Bruce Morrisette and various kinds of Parisian types. Todorov was hanging around then; *S/Z* had just come out so everyone was talking about that, and I was introduced to this world that I never knew existed. I went back to Berkeley that fall and decided to teach a course in this material and related material from the Anglo-American tradition. That's how I got into the theory business, and I was perhaps ready to do so because I had already been writing about the reader in Milton's *Paradise Lost*.

Once theory became introduced in a strong way, the theoretical perspectives began to proliferate, and one of the consequences of this proliferation was that—and this is still the case today—a general sense of the shape of the task was lost, the task of what it is we do in literary studies.

**Williams:** So you think a problem is that theory has in fact, as neoconservatives claim, taken away from the true center of literary studies?

**Fish:** No, I don't think it's a problem. It seems to me that it has produced, in the people that I see, very vigorous and brilliant investigations of issues, questions, texts, and bodies of materials that were simply not available or were not on our radar screen before. No one can any longer master it all. You can keep up to some extent, but you can't really keep up, and after a while you have to decide that you're going to stay with some topics and issues and be resigned to the fact that some very intelligent people down the hall are doing good work, but you know very little about it and really couldn't engage in an informed conversation with them.

**Williams:** Actually, one argument might be that theory provided a kind of bridge or lingua franca for literary studies, so that somebody in Renaissance could talk to somebody in twentieth-century American literature.

**Fish:** That was also true even before. New Criticism provided a vocabulary, with its notions of tension and paradox and verbal artifacts, that could be as much a part of Chaucerian criticism, as it was for a while, as of criticism, let's say, of Joseph Conrad's novels. So there was always a way, I think, that the techniques in one field could be generalized. What surprises me, though, and heartens me, is the survival through all of these changes of some commitment to close reading. I know that there are many, many complaints and laments that close reading is a lost art, but I see many people who still perform it. It still remains, at least in my experience, the most powerful pedagogical tool which can really awaken students' interest when they begin to realize that they can perform analyses of texts that remove the texts from the category of the alien and the strange, and then begin to actually understand the mechanics of how prose and verse work. Given all the changes that have occurred—some that I've participated in—this is still for me the most exciting activity. I have a new book on Milton coming out that shows me at the same old stand, vending the same old wares, and hoping that there'll be people interested in purchasing it.

**Williams:** Alongside changes in criticism, the university has also obviously changed precipitously. What do you think about the changes in the university, and what changes have you especially seen?

**Fish:** I would just point to one thing: it has become increasingly impossible to maintain the fiction that the university or even the college is isolated from social and political questions, movements, problems, crises. It hasn't been a tenable position since the sixties, probably wasn't a tenable position before that either, but what this has meant in terms of curriculum is that courses that frankly acknowledge a relationship between academic work and extra-academic life, culture, and politics are now found in every university, with the possible exception of Hillsdale College.

I think the big change in the nineties and now the early years of this century is that universities are themselves reaching out to their communities and acknowledging the necessity of coming to terms with their communities, especially in urban centers such as Chicago. And criticism is participating in this self-conscious rejection of a firm boundary line between the academic and the nonacademic, in, let's say, gay studies courses or Latina studies courses or third world literature courses. I read in *USA Today* this morning that the state of Wyoming's legislature wants to shut down the law school because one of its members has written a book suggesting that cattle should not be grazing on federal land. There's going to be more and more of that, and less and less will it be just the academic, the student, and the great book.

**Williams:** I'm surprised to hear you say that. I believe that we should see our work as being directly related to our communities—after all, public universities are by definition based on a link with their communities—but this seems to disagree with what you say in *Professional Correctness*, where you draw a fairly distinct boundary between our critical projects in literature and anything to do with politics.

**Fish:** Well, yes and no. The boundary I draw is between different forms of engagement. It's one thing to say, and to say correctly, that a scholarly analysis of grazing practices on federal land in the Southwest is addressed both to others who have written on this subject and to those in the legislature, federal government, and elsewhere, who will be influential in either maintaining the present practices or altering those practices. The question is, "When the author of that book sat down to write, what did she have in mind?" My point is, if she had in mind, "Well, I'm going to write something so that this piece of legislation will be repealed or some other legislation will be passed," then I believe that she is pretending to engage in one form of activity while actually engaging in another. It may be a consequence of her scholarly work that the arguments and analyses she offers find a political use, and she may indeed welcome that, but she has to begin, if she's doing academic work, with the intention of figuring out what is true, what are the facts of the matter as she sees them, about this question.

That's the distinction I kept trying to make in *Professional Correctness* and it was made most starkly in the context of a book written in

World War II by a very famous literary critic, G. Wilson Knight. The book was a point-for-point comparison between the scenario and characters of *Paradise Lost* and the scenario and characters of World War II. It was an effort for which one might be grateful, but it was not an academic literary effort. It wasn't something that Mr. Knight set out to do in order to advance the discussion of Milton, and in fact after World War II that book disappeared or was regarded as an oddity. That's right because it is not finally part of the mainstream progress of Milton studies. I certainly don't want to say that the work that academics do can't have a political effect—it often can have, although it's more likely in some disciplines than in some other disciplines. But I do want to hold on to the distinction between beginning your work with an avowedly partisan, political intention as opposed to beginning your work with the intention of engaging with the literature that structures the field.

**Williams:** I want to shift gears a bit and ask about your new job at the University of Illinois at Chicago. But first I'm curious to find out how you came to do what you've done. I know, since I just wrote an introduction to your work for the new *Norton Anthology of Theory*, that you grew up in Providence, "the son of a major plumbing contractor," in Nortonese, and went to the University of Pennsylvania, the first in your family to go to college. What was your path?

**Fish:** My answer to this is not going to be generalizable. And again, I would say that it would be a question better put to Jane Tompkins, who grew up in a very cultured, literary family, with poets often coming to dinner, like John Ciardi and others, a house full of books, etcetera. It was therefore natural for her to think of herself from an early time as being destined for an academic career. I didn't grow up in a household like that. I was not, as a young person, a voracious reader, and I did not take to intellectual pursuits. I just stumbled upon writing papers for English professors, both in high school and in college, finding that the papers were well received. When you're a young person and people continually ask you "What are you going to be?" or "What are you going to do?"—the questions are terrifying because they imply that right now you are nothing and that you have to find some way of being that allows you to answer those questions.

Originally I was going to be an architect because my father was in the construction business and architects hung around the house. But I don't think I had those skills. Simply because I seemed to have a knack when it came to discussing poems, I kind of slid into being an English major, and when it came time to graduate I thought, "Well, what should I do? Should I go to graduate school"—about which I knew absolutely nothing—"or should I go to law school?" So I took the law aptitude test and the Graduate Record Exams—I did better on the law test, actually—but I got fellowships to go to graduate school, whereas I wasn't going to get any scholarships to go to law school.

So I went to graduate school because someone else was paying for it. And the first year was very hard because many of my colleagues, Michael O'Loughlin and others, were true intellectuals. That is, they had, from a very early age, been thinking of themselves as persons who read widely, not simply under the pressure of an assignment, but because that is what they liked to do. Therefore they had read a great deal in many areas and I had not, so it took me quite a while to get the hang of it, and I considered quitting many times in my first year, especially on Friday afternoons when I had two back-to-back classes, one with an eighteenth-century scholar. Eighteenth century was the only area that I thought I knew something about because my two favorite instructors at Penn were in the eighteenth century, but I didn't do very well in that class. The second class, right after that one, was with William K. Wimsatt in literary criticism. There wasn't anything yet called literary theory. Wimsatt was like Kingsfield in *The Paper Chase*. He was fierce. I found my colleagues in the class so much more able to respond to the questions and so much more alert to the concerns of literary criticism. I couldn't figure it out.

My wife and I used to go to New York a lot to hear jazz music and one time we went there we dropped into a bookstore and I found this book written by Wimsatt and Brooks, *Literary Criticism: A Short History*. I looked at it, and there were all of the topics and all of the discussions and all of the questions. Wimsatt was obviously teaching the course from the book. So I bought the book, went back to New Haven, and showed it to my colleagues, and they all laughed because they all had the book. At the end of every Friday afternoon, I would say to myself, "I'm just not cut out for this," and luckily I didn't have any Monday classes so that gave me an extra day to recover. Then in the summer of that year, I sat down and made up a huge reading list, literally hundreds of Renaissance plays, and I read those, and I read *Paradise Lost* two times. I had never read it, and I've never had a Milton course. The second year, I felt very much more at home.

**Williams:** That's a great story. Now you're dean of arts and sciences at the University of Illinois at Chicago, and you're probably the most high-profile administrator, at least in the humanities, since chairing English at Duke in the eighties and nineties. I know you're in the midst of changing things at UIC; what's your rationale and what do you intend to accomplish?

**Fish:** What I like to do in administrative work is establish conditions in the workplace that allow people to use their talents and enjoy their labors, and I have been struck since the time I entered the academy by the extent to which structures in the academy and attitudes that persist in the academy tend in the opposite direction. For reasons that are certainly too complicated for me to explain in an interview, and I doubt that I could do so even if I had world enough and time, academics seem always to devise contexts for themselves that are deeply underwritten by a desire to experience pain.

**Williams:** I've had a number of other jobs, and I'm struck by how, in my academic job, the material conditions are the best I've experienced, but the ethos isn't. I'm not sure how to characterize the ethos.

**Fish:** Well, it's a form of elitism. It has to do with the phrase that perhaps does more damage than any other, at least in this context, and that is "the life of the mind." I have a general rule of thumb that if someone starts to speak about the life of the mind, watch out, something devious and perhaps dangerous is being performed and you might be its victim, because the phrase "the life of the mind," along with superficial invocations of academic freedom, are part and parcel of an almost relentless determination to ignore those features of a workplace that make it bearable for the men and women who must operate within it. There's a disdain in at least some parts of the academic world for material conditions that are humane. At times it seems that the censorious form of judgment that academics enjoy exercising seeks a physical environment that reflects the bleakness of that judgment. I have extraordinary contempt for most academic attitudes. They seem to me—this is in a way a touch of genius—simultaneously self-serving and self-defeating. They're self-defeating because they are designed finally to make sure that you never get or achieve what you say you want to achieve, and they're self-serving because in a way that failure is the goal which, when achieved, allows academics the platform of high and lofty complaint they so love to occupy. And it comes accompanied with all kinds of little sayings and attitudes, and in a way I consider it part of my work continually to puncture these balloons.

**Williams:** To close, what are you working on now? Sometimes your work is characterized, as far as these tags go, as dealing with "interpretive communities," but you've obviously done a lot since tackling that.

**Fish:** In the past few years I've been elaborating an argument that has been consistently misunderstood. Essentially it makes three points: (1) if by theory you mean the attaining of a perspective unattached to any local or partisan concerns, but providing a vantage point from which local and partisan concerns can be clarified and ordered, the theory quest will always fail because no such perspective is or could be available; (2) the unavailability of that supracontextual is in no way disabling because in its absence you will not be adrift and groundless; rather you will be grounded in and by the same everyday practices—complete with authoritative exemplars, understood goals, canons of evidence, shared histories—that gave you a habitation before you began your fruitless quest for a theory; and (3) nothing follows from 1 and 2. Knowing that resources of everyday life are all you have and knowing too that such resources are historical and therefore revisable will neither help you to identify them nor teach you to rely on them with a certain skeptical reserve; the lesson of 1 and 2 goes nowhere; if grand theories provide no guidance (because they are so general as to be empty), the realization that grand theorists provide no guidance doesn't provide any guidance either. End of story, end of theory as an interesting topic.

No matter how many times I go through these steps or respond to questions about them the same objections arise. I am told that this is cynical, but it is only cynical if the resources of everyday life do not include moral resources, as I believe they do. I am told that the position is empty, that it doesn't give any direction; but that is its point, that direction will not come from the realm of theory and that no direction comes from knowing that direction will not come from the realm of theory. I am told that the position is antiprogressive and supportive of the status quo. Actually the position isn't anything; it neither supports nor rules against any project or aspiration except the project or aspiration of grounding our decisions in something extracontextual and independent of the ways of knowing and categorizing already structuring our consciousness. I call this position "theory minimalism," and the fact that almost no one likes it and that it is continually misunderstood is in a way comforting since it means that I can go on rehearsing it forever with no fear that it will become conventional wisdom.

# 2

# Writing in Concert

## *An Interview with Cathy Davidson, Alice Kaplan, Jane Tompkins, and Marianna Torgovnick*

One of the more noteworthy—and sometimes controversial—trends in contemporary criticism has been the turn to the personal. Jane Tompkins's "Me and My Shadow" is generally regarded as a harbinger of this trend, but many other critics published memoirs and personally inflected criticism through the 1990s, including Tompkins's then colleagues at Duke, Cathy Davidson, who published *36 Views of Mt. Fuji: On Finding Myself in Japan*; Alice Kaplan, who published *French Lessons: A Memoir*; and Marianna Torgovnick, who published *Crossing Ocean Parkway: Readings by an Italian American Daughter*. In the late 1980s, they joined together to form a writing group, and this interview gives their account not only of the fact and fiction of the trend, but of the possibilities and processes of such a group.

While embraced by some, the so-called personal turn was not always met with approbation, others claiming that it did not yield legitimate scholarly knowledge or, worse, that it was narcissistic and reflected the pernicious influence of popular celebrity. But, as Torgovnick suggested in an essay, "Experimental Critical Writing" (*Profession 90* [1990]), and as the following interview makes clear, the aim of the Duke group was not confession but to revamp the staid and predictable modes of critical writing. In retrospect, this move seems part of a wider revision of High Theory, complementing "Against Theory" arguments (discussed in Stanley Fish's interview), the New Historicism, the

Photographs: Cathy Davidson (upper left), Alice Kaplan (upper right), Jane Tompkins (lower left), and Marianna Torgovnick (lower right)

more ethnographic tenor of cultural studies, and the call for more publicly accessible academic work.

Cathy Davidson was born in 1949 in Chicago and educated at Elmhurst College (B.A., 1970) and SUNY-Binghamton (Ph.D., 1974). After sojourns at Elmhurst, St. Bonaventure University, and the University of Chicago, she taught at Michigan State University from 1976 through 1983. In the interim, she also held visiting positions at Kobe College in Japan (1980–81, 1987–88), experiences that inspired *36 Views of Mt. Fuji*. In 1989 she joined the faculty at Duke University, where she is Ruth F. DeVarney Professor of English and, since 1998, vice provost of interdisciplinary studies.

A noted scholar of American literature and a prolific writer, Davidson has published *The Experimental Fictions of Ambrose Bierce: Structuring the Ineffable* (U of Nebraska P, 1984); *Revolution and the Word: The Rise of the Novel in America* (Oxford UP, 1986), an influential revisionary look at the canon of American literature; and the edited collections *The Art of Margaret Atwood: Essays in Criticism* (Anasi, 1981); *Critical Essays on Ambrose Bierce* (Hall, 1982); *Reading in America: Literature and Social History* (Johns Hopkins UP, 1989); *Subjects and Citizens: Nation, Race, and Gender from Oroonoko to Anita Hill* (with Michael Moon; Duke, 1995); *The Oxford Companion to Women's Writing in the United States* (with Linda Wagner-Martin; Oxford UP, 1995). She is also series editor of *Early American Women Writers* (Oxford UP, 1986–) and was editor of the journal *American Literature* for a decade (1989–99). Outside academic channels, she has published *36 Views of Mt. Fuji* (Dutton-Penguin, 1993); *Closing: The Life and Death of an American Factory*, with photographs by Bill Bamberger (Norton, 1998); and the anthology *The Book of Love: Writers and Their Love Letters* (Pocket, 1993). In addition, she has written for magazines such as *Vogue* and *Ms.*, as she mentions here.

Alice Yaeger Kaplan was born in 1954 in Minneapolis but also attended boarding school in Switzerland, an experience that contributed to her lifelong passion for French. Her father had been a U.S. prosecutor at the Nuremberg trials, another formative influence that, as she speculates in *French Lessons*, figures in her scholarly focus on World War II fascism. After receiving her B.A. from University of California–Berkeley (1975) and her Ph.D. from Yale

(1981), she taught at North Carolina State and Columbia universities. Since 1986 she has taught in the Department of Romance Studies and the Literature Program at Duke, and in 2000 she assumed the directorship of Duke's new Institute for French and Francophone Studies.

Kaplan's scholarly work has unearthed the permutations of French fascism, notably of writers such as Louis-Ferdinand Céline and Robert Brasillach; her books include *Reproductions of Banality: Fascism, Literature, and French Intellectual Life* (U of Minnesota P, 1986); *Relevé des sources et citations dans "Bagatelles pour un massacre"* (Du Lerot, 1987), on Céline; and *The Collaborator: The Trial and Execution of Robert Brasillach* (U of Chicago P, 2000), which was nominated for the National Book Critics Circle Award and the National Book Award, and won the 2001 LA Times Book Award for History. *French Lessons* (U of Chicago P, 1993) was also nominated for a National Book Critics Circle Award. She has also translated three works by French writer Roger Grenier: *Another November* (U of Nebraska P, 1998), a novel that chronicles the life of a Nazi collaborator; *The Difficulty of Being a Dog* (U of Chicago P, 2000); and *Piano Music for Four Hands* (U of Nebraska P, 2001).

Jane Tompkins was born in 1940 near Philadelphia and received a B.A. from Bryn Mawr College (1961) and a Ph.D. from Yale (1966). She held a series of academic jobs ranging from Hartford Community College to Temple University (1976–83); as she explains in her memoir, *A Life in School: What the Teacher Learned*, her uneven career path was the direct result of being a woman, as men were often favored for jobs. After a sojourn at Columbia University, in 1985 she moved to Duke with her spouse, Stanley Fish (interviewed in chapter 1), where she taught until 1998, when she took a professorship in education at the University of Illinois at Chicago.

Trained under the auspices of the New Critics, then in their heyday at Yale, Tompkins held to their dictum to "stay close to the text" in her early critical work, reflected in her first book, the edited collection *Twentieth-Century Interpretations of The Turn of the Screw and Other Tales: A Collection of Critical Essays* (Prentice-Hall, 1970). However, after being exposed to poststructural theory in the early 1980s (in part through attending a seminar offered by Fish), she became a prime exponent of reader-response criticism, editing the standard anthology *Reader-Response Criticism: From Formalism to Post-Structuralism* (Johns Hopkins UP, 1980). She followed this with *Sensational Designs: The Cultural Work of American Fiction 1790–1860* (Oxford UP, 1985), an influential book that reconsidered the devalued genre of sentimental fiction and fiction by women and revised the canon of nineteenth-century American literature. "Me and My Shadow" (*New Literary History* 1987; rev. 1989) recounts her turn from the intensive focus on theory; it has often been reprinted, notably in *Gender and Theory: Dialogues on Feminist Criticism* (ed. Linda Kauffman; Blackwell, 1989). Employing a hybrid of personal criticism and cultural analysis, Tompkins next published *West of Everything: The Inner Life of Westerns* (Oxford UP, 1992), and then her memoir, *A Life in School* (Addison-Wesley, 1996). On the mode of academic criticism, see also Tompkins's "Fighting Words: Unlearning to Write the Critical Essay" (*Georgia Review* 42 [1988]), and "Can We Talk?" a dialogue with Gerald Graff (interviewed in chapter 3; in *Professions: Conversations on the Future of Literary and Cultural Studies*, ed. Donald E. Hall; U of Illinois P, 2001).

Marianna Torgovnick was born in 1949 into an Italian American family in Brooklyn, New York, an experience that undergirds *Crossing Ocean Parkway* (U of Chicago P, 1994; new ed., 1996), which won the American Book Award. After taking her B.A. at NYU (1970) and her M.A. and Ph.D. at Columbia University (1971; 1975), she taught at Williams College (1975–81); *Crossing Ocean Parkway* tells of the difficult departmental politics and heartwrenching personal situation she endured there. In 1981 she joined the faculty at Duke, where she was chair of English from 1996 to 1999. She also has been a visiting professor at Princeton, Emory, and Tel-Aviv universities.

A noted scholar of modernism, Torgovnick has also published: *Closure in the Novel* (Princeton UP, 1981); *The Visual Arts, Pictorialism, and the Novel: James, Lawrence, and Woolf* (Princeton UP, 1985); *Gone Primitive: Savage Intellects, Modern Lives* (U of Chicago P, 1990); and a sequel, *Primitive Passions: Men, Women, and the Quest for Ecstasy* (Knopf, 1997). In addition, Torgovnick edited the collection *Eloquent Obsessions: Writ-*

*ing Cultural Criticism* (Duke UP, 1994); her introduction articulates the call for "reader-friendly theory," inspired by critics' obsessions, imaginations, and long-term convictions. Her books progressively instantiate such a call, shifting from more conventional, formal analysis to a broader cultural criticism ranging over art, ethnography, and popular culture as well as literature.

Relevant works assessing the personal turn include Nancy K. Miller's *Getting Personal: Feminist Occasions and Other Autobiographical Acts* (1991); the anthology *The Intimate Critique: Autobiographical Literary Criticism*, edited by Diane P. Freedman, Olivia Frey, and Frances Murphy Zauhar (1993); the collection *Confessions of the Critics*, edited by H. Aram Veeser (1996), which includes an essay by Tompkins; and Jeffrey Williams's "The New Belletrism" (*Style* 33 [1999]).

This interview took place at Alice Kaplan's condominium in Chapel Hill, North Carolina on 25 January 1994 and was conducted and transcribed by Jeffrey Williams. It originally appeared in an issue of the *minnesota review* on "States of Theory."

**Williams:** First off, what was the impetus for your writing group? What made you get together in the first place?

**Tompkins:** Well, I was in my second year at Duke and I was on an NEH fellowship and I didn't know that many people. I was writing alone and going more and more inward and feeling sort of isolated and forlorn. Many years ago I was in a similar situation when I was living in Baltimore and trying to finish a book. I had been reading Peter Elbow's *Writing without Teachers* at the time, so I called up a couple of people, both graduate students, and asked them if they were interested in doing a writing group. And that had really been a good experience for me. I finished *Sensational Designs* and they both finished their dissertations, which didn't exist when the writing group began. And then we all left and went to various points of the compass. So I found myself in the same position here and I called the two people that just came to mind. I mean, I don't remember any rationale about this. I just called Marianna and I called Alice. I'd read something of Marianna's, the Roger Fry chapter of what was then the very beginning of *Gone Primitive.* I don't know if it even existed in your mind as a book yet.

**Torgovnick:** Oh, yes. In fact, I had already written a description of the chapters. When Jane called me, I was writing a chapter on the Tarzan novels and had been thinking of asking Jane to read it. I had been going over and over the chapter—doing microlevel revisions. I had also met Alice at a party and we had had a wonderful conversation. But in the way that things often happen in universities, we might never have gotten to know one another without the writing group. So I said yes to the idea of a group, although I felt a little nervous at the prospect. My only prior experience had been trying to get readings from friends who would avoid me for two years after I'd sent them a book manuscript. All in all, I felt game.

**Kaplan:** I came in from a different angle. I teach primarily in a Romance Studies department and come totally from a French training. Anyway, I had this idea that I wanted to write about Americans' relationship to France, and at first it was a very sociological project, not an autobiographical project. I got an announcement in the mail from Jane about an American Studies discussion group at the National Humanities Center. I wrote and I said I was trying to write about Americans interested in French culture and I didn't know how to do it. I thought that learning something about American Studies would be a good idea. And then Jane called me with the idea of a writing group.

**Torgovnick:** I remember very vividly the founding meeting which was on the deck at my house. We all stated what our ambitions were . . .

**Tompkins:** What we were wanting to do . . .

**Torgovnick:** And the common element in one way or another was that we all wanted to experiment with different kinds of writing.

**Tompkins:** That's what pulled us together, gave us some sort of common ground.

**Kaplan:** And I think that's what attracted us to Cathy's work, her versatility and skill as a writer and editor.

**Davidson:** I came to Duke because this is the one university that seemed to value the full range of writing, without making a clear boundary between scholarly and creative writing. I used to write under various pseudonyms, and do fiction under one name, journalism under one name, criticism under another name. It felt schizophrenic. And then Jane and Marianna mentioned this writing group and my heart started beating very hard because I thought this would be just perfect, a great way of helping me put all my different people together in one person. But I had never met Alice, so we had this funny meeting at a restaurant where she was interviewing me. I walked into the restaurant and suddenly felt hostile because it felt like a sorority hazing.

**Williams:** You had to be initiated?

**Tompkins:** Interviewed.

**Davidson:** And I was probably very . . .

**Kaplan:** We were both very stiff.

**Davidson:** Nothing was working. I kept thinking, "I'm not going to be in this group." And then suddenly we both confessed that we didn't like a writer whom we were supposed to admire very much . . .

**Kaplan:** Who shall remain nameless . . .

**Davidson:** Who shall remain nameless . . .

**Kaplan:** We bonded over a writer that everyone admired . . .

**Davidson:** And who should have been the model for our kind of writing. And we both thought she was fake and superficial. And we bonded. And I went to the bathroom and I had to take a deep breath and I thought, "Oh my God, now I *really* want to be in this group."

**Kaplan:** That broke the ice: we finally got to where we were saying what we really thought.

**Torgovnick:** We felt that we needed another person because we were traveling too much and it was hard for us to meet.

**Kaplan:** Three is a hard number.

**Torgovnick:** We started in the spring of 1987. Cathy joined in the fall of 1989.

**Williams:** I was curious to see the author's blurb on Cathy's new book, which is different from the blurbs on a typical academic book, since it mentions that you've published in *Vogue, Ms.*, and places like that.

**Davidson:** Actually, I think the first time I ever talked to Jane was when I managed to do a review of *Sensational Designs* in *Vogue*, which I thought was a coup. That was the first academic piece I did in *Vogue*.

**Williams:** I want to ask more about the question of audience, but first, what are the logistics of the group? How do you go about it? When do you meet? How often?

**Torgovnick:** That's changed over time. At first we met episodically, maybe once a month.

**Williams:** You mean if you were working on a project?

**Torgovnick:** No. The founding rule of the group was that everybody had to bring something, a piece of writing.

**Williams:** Every meeting?

**Davidson:** Every meeting everybody had to bring writing.

**Williams:** So it would be hard to meet every week or two . . .

**Tompkins:** Maybe about every three weeks or something like that . . .

**Torgovnick:** We'd meet for a long time, as long as it took, and we frequently read things ahead of time. Sometimes we'd distribute them.

**Kaplan:** I forget when, but we decided we would read at the group and not everyone would work every time. Then we started meeting more frequently, so that we've been meeting every week with the idea that if somebody's travelling, they don't come. Now nothing works perfectly, because sometimes somebody'll have a longer piece and they'll feel frustrated that there's not enough time during the group to read it all.

**Williams:** You meet every week?

**Torgovnick:** Now we do.

**Tompkins:** One thing that happened: I remember this meeting we had at Alice's house in the summer. I think it was the first meeting of the school year. We were just back—maybe it was in August—and it was one of those times where we all kind of went out of control. We were all trying to have stuff read, and we hadn't seen each other in a long time, and we all had all kinds of agendas and hopes and desires and needs and expectations and we talked a blue streak and we all felt ravaged at the end. For me, that was a crucial experience that led to a fairly regimented format, where only two people are ever on on a given day, and we can't bring more than ten pages, or just a few more than that. When we come, we check in and say what's on our minds so we know where people are, and then we divide the rest of the time in two. The person who's stuff is being read says, "Well, let's read for so long, and then we'll have time for discussion." When the reading time is up, then the respondents, the people who have been reading, have a time period in which to give their feedback.

**Davidson:** Without interruption.

**Tompkins:** Without interruption from anybody—from the writer or from other people in the group. Then, when that's over, the floor's open, and the person who wrote the thing can say, "But I didn't mean that," or, "I took that part out," and make all the defensive moves and explanatory gestures. And then everybody jumps in, and sometimes we have a really good discussion where we move the whole thing up to another level. But the reason that we went to that was that we were interrupting each other and butting in and some people didn't get to give their feedback fully and other people talked too much.

**Kaplan:** We got some help on that. In the fall of 1992, we brought in a consultant. I had gotten some great help on the penultimate draft of *French Lessons* from the novelist Laurel Goldman. She runs fiction groups, and I had heard about these fiction groups from my colleagues, Terry Vance and Linda Orr. So she came to our group and we worked in front of her. She sat down and watched us work. She said, "You guys go too fast." And she gave us a lot of tips and ideas. One of her ideas was that if you're getting feedback, you should sit and think about it. Don't get defensive right away, don't argue, just try to soak it in. When everyone's had their peace, then you can speak. And boy I felt that took the pressure off all of us.

**Davidson:** We have talked from time to time about having Laurel come back to see how we've implemented everything. There are certain things that have worked and other things don't work as well.

**Williams:** How long do you usually meet altogether?

**Unison:** Two hours.

**Torgovnick:** We restrict that now. Some of my fondest memories were doing *Gone Primitive* when everybody was chiming in. It became very confused, but that actually moved things forward in a way that probably would not have happened if there had not been a pooling of responses. So I feel some nostalgia for the old format at the same time that this new format has worked well in lots of ways. I don't know if the format is the key thing. I think maybe the most important thing is for the group to reevaluate the format and to make changes as they're required.

**Williams:** It's been nearly seven years now . . .

**Davidson:** I don't think we would have survived if we hadn't worked with a new format. And I'm sure the format's going to change again. It's important that we all pitch in and we all say if something's not working correctly.

**Tompkins:** I wish we did more writing exercises, because we always have a good time when we do them. But we're always so eager to get what we're working on read, that we don't do them. We should build it in. We should maybe make ourselves do a writing exercise every week or every other week, for ten minutes or so.

**Torgovnick:** I thought of a really good exercise the other day. I thought wouldn't it be nice to just sit and describe a gift that we had given to one another that had caused our writing to benefit.

**Williams:** What gifts have you given, off the top of your head?

**Davidson:** I can answer that easily. I took ten years trying to write *Fuji* and couldn't figure out how I wanted to do it. And then I brought in this section about sleeping in a flophouse when I was sixteen and how this reminded me of sleeping in a Buddhist temple the first time I was in Japan. And the group said, "That's it, you've got it, that's the book." Then I wrote the book in a year. The group showed me that what I needed to do was put myself in the book in a personal and intimate way. I never would have done that without the group, so that was permission. That was a gift.

**Torgovnick:** This particular gift comes from Alice, but there are others that come from Jane and Cathy. When I first wrote on Malinowski, Alice said to me, "You've got this guy, why don't you write about his body?" And I went home and did it. I came back, and Jane gave me the gift then. She said, "Oh, this seems so much smarter than the original thing that you wrote." The idea that something could be irreverent and unconventional and also smart was a great gift.

**Williams:** That was in *Profession*, the piece on "Experimental Critical Writing."

**Torgovnick:** Right, I think that gave away one of our best exercises. That was one of the best gifts the group has given me.

**Kaplan:** The biggest gift I've gotten from the group is to stop being so secretive. That's partly from working in a foreign language all the time; I was elliptical in English. But specific things from everybody in the group: Cathy's pacing is incredible, Marianna's forthrightness, just putting her finger on it, and Jane's music. I could go on. We all have different skills.

**Torgovnick:** And the skills travel; they travel from person to person.

**Davidson:** Yes, we'll say sometimes, "Wow, that was a Marianna revision."

**Tompkins:** When I was working on *West of Everything*, I remember one day that Alice said to me, "Gee, Jane, you can do anything, you've got a license to kill." It was at that moment that I thought, I really can write this book the way that I want to write it. I really don't have to make it look like other books. So that was a gift. But more than anything, I feel

I can count on the group. I trust all of you to tell me what I need to know about my work.

**Torgovnick:** When Laurel came to the group, she asked us to decide what was the greatest satisfaction of our meetings. That was what each of us wrote down, the feeling of trust in each other's evaluation. My own feeling is that we're at another stage of critical development, probably because each of us has now completed one or more major projects. But there's always a challenge to accept the new things that people write, because one thing that happens in the profession is that people always want you to be doing the last thing that you did.

**Kaplan:** We don't always write in the first person.

**Davidson:** No, that's a mistake to think we only do personal writing. I'm doing an academic project again, a theoretical study of photography. It's not anything at all like *36 Views of Mount Fuji.*

**Kaplan:** And I did a scholarly edition of the letters Céline wrote to his publishers at Little, Brown in the thirties. The group gave me help in managing vast amounts of information in a readable way.

**Williams:** I want to ask two questions about that. I get a real sense of a common project that you have, a common goal and direction. Do you see it that way? And then I want to ask about personal writing, which I think gets a bad rap and is frequently cast as an aspersion. And it's not accurate besides; I think experimental critical writing is the better title. Anyway, how do you see your project? To reach a larger audience? Is that the motivating project?

**Tompkins and Kaplan:** It was . . .

**Torgovnick:** But I think we have reached larger audiences, so that that's not a motivating project anymore.

**Davidson:** The project I'm doing is probably going to reach a specialized audience. It's more theoretical and academic again. I'm doing a piece now on Valentino's funeral and photographic movie stills, and I know I'll feel comfortable bringing that to the group.

**Torgovnick:** I'm doing a book called *Primitivism and the Quest for Ecstasy,* which is taking me back into a scholarly mode. I think that the project now has moved from reaching a wider audience to simply being ourselves as writers.

**Kaplan:** In order to write *French Lessons,* I had to get beyond the desire to please and learn to say what I thought. That's an awful pressure to put on oneself, to please people—and it makes the writing fraudulent. In that way, simply wanting to reach a wider audience can be a block.

**Williams:** Is your project a reaction to the current scene of criticism and theory?

**Tompkins:** I don't think so. We've cemented as a group, so now, at least the way I understand it, we're here to support each other in whatever it is that each person happens to be doing. Another thing that has been really important for me—and, again, it's my interpretation—is that people grow through their writing. Where they're going in their lives and their writing are not two separate things. So it's wonderful to see different kinds of writing evolving.

**Davidson:** I don't mean to sound fatuous, but I think that we feel secure enough to take risks now, to try things that might not bring glory. That's a privilege, to be able to do writing without the goal of reaching a large audience, or of impressing anyone in your profession . . .

**Tompkins:** Or any audience . . .

**Davidson:** But just because that's what you want to do. It's wonderful to have that kind of intellectual freedom.

**Williams:** Is it a kind of return to what you got in this business for?

**Davidson:** Who can remember?

**Torgovnick:** I think one of the things that's been very important is that we each had a career before we joined the writing group. It's not like we were all novices. But I don't think the group is a return to why we had originally gotten into the profession. I think it's a utopian idea of what the profession could be that I wouldn't have dreamed when I started in the profession.

**Williams:** How would you distinguish what you do from "personal writing"?

**Tompkins:** We have encouraged each other very much to write from our own voices, because there's been an academic interdict against that. So in the beginning, at any rate, we put a lot of emphasis on that, and it took a lot of effort and courage and faith and our belief in each other. And now Alice's book is out there and Cathy's book is out there—successful examples of personal writing—so things have changed since then. You don't have to put the effort and concentration on that anymore. I'm doing a personal book right now, largely because of the group. I feel empowered to do it because of what we've done here. But we're not restricted to that.

**Kaplan:** But the other thing the label "personal writing" tends to obfuscate is that memoir is a genre, with its habits, its rules and its codes. I taught autobiography and read autobiographies for four or five years before I started *French Lessons*. It was not an unschooled, let-it-all-hang-out undertaking. What we've found again and again in our work in the group is that you have to find a formal solution to the problem of writing about yourself. It's not anti-intellectual. Writing with affect is one big problem that we've been interested in and worked on in this group. But we're also very formally aware of models in literature.

**Torgovnick:** When I was doing the Bensonhurst essay, the first extended piece of autobiographical writing I had done, I remember feeling very strongly that I did not want to feel like I was showing someone a home video of my wedding and saying, "Watch it." Memoir can have that effect; it can be boring. Or it can be chaste and have no emotional impact on the reader, and we've always been going for emotional impact on the reader. If there's going to be exposure, it needs to be exactly the right kind of exposure for you as a writer and to your audience. It's a really disciplined form of writing.

**Kaplan:** Several weeks ago Jane had a formal breakthrough in her work on *A Life in School*. It had to do with her finding a specific kind of dialogue form that really worked in one of the early chapters.

**Tompkins:** But it seems to me that there's no distinction. It's not as if over here there's form and conventions and literariness and over here there's personal hang-ups. In order for me to say something that was really important for me to say, I had to find the form that allowed me to say what I needed.

**Torgovnick:** I would even go further to say that an essay on some scholarly topic can be personal writing too. I think that the metaphor works both ways. Scholarly material has the inference of impersonality, and the problem with a lot of scholarly writing is that it seems to have been written by a computer and not a human being.

**Kaplan:** I'm working on 1945 in France, which is very historical, but my writing problems remain much the same as in memoir: leaving stuff out, being elliptical, putting in too much information, shaping.

**Torgovnick:** I think the other thing that was very helpful to me was finding out I wasn't the only one who didn't produce perfect drafts.

**Davidson:** We disproved it.

**Torgovnick:** I've done some editing since, but I had not done a lot of editing when the group started. So I was not aware how rare the writer is who produces a perfect draft. When you're in the middle of any project, you have these doubts about whether it's going to work and it feels like you've never had so much trouble before, but if you look back at all of those drafts, which are records of the difficulties you have had . . .

**Kaplan:** The group is very good for seeing how someone else struggles to get a piece right and seeing someone else's process.

**Davidson:** And we get great suggestions from the group and we rejoice when it hits . . .

**Kaplan:** When someone takes the revision and really runs with it and comes back to the group with something wonderful, I think for me that's one of the most magical things about the group. Someone can be totally off, the group then gives criticism and they feel terrible, and they'll come back with a revision and the group will just say, "You did it," and really be joyful that someone's had a breakthrough. That's the most communal sense operating in the group—the pleasure that someone took our suggestions and got further because of them. And I think we all feel a real sense of pride when it happens.

**Torgovnick:** That's the usefulness of a group. It takes an activity which can be solitary and puts it in touch with other people. It's a long process to achieve a book.

**Tompkins:** Or even an essay.

**Williams:** Have you ever counted hours?

**Davidson:** Oh, I think that would be terrible.

**Williams:** Ten hours on a bloody paragraph . . .

**Kaplan:** And then other things write themselves.

**Davidson:** One chapter in my book I wrote in the morning just because it was my turn to go before the group and I had to have something. I brought it and thought it was terrible. The group loved it and I now think it's one of the best chapters. On the other hand, the introduction I wrote about six hundred times. There aren't rules. I don't think you ever fully learn the lessons, and you have to keep relearning them. You learn certain tricks and certain repertoires, but you forget them too or you have to learn other ones for other situations.

**Tompkins:** Or you have to find them out all over again.

**Davidson:** And sometimes it's painful. That's the thing with writing.

**Tompkins:** What I love is when—I've been writing this column for a newspaper—

**Williams:** Do you write it regularly?

**Tompkins:** Yes, once a month, and sometimes I bring my column, and Cathy walks in and says, "Take this paragraph and put it here, and take this paragraph and put it there, and you don't need to say this anymore, and beef this up a little here, and you've got it, boom, boom, boom, boom." It's sort of like going to a specialist with a broken thing, and they take their tools and it's in shape. Marianna will always find where the fat is, the stuff that doesn't have to be there. She just has an unerring eye.

**Torgovnick:** The flip side of that, though, is that sometimes you expect the group to perform miracles and it can't.

**Tompkins:** You have to do the evolution yourself.

**Kaplan:** That happened to me very much at the end of my book. I got up to a point where the group had read so many drafts, they couldn't help me anymore.

**Tompkins:** Maybe we should tell you about our marathon sessions. There was a time earlier in the life of the group when Marianna, Alice, and I all had completed manuscripts. They were at various stages of being ready. Marianna's was the closest, then mine, then Alice's. I was in California that semester, and at a certain point we mailed each other our manuscripts and I flew back and we had a two-day marathon session.

**Williams:** Did you stock in provisions?

**Tompkins:** We went through each manuscript . . .

**Torgovnick:** Chapter by chapter. It was wonderful . . .

**Tompkins:** And we recorded the whole thing so that we would each have a tape to listen to when we wanted to go back and make revisions. We were sort of exhausted and exhilarated at the end because it was so much work, but it was fantastic.

**Kaplan:** And then we did something similar with *Mount Fuji*, we had one that was several hours . . .

**Torgovnick:** We have an open-door policy to marathons, although they require advance warning. But it's really an invaluable experience to have people read your book, giving you one more chance before it's going out in the world. When the book goes out in the world, you get a different level of feedback.

**Williams:** To shift gears a bit, I want to ask how you see what you do in relation to other tendencies on the current scene—to, say, confessional criticism or other kinds of critical writing. Do you have comments on why so many people are doing this at the same time—for instance, Nancy Miller in *Getting Personal*, or Lentricchia in *Edge of Night*? Besides those, it seems to me that there are a lot of new kinds of critical writing, like Michael Bérubé's pieces in the *Village Voice* or Avital Ronell's *Telephone Book*.

**Tompkins:** That's a big question.

**Torgovnick:** I don't feel I can answer that question. I haven't thought about my writing in relationship to those books.

**Davidson:** I share Marianna's unease about situating my writing in relationship to the field right now. But I certainly remember the first time I read Barthes's *Mythologies*, realizing that I could write a kind of criticism that's different from the kind I'd been taught in graduate school. From Barthes I learned a new world of voice and eloquence and passion and wit. In some way, that became a model for me. I don't know that many people would think that was personal writing, but it just felt connected and passionate . . .

**Kaplan:** Miller has a lot to say about Barthes in *Getting Personal*.

**Davidson:** He wrote so beautifully. So that was important for me to feel that kind of freedom. I'm not sure I like the personal or not-personal distinction, especially when you're talking about Ronell or Bérubé, who are very different from each other and very different from what we're doing too, but that sense of freedom and that sense you can explore different voices is crucial. It's important to realize you can write intelligently and not use what I'll call the footnote voice. It's part of the poststructural moment . . .

**Williams:** The post-poststructural moment . . .

**Davidson:** The post-poststructural moment. It's very exciting.

**Williams:** What's your read on the scene of criticism right now? It seems to me that we're in a different moment now than we were ten years ago, sort of the last gasp of High Theory.

**Tompkins:** I'm not so sure.

**Torgovnick:** I don't think you can be sure about the end of theory.

**Kaplan:** I don't know about the division you're making between personal writing and theory. There's something in me that really resists it.

**Davidson:** In Barthes, there's both.

**Torgovnick:** Some of the biggest compliments I got about *Gone Primitive* were when people told me I had done theory and personal writing. So I don't buy the distinction.

**Kaplan:** I got a lot out of a book that was a general audience book, which was Carolyn Heilbrun's *Writing a Woman's Life*. I read that several times while I was writing *French Lessons*. But also I read technical essays about language acquisition and novels about "métiers," like Richard Ford's *The Sportswriter*.

**Williams:** You were saying before that autobiography is very much a form, so the personal is a formal category that's not necessarily opposed to theory. About the current state of criticism and theory, what do you think of the things you see at MLA? If you go to MLA, what are your reactions?

**Davidson:** I'd say mixed. I go to MLA and some things bore me to death and other things I find exciting.

**Torgovnick:** There's a lot of interesting stuff going on at MLA. I think that cultural studies has been a significant infusion into what we used to think of as MLA. One of the things which happened really effortlessly was that the subject matter available to literary people has become so much greater.

**Kaplan:** One thing that's happening in my own trajectory, when I was a graduate student I read almost uniquely theory, and now I'd say I read a whole lot more fiction. And it's probably because I got very interested in problems of form, so I wanted to see how writers created form. It's enriched the kind of writing that I've been doing, more literary writing. It's also enriched my teaching. I read different kinds of criticism now; I've gone back to some of those French close readers of literary texts and rediscovered rhetorical and genre criticism.

**Torgovnick:** I had a special fixation on fiction when I got out of graduate school. I'm reading more nonfiction now. I still read novels, but I've gotten great pleasure recently from writing about land, for instance, a book called *Dakota* by Kathleen Norris. And I read Norman Maclean's *Young Men and Fire* and I got a lot of energy from that. The boundary between fiction and nonfiction has broken down to some extent and a lot of people write nonfiction with the energy that goes into fiction. That's another very important thing that we've all been working on, how to bring that kind of energy to criticism.

**Williams:** That brings up another question. Is what you're doing a "new belletrism"? (That's my phrase, and no doubt a charged phrase.) Or is it a return to literature? That's perhaps salutary in some ways—God forbid professors write the way they usually do. On the other hand, is this return to literature or a more self-consciously literary writing a return to a humanistic or belletristic ethos? What are the politics implicit in it?

**Tompkins:** Well, I'll speak for myself. Writing in the personal mode has freed me up as a writer and has made me feel that I could do more with the medium. Maybe as a result of that, or because I feel much more in touch with myself in doing this kind of writing, I'm more interested in literature. That is, I'm more interested in the imaginative and creative and magical properties of literature than I was for a long time, doing theory and more politically oriented thinking about it. So that's my trajectory, but it doesn't have any agenda attached to it that I'm aware of. It doesn't mean that I have to read only literature or teach only literature anymore. In fact, in the last course that I taught, I taught two classical literary texts and the only writing that people did in relation to those texts was creative writing or creative living. It's another dimension of literature to which I've returned. I don't even know if I should say returned.

**Davidson:** "36 Views of Mount Fuji" comes from Hokusai, an early nineteenth-century printmaker, who's taking his inspiration from much earlier Japanese and Chinese sources that resonate with our poststructuralist concepts of relativism and perspectivism. I don't know if I would talk about my interest in writing about Japan in that particular book as humanistic. Zen is very postmodern. I'm just not sure about those kinds of equations of the personal with a certain kind of political agenda. Certainly there is a big political agenda in that book as well as the personal agenda. So for me those oppositions don't hold.

**Torgovnick:** You're making me feel as if we need a name for what we're doing, because otherwise somebody else is going to give us a name. I think we've been resistant to giving it a name, but coming off these two comments I would say that to me it's a big mistake to put a divide between criticism and writing. One of the things in which I've found great pleasure is when people ask about the creative process that goes into writing criticism. For me it comes back to feeling that criticism is a form of writing . . .

**Kaplan:** I don't know how I could go back to a time before I studied deconstruction or before I was aware of theory, which woke me up and made me excited about the world and made me see things in terms of signs, and feminism, which made me see myself as constructed. All the things about theory I had learned went into writing a memoir about the construction of my cultural self in the world. So, to call that

. . . You know, when I think of the old humanism and the old belletrism, I think of a kind of dreary literary history where it's just the theories of guys in salons talking to each other. I mean, I love certain kinds of philology. I think Leo Spitzer's essay on *Phèdre* is one of the greatest pieces of literary criticism ever written, but calling somebody a humanist in the age of theory is an accusation, no?

**Williams:** Twenty years from now, couldn't people say that you were in a salon?

**Davidson:** I don't know, I kind of like the idea.

**Torgovnick:** I don't have any problem with being in a circle. I think we probably do represent a movement and we are passing up a power move in not naming it. It's a temptation that women have always succumbed to, not naming the movement, and then some man comes in and names the movement.

**Davidson:** We'd better come up with a name.

**Torgovnick:** Personal writing is not it. Integrative writing—I think it's a model of integration . . .

**Tompkins:** But at the same time also permitting fragmentation, permitting lots of different selves, or different aspects of the self . . .

**Torgovnick:** Creative criticism or writerly criticism?

**Davidson:** I like creative criticism or writerly criticism better than personal criticism.

**Torgovnick:** Me too.

**Tompkins:** One thing about graduate students these days is that most of them are poets or closet poets. Last year, it seemed to me a pretty large proportion of the first-year students were writing poetry. I don't think that's just our students either. There's a tremendous desire on the part of graduate students, and undergraduates too, to do writing that's more creative than the standard critical essay. And they have to lead these split lives or even be ashamed of what they write. I'm sorry, that's really wrong. The profession has shut itself off from a tremendous source of energy, and that just can't go on anymore.

**Torgovnick:** I think that's true, but there's another side. We were the victims but also the beneficiaries of a particular kind of education. We got certain kinds of background that our students don't always get.

**Tompkins:** You mean in writing? In studying?

**Torgovnick:** In studying, in actual content. One of the things that one notices is that there's a tendency to write and construct theory without having some of the background first, and that's not something that I especially want to encourage. There's an imaginative relationship to the material which I think should be encouraged, but I think that certain forms of material demand a particular level of knowledge.

**Kaplan:** It's hard to teach today. In my field there's a crisis because of course France is no longer the center of the universe—or even of Europe! The whole corpus has expanded to include all the Francophone countries, so the amount of knowledge required has become huge and the faculty don't always have the expertise to respond to what the students want.

**Davidson:** One of the reasons I'm excited about teaching and the profession again is that I'm teaching a photography course and my students know more than I do about the technology of the camera and even about media more generally. They're visually and media literate and sensitive. It's exciting to go into the classroom. We spend part of each class not only reading texts about photography, whether it's fictional texts or theoretical texts, but we look at photographs, and my students see differently than I do. It's a different background. Their vocabulary is different. I leave class feeling energized.

**Torgovnick:** On the other hand, there are different kinds of problems. I think it's tough to teach graduate students well; it's tough to read dissertations; it's tough to know exactly what kind of advice to give them. It's hard because today there's a very different landscape from the one that we came up in, not that the one we came up in was all that easy . . .

**Davidson:** No, it wasn't easy . . .

**Torgovnick:** It was a hard one. But this is hard in a different way. Things become familiar and old hat with so much speed.

**Williams:** That brings up another point about politics and the profession. It seems to me it's a beleaguered profession. What was the landscape like before and how do you think it is for students now?

**Davidson:** Undergraduate or graduate students?

**Williams:** Both.

**Davidson:** I think in English and probably in French too, on the graduate level, it's one of the worst job markets that's ever been, at least since World War II, so there's the blatant problem that some of these brilliant people are writing dissertations and not getting jobs.

**Kaplan:** And it was supposed to be different.

**Williams:** There were predictions that it would change in the early 1990s.

**Davidson:** It should be different. The retirements have happened. That's why we're all so overworked. It's happened. People are retiring but not being replaced.

**Kaplan:** And the economic crisis.

**Torgovnick:** Universities are about three years behind the general economy, so I think we'll see a reversal. There's a lot of waste going on. There are students who I think are much more talented than I was at their age and who are really struggling.

**Tompkins:** I feel sad that the students have to spend so much time thinking about the profession and how they're going to get a job. From day one, they come in and they're thinking about the job market, and they're twisted out of shape by it. It's awful.

**Torgovnick:** We were touchingly naive in lots of ways. I remember we compared our professional careers and it's miraculous that we survived. We took crazy and idiosyncratic routes.

**Kaplan:** Now, the pressure to publish while they're still in graduate school, it's terrible . . .

**Tompkins:** And to be up on everything. They're so afraid not to speak a language of expertise, a technical language . . .

**Williams:** For me, it's a pressing political issue. It seems to me that we're in a devastated profession, that eats its young, although one of my friends says it's a profession that leaves its young out in the desert to starve . . .

**Tompkins and Kaplan:** Both are true.

**Torgovnick:** We can change that if we exert constant pressure, but it's going to take a lot of pressure and faculties oftentimes don't have the will for it. When I go around the country, I urge faculties, "Do not accept higher teaching loads, do not accept larger classes, do not allow young people to be squeezed out." That's part of our responsibility if we teach and are in the profession. But the other thing is the relaxing of the retirement age. I guess it will benefit us at a certain age, but what is it going to do to all the kids who are waiting for jobs that aren't going to be opening up? It's really quite appalling.

**Williams:** I recently read a statistic that faculties are something like 50 to 60 percent full-time and 40 to 50 percent part-time. This fits the general post-Fordist reshuffling of labor: part-timers are very cheap, no benefits, so it's an effective employment practice. But universities used not to do that; it used to be something like 90 percent full-time. How about if we pick up one point from before, relating to the question of politics? You had mentioned, Cathy, that your book is very definitely informed by feminism, so it has the vista of feminist politics . . .

**Davidson:** Yes, but not just feminist. It's informed by a constellation of my own personal politics, antiracist politics, multicultural politics, feminist politics, and there's an economic agenda that I put forth. There are a lot of different levels of politics. I'm a political person; politics are a passionate part of my life. One of the projects I'm doing now is with a photojournalist who's photographing the little town of Mebane in North Carolina, which has been hurt by a plant closing. He's doing the photojournalism and I'm doing the text for this book. We're looking at what happened to Mebane, people who were put out of work when the White Furniture Company went out of business. So that kind of politics is important to me, too.

**Kaplan:** Do you want more testimony?

[Cathy Davidson has to leave for a meeting at this point.]

**Williams:** It seems to me that feminism enables the way that you write.

**Kaplan:** Well, on a political level, my work has been antifascist, in *Reproductions of Banality* to the work I did in *French Lessons* about Holocaust revisionism, and on a personal level working through my relationship to my father, who was a prosecutor at Nuremburg. The feminism there is deep; it's not programmatic—it has to do with fathers, mentors, and what it means for an intellectual woman to have an ambition.

**Torgovnick:** My own trajectory has been more concerned with processes of making meaning, although I would not have put it that way early in my career. There certainly was a time when I was upset that the process of making meaning in art did not have to do with politics, but I'm increasingly aware that there is no separation between the two. I have always thought of myself as a feminist but certainly not as a programmatic feminist, and I think a lot of the recent work I've been doing, a lot of the essays in *Crossing Ocean Parkway* are about various roles that women play in life, both in the family and professionally.

**Tompkins:** My turn. I used to be interested in politics. I don't know how to describe . . .

**Torgovnick:** You're interested in emotional politics.

**Tompkins:** Well, I was heavily into canon formation when I wrote *Sensational Designs* and believed strongly and still believe that the books that are taught in school send strong messages about who's powerful in the culture and who gets listened to and who can be respected. But my own interests have evolved from institutional polemics to personal development and exploration. I put large portions of my life on hold to become professionally successful and now I'm making up for that and doing a lot of work on myself. So I'm not involved in critical debates all that much. *West of Everything* does have an agenda in the sense that it's taking a feminist perspective on fiction and cultural narratives that were written for men and about men. Basically my thesis there was that in order to think of themselves as persons who could command respect and be successful in our society, men have had to shut down on their emotional lives. The western hero was a model for how to tough it out in this kind of world. After I wrote the book I discovered that I wasn't just writing about men, I was writing about myself. I'd had to become a man to do what I'd done.

**Williams:** Hence why you cook breakfast at Wellspring grocery on weekends, as all the local graduate students tell me?

**Tompkins:** I needed to get out of an academic environment to continue this process of self-recovery. Spiritual life has become important to me. I'm writing about my experiments in the classroom now, where I try to step out of a position of authority and get the students to take over and become responsible for their learning. And I've been trying to understand my own formation as a child in school, how I've been imprinted by authority, where my fears come from. I guess in some sense there could be a systematic or political outcome, at least as far as the way our school systems are organized, but right now I'm not at that level. I'm just trying to find out what happened to me, in order to understand myself.

**Williams:** To close, what is everyone working on now?

**Torgovnick:** *Crossing Ocean Parkway* is coming out in the fall . . .

**Williams:** I read "Slasher Stories" last night and it almost made me cry.

**Tompkins:** Well, there you go . . .

**Kaplan:** That's a goal each of us has worked toward, to move people in different ways.

**Torgovnick:** It's a book written from an Italian American female point of view. Half the essays are autobiographical with some cultural focus, and half of the essays are cultural with some autobiographical perspective. I'm aiming for the warm and the touching and the integration of personal history and intellectual interests. The project I'm in the middle of is called *Primitivism and the Quest for Ecstasy*. It began as an extension of *Gone Primitive*, but it's much more about primitivism as a displaced form of spiritual expression. I'm dealing with a lot of contemporary phenomena, like body piercing, and then particular case studies, like Georgia O'Keeffe and Dian Fossey. What I'm talking about is a kind of symbolic primitivism, an attraction toward land and animal life, and the desire to obliterate the concept of the self in relationship to the rest of the universe, which is a very deep pattern in religious experience. But it doesn't seem to find fulfillment in our culture, at least within religious institutions. So in our culture it seems to be channeled as a form of primitivism.

**Tompkins:** Didn't you work on Native Americans?

**Torgovnick:** In *Gone Primitive*, Africans were the primary example of the primitive, but in this book Native Americans are the quintessential example of the primitive, in part because I'm talking about a U.S.-based phenomenon.

**Kaplan:** I'm just starting some new things. I do have something coming out this summer, an issue of *South Atlantic Quarterly* on Céline's American career, which I've coedited with Philippe Roussin, a colleague at the Centre de recherche sur les arts et le langage in Paris. I'm starting a new book project on the year 1945. That was the year of the liberation and the year a young writer named Robert Brasillach was executed for collaboration. It's very interesting to work on a fascist, closet gay, very sentimental in his fiction but really a very cruel guy who denounced Jews and Communists. So I'm interested in that whole culture and how all the intellectuals in Paris positioned themselves in 1945 at the end of the war. Some of them were scrambling to save their asses; they were fighting to see who was going to lead the new generation—a very, very rich moment, and very confusing. So I want to write a book that will be lively. It's not going to be personal but I want it to have all the energy that a personal book would have. I also think that I might have a novel in me at some point in the future. After writing *French Lessons*, I got interested in writing dialogue and fiction.

**Williams:** It doesn't seem as unusual in French intellectual life, one is able to write novels . . .

**Torgovnick:** Just watch. Lots of people have done them under different names . . .

**Kaplan:** That's true in France, but the French make a really strong division between their persona as critics and their persona as novelists, whereas I don't believe in that . . .

# 3

# Only Connect

## *An Interview with Gerald Graff*

Gerald Graff has persistently upbraided literary studies for its disconnections—of literature and criticism from society, of academics from intellectual community, and of students from a coherent curriculum. Countering what he sees as a common American tendency to avoid conflict (as he discusses here), he has famously advocated, in his succinct motto, that we "teach the conflicts." Rather than seeing debates over the canon, theory, "political correctness," or other contentious issues as a problem, in *Beyond the Culture Wars: How Teaching the Conflicts Can Revitalize Higher Education* he argues that they are a pedagogical resource to be exploited rather than hidden.

While he has been a prominent member of the "theory generation," Graff is an iconoclast and does not readily fit into any definable camps. Like Richard Ohmann (interviewed in chapter 4), Graff turns critical theory on the university itself, examining the institutional structures, history, and pedagogy of English departments and forging a historically inflected and polemically charged study of the profession and institution of literature. His *Professing Literature: An Institutional History*, regarded as the standard history of the discipline tracing debates between scholars and critics since the nineteenth century, takes to task the very institutional structure of "field coverage," which essentially quarantines individual scholars.

Like Augie March, Graff is a loyal Chicagoan, born there in 1937, educated at the University of Chicago (B.A., 1959), and, after brief sojourns at Stanford (Ph.D., 1963) and the University of New Mexico (in his first teaching job, 1963–66), carrying out his teaching career at Northwestern (1966–91), the University of Chicago, where he held the Pullman Professorship (1991–98), and the University of Illinois at Chicago, where he is dean of undergraduate curricula (1999–) and where he joined Stanley Fish and Jane Tompkins.

At Stanford, as he recalls here, Graff did graduate work with the New Critic Yvor Winters and the New York Intellectual Irving Howe; his first book, *Poetic Statement and Critical Dogma* (Northwestern UP, 1970), which takes to task the New Criticism and other approaches for undermining "the power of language to connect us with the world," stemmed from his dissertation written under their direction. See also Graff's account, "Yvor Winters at Stanford" (*American Scholar* 44 [1957]; rpt. in *Masters: Portraits of Great Teachers*, ed. Joseph Epstein [Basic, 1981]). In the provocative *Literature against Itself: Literary Ideas in Modern Society* (U of Chicago P, 1979; with a new preface, Ivan Dee, 1995), Graff turned his sights to contemporary theory and its focus on language. A companion collection (coedited with Reginald Gibbons), *Criticism in the University* (Northwestern UP, 1985), focuses on the present divide between literary journalism and academic criticism. Alongside *Professing Literature* (U of Chicago P, 1987), Graff compiled (with Michael Warner) a collection of historical documents, *The Origins of Literary Studies in America: A Documentary History* (Routledge, 1988). "Criticism since 1940" (coauthored with Evan Carton), in *The Cambridge History of American Literature*, Vol. 8 (1996), synthesizes Graff's views of the cycle of conflicts in and the "academicization" of criticism. Deploying his conflictual model from *Beyond the Culture Wars* (Norton, 1992), Graff has also coedited (with James Phelan) two casebooks, *Adventures of Huckleberry Finn: A Case Study in Critical Controversy* (Bedford, 1995) and *The Tempest: A Case Study in Contemporary Controversy* (Bedford, 1999). Most recently, *Clueless in Academe: How Schooling Obscures the Life of the Mind* (Yale UP, 2003) gives his further prescriptions for clarifying academic work and connecting it with the world; an excerpt appears as "Scholars and Sound Bites: The Myth of Academic Difficulty" in *PMLA* 115.5 (2000). See also Graff and Tompkins's dialogue, "Can We Talk?," in *Professions: Conversations on the Fu-*

*ture of Literary and Cultural Studies* (ed. Donald E. Hall; U of Illinois P, 2001); Tompkins advocates cooperation rather than confrontation.

This interview took place on 17 June 2001 in Gerald Graff's office at UIC. It was conducted by Jeffrey Williams and transcribed by Laura Rotunno, a Ph.D. student at Missouri and the managing editor of the *minnesota review*. It originally appeared in an issue of the review on "50s Culture."

**Williams:** Your early work is very polemical, and you generally attack literary critics for their detachment from society. In *Poetic Statement and Critical Dogma*, you take on the New Critics, and in *Literature against Itself*, the new developments in theory. In fact, when I started reading theory in the mid-eighties, you were known as an enemy of theory. But, later on, you became a proponent of theory. How did you come to be a supporter of theory?

**Graff:** Actually, I was always a supporter of theory, even before it was called "theory." My 1963 doctoral dissertation was on poetics. What I attacked in *Literature against Itself* were certain new forms of theory—deconstruction, postmodernism, poststructuralism, cultural radicalism, etcetera, which after 1975 or so became equated by a lot of people with "theory" *tout court*.

I did revise my views quite sharply in the mid-eighties, though, when I had read more deconstruction and poststructuralist theory and began to realize they were not what I had thought they were. I had mistakenly conflated Derrida, for example, with sixties subjectivist radicalism, relativism, and irrationalism. The turning point was working as editor with Derrida on the Northwestern University Press edition of his *Limited, Inc.*, an experience that made me realize that I'd confused his ideas with vulgarized versions of deconstruction promoted by some of his followers and then attacked by his critics.

Another thing that led me to change my mind was being reviewed favorably by neocons who obviously had no idea what they were talking about when they pontificated about the horrors of current theory. That and going to conferences where I met some of the theorists I had savaged and realized that I found them a lot more interesting than many of those who agreed with me.

On the other hand, I think I was right in some of the objections I made in *Literature against Itself* about some of the uncritical claims of subversiveness made by some forms of theory and how these forms dovetail with the spirit of consumer culture. Most of Alan Sokal's and Allan Bloom's arguments, for example, are present in *Literature against Itself*, but I don't get credit for that kind of critique anymore since I've moved on to other things.

**Williams:** To take a couple of steps back, I want to ask about your intellectual formation. You grew up in Chicago, went to the University of Chicago in the fifties, and other than a loop out west to Stanford for grad school and a couple of years in your first job at New Mexico, you've stayed in Chicago. That seems unique; I mean, I doubt many academics end up getting a job where they grew up. What was it like growing up in Chicago? Has it rooted you politically in any particular way?

**Graff:** As I think of it, my Chicago background, growing up hanging out in the neighborhood, playing sports, and being alienated from school and book culture, gave me a certain "outsider" perspective toward academia and the aestheticism of literature departments that I've cultivated in my work. This perspective has become especially important to me as I've gotten more and more into writing about education, since I think of it as providing a link and a bridge to the many students who feel themselves to be outsiders to the intellectual culture of academia.

I think this "outsiderism" also underlies my ambivalence toward the academic Left, whose causes I tend to identify with but whose styles and attitudes often put me off. But this may be as much a generational as a regional matter. Being born in 1937, I'm part of an in-between generation, I think: too young to have been a New Critic, but too old for the counterculture, poststructuralism, etcetera.

**Williams:** I was interested to learn, when I wrote about your work for the Norton theory anthology, that while you were at Stanford, you did your graduate work with Yvor Winters and Irving Howe. What was that like? How did they influence you?

**Graff:** Both provided me with great—though very different—models of "committed" intellectuals, Winters as a moralist, Howe as a political critic. I, a fifites kid, was very apolitical in those days and found Winters easier to get a handle on and imitate than Howe. Both were powerful men who projected great confidence in their views, but Winters was overwhelming, a kind of Dr. Johnson type in the Great Man mold. I became fascinated by him, read everything of his I could get my hands on—his poetry as well as his criticism. At first I felt challenged to try to find a chink in his theoretical arguments about the nature of poetry; it was through Winters that I found out that there were exciting debates about such questions. Gradually, after a period of arguing with him in his office—or of me proposing arguments and he patiently explaining why I was wrong, as he had shown at length in this or that book or essay that I should go back and look at—I succumbed and became a card-carrying Wintersian, as the type was called at Stanford. I wrote an essay about this captivation with Winters and my subsequent efforts to get out from his shadow.

Howe was more strange to me—the first New York Intellectual I had seen up close and personal. I still picture him in his small office at Stanford, his books (mostly paperbacks) in piles on the floor, and him banging away at a little typewriter propped on one of the piles, pounding out his latest piece for *Dissent* or *Partisan Review*, I assume, though I don't think I knew much about those journals then. In any case, having Howe and Winters on my dissertation committee gave me two excellent models of critics who believed above all in the relevance of literature to life, and in those days (circa 1960), in which literary studies was still under the sway of the New Criticism, that meant a lot. Howe and Winters had assimilated the close reading techniques of the New Critics but extended them in broader political and moral ways. That, I guess, is how I think of their effect on me.

**Williams:** After *Literature against Itself*, you moved on to do *Professing Literature*. I can see how it's consistent with your earlier work, both in taking a metacritical view (you've rarely written on literature, but primarily on criticism, theory, and our professional practices) and in looking at how the academy affects literature. But, still, it's relatively unique; other than Ohmann's *English in America*, there were not many people focusing on the disciplinary history of English. What prompted you to do it? And what was the state of institutional studies when you took it up?

**Graff:** There were things like William Riley Parker's fine essay "Where Do English Departments Come From?" which I had stumbled on through my colleague at Northwestern, the late Wallace Douglas, who also directed me to some histories of English departments. (He also cowrote one of the chapters in Richard Ohmann's *English in America.*) One that was very helpful and that I ended up drawing on a lot was of Indiana University. And there was, of course, Ohmann, even though I didn't praise his book as much as I should have in *Literature against Itself.* What for me was great about Ohmann was that he wrote about department meetings and stuff that would happen in the corridors—the unofficial aspect of academic life that no one was talking about then but that he saw was very important as an index to what was going on in the institutions.

Let me back up. In the early eighties, I began accumulating materials toward some kind of history of English studies, probably as much as anything out of a sense of confusion about why I was doing what I was doing and where this institution had come from. I had the sense the profession must have lost touch with what it was doing at the beginning and I wanted to know what that was. So I had accumulated a lot of information, but I didn't really have a way of telling the story. The initial manuscript that was sent to the University of Chicago Press told the story as one of decline, decline into the incoherence of poststructuralist theory, deconstruction, and so forth. But I didn't have a lot of conviction in that. For one thing I didn't believe that things had been great at some point and then fallen off. But in any case, what held the book together was a story of decline or deterioration into incoherence.

Chicago sent the manuscript to Jonathan Culler, and Culler said in his reader's report that while there's a lot of interesting stuff here, it's unfortunate that Graff uses it all as another stick with which to beat poststructuralism. He also noted that by then a lot of people were already doing that, and we didn't need another pessimistic story. What Culler said was very good; often you get criticism that you agree with but needed someone to say.

Another idea that was swimming around came from Christopher Lasch. He had been at Northwestern in 1966–69, and I became friendly with him and read all his stuff. He was somebody who helped me shape some kind of political perspective, and he was also a very solid academic historian and social thinker. Lasch had always talked about American culture as a culture that evades conflict. I had noticed this theme in his work, that American culture for various complicated reasons fails to come to terms with conflict. This was the Lasch of *The New Radicalism in America* and *The Agony of the American Left*. Anyway, that theme stuck in my mind and somehow, when I got this response from Culler, I got the idea that what I was telling was really a story about conflict that had been evaded. And I began to feel that this failure of our profession to confront our conflicts was connected with the murkiness about what it is we do. We adopt a pluralistic model that lets us study literature in any number of ways, but by not coming to terms with or asking students to come to terms with the conflicting approaches or conflicting readings, we evade questions about what it is we are doing.

**Williams:** Hence "teaching the conflicts," the phrase you're probably most known for. Hearing you mention pluralism, I can't but think of the Chicago critics and ask whether it was a reaction or an answer to the Chicago school?

**Graff:** I had never identified with the Chicago school, and I guess I still don't. In a way I can see how there is a certain emphasis on debate and negotiating various pluralistic differences that I might have caught from the Chicago atmosphere. I had read some of R. S. Crane, and he became important to the story. I liked the kind of incisiveness and the kind of argumentative edge that a figure like Crane had.

**Williams:** *Professing Literature* came out in 1987, but I don't think it's been superseded. Do you have any updates or revisions that you'd make now?

**Graff:** Well, Chris Baldick and Terry Eagleton were writing good stuff around the time that I published *Professing Literature*. Now, I like David Damrosch's book *We Scholars* a lot. It's a critique of the isolationist individualism of the profession. Guillory's *Cultural Capitalism* is obviously important, and Bérubé's work on public intellectuals, and some of your own essays are important, especially in thinking out the political ramifications of our institution. John Brereton has produced an excellent documentary history of composition studies, *The Origins of Composition Studies in the American College: 1875–1925.*

**Williams:** Besides "teaching the conflicts," "field coverage" is another phrase that you're known for. It nicely characterizes both the cornucopia and the isolating structure of English departments. Now it seems that everybody claims to be doing cultural studies, and interdisciplinarity is a buzzword, which promises to break down field divisions. On the other hand, when we hire people, we still apportion them in literary fields in basically the same old ways. Do you see field coverage dissipating under the auspices of cultural studies and interdisciplinarity, or do you see it as still entrenched?

**Graff:** No, I don't see it dissipating at all. The idea of coverage is rooted in something more primary, which is the fact that the basic unit of pedagogy is the course, which stands alone and is not connected to any other course. I have a chapter in *Beyond the Culture Wars* called "Other Voices, Other Rooms" about "the course fetish," the tendency to conceive of education as basically a series of courses that aren't connected with each other. I think it's deeply ingrained in our professional unconscious that teaching is a solo performance done pretty much in isolation. The notion that an education will consist of a series of courses that aren't in dialogue with each other goes hand in hand with the field coverage model.

This is part of my argument that I don't think I've gotten across very well. I'm trying to take another shot at it in the new book that I'm finishing called *Clueless in Academe*. The subtitle is *How Schooling Obscures the Life of the Mind*. I feel my real subject all along has not been conflict but confusion and cluelessness. It's in *Professing Literature* and everything that I've written recently: the gulf between academics and nonacademics, which I think has always been huge and is getting huger. My notion is that the incomprehensibility of academia is not because of jargon or technical language, which is superficial, but because we chop up an intellectual culture into courses and, to some extent, disciplines and subjects. I'm not against courses or disciplines or subjects—there have to be some of these—but when you don't connect them you render the whole thing incomprehensible.

You've written very interestingly in the *Institution of Literature* volume you edited about the famous Kenneth Burke quotation about the conversation. You come to a parlor, you come late, and everyone is arguing about something. At first you don't know what the argument is, but gradually you jump in and then you are part of it. I think that is where intellectual life ultimately is and what a school should look like, a connected conversation. It's the conversation that connects academia ultimately with what's outside academia—the popular media and so forth. A disconnected curriculum wipes that conversation out of view or cuts it up into such disconnected fragments that it's unrecognizable, certainly not visible as a conversation.

**Williams:** But Burke's room doesn't have much connection to the outside; it's a self-contained conversation. Frequently I hear academics say "academics do this," directed at other academics, when they too are academics in their own rooms. I've had a number of other jobs, and I don't find the academic world any more cut off than if you worked in a hospital or other institution. Each institution has its own internal code, but you still get your coffee at the deli down the street.

**Graff:** But there's a sense in which academia pushes obscurity to another level. Take a hospital: it's true that we don't know the kind of biochemistry or whatever it is that doctors know about, but we do at least have some working conviction about what a doctor is for. That is, there is a certain commonsense understanding of what doctors do. So while, you're right that academics aren't any more specialized or esoteric than any other modern occupation, there's nevertheless a certain understanding of the function of those occupations, of what a doctor's for, what a linebacker's for, what a policeman is for. By contrast, people don't know what a humanist is for, though they have more of a sense of what a management professor is for.

**Williams:** I think the same applies to us. We teach verbal skills, as well as the appreciation of culture, in the public view.

**Graff:** Yes, but our basic practices—the analysis and interpretation of texts, or the rationale for those practices—are not at all understood. And why should they be, since we don't really discuss such questions very publicly?

**Williams:** I don't think people think our job is the analysis and interpretation of texts, but that we're here to teach writing and to develop an appreciation of great works of literature.

**Graff:** But that's my point: there's a wide gap between what people think we're about and what we think. Of course, it depends on who the "we" is. There's a kind of nebulosity about what the cultural fields do that makes them more obscure than even the sciences, which have a kind of technical rationale. That's crucial to my argument—that we are qualitatively more incomprehensible than your average garden-variety incomprehensible professional. We don't even think about it; we don't talk about it, or else we assume our incomprehensibility is a normal thing, perhaps even a sign of our distinction.

**Williams:** Bruce Robbins talks about how professionals project an outside world that they both appeal to but separate themselves from. In more rhetorical terms, what you're saying is a kind of jeremiad, that we've fallen away from our connection to the world.

**Graff:** Actually, Robbins's work is important to me, and because it's *not* a jeremiad. In *Secular Vocations,* he argues that we've exaggerated the outside-inside distinction, the idea that once professionals have become insiders, they exclude outsiders. That's become one of the common "decline" theories: that we've grown away from the outside public. He argues that, on the contrary, any successful profession has to internalize the outside perspective in order to be useful to its clients. And I argue virtually the same thing, that the work that has most influence on our field among insiders is work that incorporates some outside perspective. Ohmann would be an example. Ohmann decided to look at English studies from the perspective of an outside political critic who was also an insider. So I'm not trying to bash the insiders from the point of view of the outsiders; I'm trying to rethink the institution as a hybrid interplay of insider and outsider.

**Williams:** I think the problem is a structural one, that we judge ourselves and accrue professional standing based on research rather than teaching. But the teaching rationale has always been our public rationale—I'm sure it's declared to be in our universities' mission statements—and in fact the vast majority of us at state schools experience a more direct idea of teaching.

**Graff:** Okay, except that we might disagree over how specialized and narrow the research model is now, and therefore how far research really does clash with teaching. I make the argument that successful research now has to have some public impact—in order to get funded, for example—and that this fact makes research far more *teachable* than it once was.

In 1910 or 1920, the basic research topic in an English department was, for example, the syntax of *at* and *ana* in Old Icelandic or something like that, the more specialized the better. If you made broad general claims, you sounded like a journalist or a dilettante. It seems to me that today younger professionals in the humanities are encouraged, sometimes overencouraged, to get at the big picture right away. People ask, how is your research really going to change the way we think about health care or gender or sexuality? While we weren't looking, the model of what counts as successful research changed. In *Clueless in Academe,* I quote a phrase of yours, the "journalization of criticism," that nicely describes what is happening. Critics—Eve Sedgwick is a good example whom I cite—write academic criticism, but of a kind that makes big quasi-journalistic kinds of claims. Though academics like Sedgwick are not accessible to wide publics, the kinds of claims they make are much more big-picture claims than the syntax of *at* and *ana*, and they get translated by journalists for news and feature articles. The research model has been blown apart and is being replaced by a public intellectual model. But we don't realize it yet and we still write and operate in ways that don't take into account how these big-picture issues have taken over research. The point about teaching is that, insofar as research is now broad-gauged, the old conflict between research and teaching lessens.

**Williams:** You've written a lot about teaching—unlike most people who write on theory—and you mentioned to me that you recently wrote a piece with Jane Tompkins and have sat in on each other's classes since coming to UIC. One thing I was struck with in reading "Taking Cover in Coverage" is that your conflicts model is a kind of rough sport model. You like the contact. But if you read Tompkins, she would say this is the model that damaged her and that it has a masculinist bias. Not everybody likes sports. How have you worked it out with Jane Tompkins?

**Graff:** Jane and I are team-teaching these very issues right now. I have quite a bit in *Clueless in Academe* about them: Is argument male? Is it ethnocentric? In a certain sense it obviously is, but it doesn't need to be. Jane and I talk about this in our dialogue called "Can We Talk?" She argues that, before we can have good talk, we need to create safe zones where we feel enough trust in each other, enough nurturance. We aren't going to have good talk if we feel the person we are talking to is always ready to stick the knife in, in a very gendered way. My response is to ask, "When are we going to have a safe zone? When will we know, are we safe yet?" If we wait until there is a safe zone, we are never going to have good talk, so it becomes circular. I have a long chapter on Deborah Tannen called "Two Cheers for the Argument Culture," in which I grant what Tompkins, Tannen and other feminists have been saying, that the conditions of academic debate and public debate are often deplorably thuggish, more like insult or mud-wrestling than serious attempts to engage with others. But I point out that Tannen and Tompkins themselves performatively show the necessity of entering into debate culture. They themselves are very much polemically engaged, and their gender concerns become part of the debate.

By the way, I've found in teaching my freshman course here at UIC to students who are not sure they want to jump into intellectual life that the question to debate or not to debate is one that really engages them. The ethnic issue emerges: Is there something antidebate about Asian culture? Some Asian students say, "Yeah, I grew up in a home where we did what our parents told us and I think that's the right way." Others, however, reply, "No, to get anywhere in the U.S. you've got to have an argument." So a very interesting argument breaks out about argument. It's generally my tactic to say, "If you think debate is problematic, then we have to make that part of the debate." That, it seems to me, is what a good debate does: reflectively generate a discussion of its own conditions and possibilities (which I take to be one of the messages of poststructuralism). I do think that the challenge from feminists to conflict models is important, but I see the feminists themselves involved in a contestatory-conflictual model of one kind or another. Or maybe they're trying to change the dynamics of contestation from within, which is fine, but some kind of contestation is still part of the game.

**Williams:** One thing that I admire about your work is that you're actually putting your money down, applying what you think about education to what you do. Maybe you could talk about what you're doing in your program here as a dean at UIC. You also mentioned earlier that you have started sitting in on other people's classes, not to evaluate them but to see what other people do.

**Graff:** As I've already suggested, my premise—and I said this in *Beyond the Culture Wars*—is that though we like to refer to an "academic conversation," students don't really see a conversation. They see individual profs whom they might have conversations with, but the conversation or interaction among professors and scholars is effaced. I think it's very hard to learn if you are always experiencing authority as a series of monologues or isolated glimpses.

**Williams:** Students do seem aware that one professor might be utterly different from another professor, and that they have to say different things in class or on a paper to get a good grade.

**Graff:** Yes, the quicker students not only immediately see that their profs are different. They also see how and what's at stake in the differences. But most can only cope by adopting the strategy of doing whatever each prof "wants" in succession.

I've started to call what I want a comparative curriculum, not so much a conflictual curriculum. When we isolate one course from the next, we shut down the comparisons and contrasts. We not only obscure our conflicts from the students—I have spent a lot of time griping about this—but we also hide our agreements. In fact we ourselves often don't know whether we agree or disagree. How do I know whether I agree with Fish? I don't see what he's saying in his class; he doesn't see what I'm saying in mine. A lot of times it's hard enough to tell whether you agree or disagree with your colleague even when you try to talk about it. So—this is the argument I am pushing—unless we structure education in a way that allows students to perceive (and enter into) the interactions among positions, methods, and assumptions, their chances of entering our conversations—and us entering theirs—are limited. Our isolated dynamic basically perpetuates inclusion and exclusion. The excluded are not going to be able to get in on the game until they have the game represented to them in a way that is more connected and makes sense.

Now, how am I trying to do something about this at UIC? Well, not entirely through my instigation—it has more to do with worries about retention—but we are moving to a learning-community model. Next year for freshmen we're instituting thematic clusters of courses. Jane Tompkins and I are both involved with this project. There will be ten cohorts of twenty-five students each taking the same courses—the same English course, the same communications course, the same chemistry course. I wrote about these learning-community models at the end of *Beyond the Culture Wars*, and we are going to try to put the idea into effect. I think it could help a lot. I have a palpable sense from teaching freshman here—mostly working-class kids, first-generation academics—that they are ground to pieces by having to meet different demands of different courses that aren't correlated, and their whole sense of belonging to an intellectual community is wiped out. The course disjunctions materially impair their ability to make sense of education, and to get through it successfully.

**Williams:** It's also a material issue; a lot of them are probably working part-time jobs.

**Graff:** All the more reason to help them integrate their studies. Kids who work thirty to forty hours a week need a more focused curriculum and more help in putting it together. A lot of what I was teaching in English, I think, would have helped them in chemistry or physics or in someplace else. But I was in no position to provide that help because my course was segmented off from the rest. So I think the learning community will help.

Another thing I am promoting at UIC is undergraduate research. We've had two undergraduate research conferences in the year and a half I've been here, and they've been spectacular. I think undergraduate research is going to be one of the big trends in education in the next few decades and will illustrate the obsoleteness of the research-versus-teaching opposition that I spoke of a moment ago. It doesn't make any sense to keep undergraduates out of research. One thing I noticed is that, when undergraduates become coresearchers with a professor, the usual adversarial relationship dissolves. We're working on the same team together and it's great. I would love to help bring about a situation here where every UIC undergraduate would be expected, as part of their education, to get involved in a research project with a grad student or professor. The sciences are way ahead of the humanities in this respect. Kids are doing science fairs in high school. In the humanities we are still hiding our research, even though we're doing research on hot-button topics—gender, race, class, and so forth—that are ripe for bringing undergraduates in. That's the real paradigm shift: to wipe out the old idea that research is for graduate students and not for undergraduates.

I think another barrier that is crumbling is the one that has separated the high school and the college. The pressures to improve lower schooling in America and the pressures for greater accountability, whether you like it or not, are bringing the high school and the college closer together. Some younger academics are taking the lead and working with high school students and high school teachers. I think that's a tremendous opportunity. It's also obviously a potential trap, since one could say, "Well, you're no longer going to be able to collect your salary by just teaching four courses or six courses; you're going to have to go out and do more." High school outreach could become a way of squeezing more work out of people for less money and further proletarianizing the professoriate. On balance, though, the collaborations arising between colleges and high schools seem a very promising thing.

**Williams:** To look backward instead of forward, I'm struck by the fact that the generation of people who brought us the thing called theory—you, Fish, various other people—are coming to the end of their careers. Theory was the name of the game, whereas now it doesn't seem to be. What do you make of what's happened to theory?

**Graff:** Well, I guess I wouldn't say that it's no longer the name of the game. I suppose what's set in in the last ten or fifteen years is something like what set in with the New Criticism. New Criticism didn't go away; it became part of "normal science." It's the bedrock practice of most teaching; it's still predominant in the schools. I think that something similar happened with theory. If theory no longer seems au courant, it's because it's been naturalized, normalized, so that we take for granted certain notions of interrogating concepts. It's taken for granted that "literature" is no longer seen unproblematically as a thing that isn't in some way produced by institutional conditions and historic variables. But current academic scholarship is still very much operating within the kinds of paradigms that were set by the theorists, don't you think?

**Williams:** Yes and no. I would agree that theory has permeated our discourse, but, on the other hand, I see a turn to a more belletristic rationale—what I've called "the new belletrism." That isn't quite as positive or celebratory as seeing a turn to the public intellectual.

**Graff:** I tried to talk you out of calling your essay "The New Belletrism," because "belletrism," it seems to me, invites confusion. I think what you were describing is not belletrism so much as a closing of the gap between academic writing and more publicly accessible kinds of writing—journalism as well as personal writing and autobiography. Your phrase "the journalization of criticism," I think, names the phenomenon a little better. And I have been trying to argue in the new book that professors and journalists are now in the same game. In fact, that's one reason why professors and journalists are often at odds. Whereas at one time they looked at each other from a distance with a kind of mutual scorn, I think now the scorn is rooted in how close they are, as competitors in the cultural explanation business. And this is more or less inevitable once academia took on, in a big way, the business of explaining the contemporary. Scholars now—even people working on the past, like Greenblatt—reinterpret the past in the light of the contemporary. We are much more involved than academics were fifty or sixty or a hundred years ago in being explainers of contemporary life. And that's why we're quoted so often, why academic research is quoted so often, even by journalists; we're in the same ballpark. That may have been, in some ways, a reaction against the kind of esoteric qualities of theory, but you could also see it as a move toward taking those esoteric theories and turning them into more journalistically accessible terms.

Let me cap off this discussion with one example. *Nightline* did a program a couple of nights ago on an archaeologist, who, through analysis of ancient relics going back millions of years, has come out with the argument that the image we have of prehistoric man—the caveman classically depicted in *National Geographic*—is wrong. The assumption was that their economy and survival were based on the men going out and slaying big animals—throwing their spears into huge mastodons—which meant that male strength was extremely important, and that the women huddled together and raised the babies and did a little farming. Well, these scientists now claim that's nonsense. In fact, the evidence suggests that primitive economies were based on hunting down rabbits, getting them in nets and skinning them, and that women and children were doing this as much as men. They would have been crazy to take on mastodons and huge beasts when they could live quite nicely on rabbits. *National Geographic* wrote them up because it's an important discovery, and they printed this picture which shows the women and the children with the men trapping rabbits, but in the background you still see men throwing spears into mastodons. And the scientist explained, "Well, we went to *National Geographic* and told them, 'Look, the men with the mastodons, they didn't do that; it didn't work that way.'" And *National Geographic* came back and said, "We're sorry, but we have to report it that way, that's what we're all about."

Here's a wonderful example of what theoretically inclined people have been talking about for years: that representation is a site of struggle, that conflicting representations affect the construction of reality and history and make up the fabric of reality and history. I don't know if the archaeologists were influenced by these theories of representation, but, whether they were or not, this is an interesting example of how journalism is beginning to absorb academic theorizing about the contested nature of representation. The question was quite explicitly posed on *Nightline*: is the myth of the caveman based on a sexist attempt to glorify the old heroic male role? So I see that kind of dissemination of theory as an example of where things are going, and, given the economic plight that universities are in, maybe that's a good reason for going in that direction.

# 4

# English in America Revisited

## *An Interview with Richard Ohmann*

Richard Ohmann has been a unique voice in American literary studies. His *English in America: A Radical View of the Profession* pioneered the study of academic institutionalization and professionalization, inaugurating a strand of criticism that only came to the fore two decades later, in the work of Gerald Graff (interviewed in chapter 3), Bruce Robbins, Evan Watkins, John Guillory, and others. Against the typical, Arnoldian justification that English exists to inculcate the appreciation of timeless works of literature, Ohmann points out other, less advertised functions: "We also discipline the young to do assignments, on time, to follow instructions, to turn out uniform products, to observe the etiquette of verbal communication." Further, despite the ideology of equal opportunity, "we eliminate the less adapted, the ill-trained, the city youth with bad verbal manners, blacks with the wrong dialect . . . and the rebellious of all shapes and sizes." Examining the facets of English from composition to the university's role in the "military-industrial complex," Ohmann issues a damning critique of the institution of English as an "instrument" to "maintain social and economic inequalities," a critique that only seems more relevant today, given growing disparities of wealth in the world, the corporatization of the university, and the wide gap between full-time and term labor there.

Turning from English departments to American culture at large, Ohmann has also forged a distinctive kind of American cultural studies, notably in *Selling Culture: Magazines, Markets, and Class at the Turn of the Century*, as well as in numerous essays. Persistently exposing how literature is not an autonomous aesthetic object but is thoroughly embedded in capitalism, in *Selling*

*Culture* Ohmann examines the links between the rise of popular literary magazines and the rise of advertising in the late nineteenth and early twentieth centuries.

Ohmann's work does not readily fit in the standard schools of contemporary criticism. Like Noam Chomsky, Ohmann has maintained an independent, unrelentingly critical, radical position; like Paul Lauter (interviewed in chapter 7), his work might be aligned with the Left, but it stems from the sixties sense of a "ruthless critique of all things" rather than from a doctrinaire Marxism. In one way his still timely *English in America* fits in the iconoclastic tradition of American social criticism of the university, started with Thorstein Veblen's *Higher Learning in America.*

Born in 1931 in Cleveland, Ohmann received his B.A. from Oberlin College in 1952 and his Ph.D. in English from Harvard in 1960. He taught at Wesleyan University in Connecticut from 1961 until his retirement in 1996, also serving in various administrative positions. Befitting his time and training, Ohmann's early scholarly work focused on literary style in figures such as George Bernard Shaw, but through the 1960s he explored new theoretical approaches imported from linguistics, and he was one of the first American scholars to introduce speech act theory to literary criticism. Deeply influenced by the social unrest and leftist politics of the late 1960s, as he recounts here his work again shifted to examine the social and political issues involved in the study of literature.

Ohmann's early work includes *Shaw: The Style and the Man* (Wesleyan UP, 1962); the edited collection *The Making of Myth* (Putnam, 1962); two coauthored textbooks on rhetoric and composition; and several influential essays employing speech act theory to analyze the style of literary works. From 1966 through 1978, Ohmann also edited the influential National Council of Teachers of English (NCTE) journal, *College English,* sponsoring innovative issues on feminism, gay studies, and other topics (also resulting in the collection, with W. B. Coley, *Ideas for English 101: Teaching Writing in College* [NCTE, 1975]). *Politics of Letters* (Wesleyan UP, 1987), a collection of essays, complements *English in America* (Oxford UP, 1976; reissued by Wesleyan UP in 1996 with a foreword by Graff and a new introduction by Ohmann). Representing over fifteen years of research, *Selling Culture* (Verso,

1996) culminates his look at larger literary culture. In a related effort, Ohmann edited *Making and Selling Culture* (Wesleyan UP, 1996), which includes interviews with publishers and filmmakers as well as academics.

Fugitive essays relevant to this interview include "English after the USSR," in *After Political Correctness: The Humanities and Society in the 1990s*, ed. Christopher Newfield and Ronald Strickland (Westview, 1995); and "Graduate Students, Professionals, Intellectuals," *College English* 52 (1990). For two notable responses to *English in America*, see chapters in Graff's *Literature against Itself: Literary Ideas in Modern Society* (U of Chicago P, 1979), which criticizes its radicalism; and in Stanley Fish's *Doing What Comes Naturally: Change, Rhetoric, and the Practice of Theory in Literary and Legal Studies* (Duke UP, 1989), which criticizes its inherent antiprofessionalism.

This interview took place on 22 December 1993 in Richard Ohmann's office at the Center for the Humanities at Wesleyan University in Middletown, Connecticut. It was conducted by Jeffrey Williams and transcribed by Jan Forehand, an assistant to the *minnesota review* while a graduate student at East Carolina University. It originally appeared in an issue of the review on "Institutional Questions."

**Williams:** The question I want to start with is about *English in America*, which strikes me as having been ahead of its time in dealing with issues—like institutionalization and professionalization—that are very current now. What was the field like when you wrote it?

**Ohmann:** I remember when I came to think that I was writing a book—rather than just the stray article—and I knew that I wanted to write about the institutions of English, I looked around to find out what the historians and the sociologists had said about departments, and I was astonished to find that they had very little to say at all. There was literature on professionalism that was some help, especially an older scholar named Everett Hughes, but the sociologists were remarkably silent about departments—the institutions in which they themselves and we work. So I felt that I was making it up as I went along, clearing the brush, and I'm sure that the path was erratic, but it was a kind of a path. I don't claim credit for all of the explosion of interest in professionalization in the institutions of the academies, but I think that what I did in *English in America*, along with work that was under way simultaneously by Burton Bledstein and by Magali Sarfatti Larson, really opened up a field of inquiry and exhibited a certain political urgency in doing so. So I'm satisfied about that, though I have not read parts of *English in America* during the intervening eighteen years, and I'm sure that there are parts that I would find very embarrassing now if I read them again. But some parts of it seem to have set some energies going for people in our field or in other fields—the section on composition and the sections on departments especially.

**Williams:** Michael Sprinker once told me that it changed the way he looked at the profession and in some ways brought him to Marxism.

**Ohmann:** Really? You said it was a work that was slightly ahead of its time, but in another way, it was entirely part of its moment, which was really a few years before it came out. That was the time when a whole bunch of people in the U.S. were engaging in a ruthless critique of all things existing, to use one of my favorite phrases, and when it seemed as if every day when you went to a meeting, new knowledge and thought opened up, and it was very exciting. There's no possibility that *English in America* could have turned into what it was without the Radical Caucus of the Modern Language Association, without the New University Conference, and the people in literary and cultural studies who had small meetings within the bigger NUC meetings and astonished ourselves mutually with the way we were looking again at the work that we did. In short, its ideas came out of the politics of that time and the efforts of mostly younger intellectuals. I was the one, as it turned out, that specialized in departments and the institutions of writing instruction, but the book itself, as can be said of almost all books, can best be thought of as a kind of collective project, or the result of a collective project of that time. It was unthinkable without The Movement, as we used to call it.

**Williams:** What do you think of the current concern with these issues?

**Ohmann:** I hope that there is more and more of it. I value very much things that people like Evan Watkins and Bruce Robbins and Jim Berlin have done. They've gone, in some ways, well beyond what I did, and it seems to me that there are also a lot of historical studies of the discipline and institutions, especially of writing. People like Robert Connors have been grounding the kinds of points at which I more or less conjectured about the history of composition, both in *English in America* and in *Politics of Letters*.

**Williams:** How did you come to do this kind of work, to be interested in the things you deal with in *English in America*?

**Ohmann:** The simple answer—it's a double-barreled answer—I was increasingly discontent and uneasy with what we were doing in our own rush toward fuller professionalization and specialization in the early sixties, and I was angry about race and militarism and class in our country, and those two strands fused for me. I turned back to look at our work in light of the critiques that were being staged of American power around the world—the Vietnam War and racism, and then a little bit later, male supremacy—so those two things simply came together because I needed to know why I was doing the things I did and what they were contributing to, or how they were critical of, the uses of power in the country that I was contesting more openly in the field. I never thought I was writing a book. In fact, I've never in my career so far set out to write a book and written it. The ones I've set out to write, I haven't written. The ones I've written, I did not intend to write.

**Williams:** Really? What were you planning on writing next?

**Ohmann:** I gave talks and wrote articles about particular questions and eventually I began to see that these could be part of a kind of an overview of our profession. And some time around 1974 I decided that I would turn that into the book. In the material you sent me, you asked a question about writing style, and I think that one of the ways I came to the kind of—we'll say "conversational"—style I now like and try to use is that so much of that writing was addressed to particular moments, crises, occasions, and it came out of a ferment of, well, anger, among other things. I wanted to write with a certain energy, as if there were real people there reading it.

**Williams:** What's the connection with *College English*? You were editor for a time; could you fill in that background? It seems relevant to this question of writing style, since it reaches a larger and more general audience than most other journals except maybe *PMLA*.

**Ohmann:** Oh, absolutely. It probably has about fifteen thousand readers. Well, *College English* was very important to me. I feel it was more important to me, in a sense, than I was to it, though I am proud of what *College English* was during those years. It seems to me now that an editor would have had to be an idiot at that time not to produce an interesting journal—partly because of the ferment that I talked about earlier, and partly because things just came in. We got articles from

Oregon or Arkansas or from a person you'd never heard of that gave the "Gee whiz, Marge, look at this" effect, as an editor of the *National Inquirer* put it. It was exciting. Don Gray, who was the editor after I finished, told me once that he had looked back over a number of the issues during my editorship and thought that material like that just wasn't coming in. Of course, we did do some soliciting and farm out some edited issues so that we were active in cultural production there. But also, we were learning a lot and having our eyes opened. Most of the writing had a certain intensity—not all of it in the conversational voice—but with energies that were not conventionally academic, so I'm sure I learned something from the writing that came in to *College English* at that time, too.

**Williams:** How did you come to be affiliated with it? Was it the interest in teaching?

**Ohmann:** Well, when I was a graduate student and a teaching fellow at Harvard, there were two or three journals around the staff room, the place where the TAs hung out, and one of them was *College English*, and I realized then in the late fifties that in each issue there was usually something that I was interested in, maybe that I could use in my own embryonic teaching efforts, and that it was different from *PMLA* and *JEGP* and so on, and I kind of liked it. So I went to a couple of NCTE meetings, but I was more active in MLA before 1966. *College English* is the journal of the college section of the National Council of Teachers of English; the college section committee picks its editor. They opened up a competition in 1964 when Jim Miller at the University of Chicago was about to end his term, and they asked me if I wanted to apply, and I put in an application and got the job. And then history took it up. I mean, I had a prospectus in *College English* sometime during 1965, and it was, I think, much more oriented toward theorizing everything, theorizing literature, the profession, language, and so on, than it was toward political intervention.

**Williams:** Some of your early stuff—some of the citations I've seen—deals with linguistics.

**Ohmann:** Yes. I did two bodies of work early on. One had to do with stylistics and was grounded especially in transformational grammar, and the other had to do with pragmatics and was grounded in speech act theory, and there was some overlap between the two. I still retain an interest in speech act theory, though I don't practice it very extensively anymore. So those were my interests, and by the time I became editor of *College English*, I was disturbed, as I mentioned earlier, by the seeming juggernaut of professional expansion and the kind of irrationality of some of the practices that were developing—that is, too many books to read and books read only by eight people—which became, if anything, more extreme. But events took their course and *College English* turned out very differently from what I envisioned.

I mentioned that there were guest-edited issues, some of them especially important, including one of the first issues of feminist criticism and critique, about 1970.

**Williams:** Who edited it?

**Ohmann:** Elaine Hedges and Susan McAllester. And there was one that Ira Shor and Dick Wasson edited on Marxist criticism, which was one of the first such issues that came out. Another was an issue in 1974 edited by Louie Crew and Rictor Norton called "The Homosexual Imagination," which was the first issue of a scholarly or professional journal ever on that subject.

**Williams:** Long before Eve Sedgwick . . .

**Ohmann:** Long before Eve Sedgwick. That was the only time that the people to whom I theoretically reported—the College Section Committee—raised objections to anything I was doing in *College English*. They didn't mind the Marxists, the anarchists, the feminists, and so on, but it deeply upset them that the homosexuals were now in *College English*. But they didn't try to fire me.

**Williams:** Really? There was grumbling?

**Ohmann:** Oh, yes. Some people did not want that issue to be there. And now it's twenty years later, and I'm going to chair a session of 4Cs this spring that celebrates the twentieth anniversary of "The Homosexual Imagination" in that issue of *College English*, which is an indication of how things can turn around.

**Williams:** Speaking of changes in the profession, how would you update *English in America* now? Obviously, you talk about some of the same things in *Politics of Letters* and some articles I've seen, but what would be one angle you would take now to update it? Any afterthoughts on it?

**Ohmann:** Well, there would be no simple way to update that book, except by looking back critically upon it and attempting some kind of dialectical interaction with it. There are parts of it that, if it were to be reprinted, would probably just have to be scrapped. But even in some of those portions of it—the last three chapters, for example, where I made distant and conjectural forays into issues of knowledge and power—even those parts were generative for me—things having to do with technology and the environment and the challenges to the biosphere, the particular way that our society had and to an extent still has of generating and deploying knowledge that serves capital and profit. It's just that I wasn't very well equipped to write about those things at that time.

**Williams:** I was wondering when I first read it, because it seems implicitly Marxist in that you work out, for the most part, how English education is an ideological state apparatus . . .

**Ohmann:** That was not available to me as a Marxist critique then. That is, I did not know Althusser, and I hardly knew the Marxist classics. I knew at that time some writing by radical political economists and other radical groups within the U.S. academic professions. Just at the time that *English in America* came out, I was working with study groups, with faculty members and students, to learn Marxism. The kinds of language and concepts that were available to me then had to do with power elites and the power structure and the technostructure, things of that sort. I mean, it turned out, of course, that Marxism tremendously enriched and deepened for me those sorts of perceptions and arguments, but it really joined in afterward. There was another part of that question.

**Williams:** Yes, how would you update it? There are different factors on the scene now, obviously, and there are different contours of multinational capitalism that have been played out.

**Ohmann:** I couldn't, without rebuilding the entire architecture of the book, in the light of what happened later. Incidentally, within two or three years of publishing *English in America,* I had read some things that would have made a big difference had I known them at the time. Braverman's *Monopoly Capital* especially was a crucial text for me in rethinking work. I was reading those books about 1976 or 1977 with study groups, and there was probably nothing more important for me than Braverman in deciding that I was willing to try to be a Marxist. But then, on top of that, of course there have been major changes in the positioning and structure of the professional managerial class . . .

**Williams:** Which wasn't even a phrase at that point . . .

**Ohmann:** No, that wasn't available to me. The Ehrenreich article came out after that. Anyway, there were new structures and processes, and there was also new writing about that class, which would have related if I had had it available. Nonetheless, *English in America* is tentative and hesitant and in some ways rather crude about the way that a certain section of the PMC, mainly people who teach English, work for capital. There's little there beyond saying we teach students to be obedient and punctual and so on . . .

**Williams:** Neat manners and handling memos . . .

**Ohmann:** Right. Those things are really more about how the PMC reproduces itself than they are about how we discipline the proletariat; those things have been theorized better, and I would want to talk about that. I definitely want to talk about the evolution of late capitalism, post-Fordist capitalism, with the help of people like David Harvey, whose book *The Condition of Postmodernity*, when I finally got to it a year and a half ago, helped me think about these things a lot. I sometimes write now about the regime of flexible accumulation and the development of highly mobile forms of capital, credit, and so on, intensely innovative production, with technology, and especially the creative uses of flexible pools of labor all around the world, as characterizing the situation we find ourselves in now. It's remarkable the extent to which, as I've written in an article called "English after the USSR," you could understand some of the things that have been happening in the academic workforce, English especially, as homologous to those developments from Fordism to the regime of flexible accumulation. We were a little laboratory for the use of mobile, exploited, part-time, flextime labor.

**Williams:** All under the optimistic auspices of giving people more opportunities.

**Ohmann:** Absolutely. There's no law that forbids you to teach eight courses a semester at seventeen hundred dollars a course at eight different colleges.

**Williams:** I have a former student who is getting his Ph.D. at the University of Maryland and he teaches three different courses at two local colleges, which I think is horrible. I mean, the profession has abandoned him.

**Ohmann:** It's terrible. Jim Slevin wrote an article about this in *The Politics of Writing Instruction*, which lays out the dismal facts and proposes professional remedies—not exactly unionization, but banding together to fight administrations to end this scandal. I don't think that's easy to do. I don't think it's possible to do without a much more integrated, national, politically savvy organization of academics. The attractions of this kind of work policy to administrations are simply too overwhelming. I've been serving as a consultant to one of the State University of New York colleges for the last three years, and between my first visit there and my second visit there, the seven or eight full-time, non-tenure-track faculty members, who had benefits and decent salaries and who were doing most of the composition work, had disappeared entirely, to be replaced by a group of part-time adjuncts at a salary something like the one that I mentioned, seventeen hundred dollars a course. I'm talking about a very remote place in upstate New York where they've been able to find a phalanx of adjuncts at those salaries to come in and teach. I spoke about this with the dean on my last visit there, and he said that even now this college was not up to the benchmark for the SUNY system, meaning that it didn't have as many adjuncts in relation to tenure-track faculty as the average for the entire system; therefore, it had to do more of this. These are budget-driven decisions, and the ethics of them can easily be adjusted—tempered—by the observation that there are people out there who are willing to do this work. But it's a very serious obstacle to organizing professionally and politically because we do have these increasingly divided groups. Anyhow, it was dumb of me in *English in America* not to have paid attention to the job crisis, which already existed. In fact, the job crisis in English burst upon us in 1969 at the MLA convention in Denver.

**Williams:** It was my understanding that it was much later, in 1975 or so. You mentioned, in a piece that I just saw in *College English*, "Graduate Students, Professionals, Intellectuals," that the situation you came out of was a lot different because jobs were so plentiful.

**Ohmann:** They were plentiful up through 1968, and then our field participated in the tectonic plate shifts that Harvey describes in his book. That is, all those changes that you can mark from about 1970 included, as a very, very minor part, the job crisis in the humanities, especially in English. The 1969 MLA convention was supposed to have been held in Chicago, but because of what happened at the Democratic convention in 1968, a number of organizations were boycotting Chicago, and MLA was persuaded to do that and went to Denver instead. MLA had never met in Denver or such a place before. The Radical Caucus people went out there expecting to carry on inquiry and provocation and disruption in the same ways that we had in 1968 in New York, and to an extent, we did. But suddenly, on the first day of the convention, there was a new organization. It was called the Job-Seekers Caucus. Graduate students who were finishing their Ph.D.'s and had no historical reason to expect that there wouldn't be more jobs, found that there were no job interviews, a lot of jobs had dried up—a situation that has continued for the intervening twenty-four years with small oscillations one way or another.

So that was definitely out there in professional space to be charted. I can't remember whether I even alluded to it in *English in America*, but the general critique that I staged was one of an affluent profession which is able to take advantage of a historical conjuncture to strengthen its own position, and that was true for the tenure-track and tenured people, but meanwhile the peripheral army of the unemployed was being recruited right then in a very big way. I would want to talk about that in an updated edition. I might also mention another consequence for our field: the college in the SUNY system that I alluded to earlier has essentially no one in the English department, except for the very recent hires, who came there after about 1970. In 1970, after expanding for fifteen years from an old normal school into a rather large college, the money began to run out. They participated in the job crisis that began in the sixties, so there were no more additional positions. Most of the people who were hired then got tenure between 1970 and 1975. That, in itself, is a minor problem for English departments all over the country—too many of my generation are occupying the tenured jobs.

**Williams:** I realize that it's a complicated set of factors, but what is the political stake of that pool of unemployed? I mean, is it some sort of deliberate emaciation of intellectuals, or just a function of the job market and post-Fordism?

**Ohmann:** That's such a complicated question; let me just say that there are contradictory forces at work here. One is that because the jobs are so few and the stakes are so high for graduate students and untenured faculty members, there are some pressures to do whatever it is that needs to be done in your particular institution, and that may be a repressive influence, but at the very same time, the little victories of the last twenty-five years are nonetheless victories, and intellectual work of the sort that you and I do now can also claim its own rewards. That is, you can get tenure for being a feminist, a queer theorist, or a Marxist, so I don't think that there's a simple way that the two-class system in our profession is going to play out in terms of intellectual work.

But it's such a hard question to think about politically. You asked me in the questions you sent about what chances there are for political work in the academy; it's very hard for me to think about that question as a labor question. I know that's only part of what you meant, but it seems to me that this sort of dual labor system, which has been developing and strengthening for twenty years or more, is basically in all sectors and all economies. It's worldwide, and the breakup of so-called actually existing socialism is just going to mean further possibilities for maquiladora schemes, and the farming out of labor processes, and places where people are very poor in what used to be the second world, as well as what used to be the third world, and of course many parts of the United States of America. So you can't look at your unfortunate younger colleagues who are adjuncts and exploited graduate students and think of the chances for improving their and all our lives without thinking about the people who are assembling electronic devices in Mexico and the Philippines and so on, about the new knowledge markets of various sorts that have developed all over the world. It's a challenge that far exceeds my powers of analysis, but I am convinced this can't be solved within English as a profession.

**Williams:** What do you think about the prospects for the new university and for the corporatization of the university?

**Ohmann:** Here again, this is an important subject, and it's one that's beyond my grasp at the moment. David Noble, who wrote *America by Design* and some other really important books, is suggesting that the universities essentially are getting out of the education business now.

**Williams:** And what are they in now?

**Ohmann:** Well, contracting more and more. I was talking with an anthropologist at Berkeley, and he told me that about 75 percent of the University of California's budget is money that does not come from the State of California.

**Williams:** It's from grants and contracts?

**Ohmann:** Grants, contracts, federal money, tuition. There are also ways in which knowledge and learning are being packaged and sold entirely outside the university system, so that universities will have to compete with things like IBM, Whittle Communications, Channel 1. Companies are spending more and more on education of their own people, I guess I should say training, that is, retooling employees with the kinds of knowledge that they will need as new technologies get in place. And then the states and municipalities and probably even countries compete to attract capital increasingly by offering a pretrained workforce to companies that will move in. South Carolina did this with BMW—I talk about these things in "English after the USSR." Universities cannot take for granted anymore, really, that they are the main purveyors of knowledge, theoretical or useful, to our society or to the world. Public schools are going to be competing more and more with these other agencies, and I think that the ideal of the university, which was always belied by circumstances but was nonetheless not a bad ideal, will have a harder time flying as an ideology and certainly as a practice in the future.

You asked, and I think rightly so, what were the universities doing before, and you mentioned class reproduction. Yes, they were always doing class reproduction.

**Williams:** Although most people just didn't go to the universities before. I think in Graff's book *Professing Literature* there's a statistic that only something like 2 percent of the population went to university in, say, 1900 to 1920.

**Ohmann:** A little earlier. The PMC established and expanded its class position in connection with the growth of the university—two things that are inseparable—and our class helped make the universities invaluable to the entire economic system. Now, universities are still certainly in the business of class reproduction.

**Williams:** On the other hand, one could see it as providing more possibilities for working-class people to go to a university and be trained for bourgeois life.

**Ohmann:** That happened a lot in the postwar period, and there are millions of students in community colleges and in state colleges now and in the elite colleges who are the first in their families to go to college. The hegemonic process works in part because some of those people do in fact achieve their ambitions and their parents' ambitions. The ideology of equal opportunity would not be so durable an ideology unless there were some truth in it. I think the truth is going to diminish and that the promises being implicitly made to working-class students, that if they work hard in education, they will be able to climb above their parents, are increasingly false promises. This, too, is inseparable from the separating out of the world's workforce into core workers and peripheral and flextime workers. I think that more and more of those working-class students who go to our colleges will find themselves driven toward very job-specific training. And it's also getting harder and harder for them to go to college at all. I don't know the specifics on this, but I bet that more are choosing other ways of moving into the job market now than just a few years ago.

**Williams:** Right, there's been a severe reduction in financial aid programs and things like that.

**Ohmann:** Reduction of financial aid, the increases in cost of public and private institutions, the cutbacks in universities, which are making many students take six years to complete the B.A., partly because the courses that they need to get through their majors aren't there at the right time, partly because they have to keep dropping out to work. It's getting tougher . . .

**Williams:** There's a sweatshirt at my school that says on the back, "ECU, the best five or six years of your life."

**Ohmann:** There you go. I don't think the universities will play quite the role, either, in preserving the porosity of the class structure as they have in the past or sustaining the ideology of equal opportunity as they have. But, on the other hand, they of course will go on, at least for a while, playing several important roles: one is to reproduce the professional managerial class and the bourgeoisie. Even with the exorbitant cost of education at places like Wesleyan, they still, knock on wood, have plenty of applicants who want to come here and are qualified to do it. The colleges and the universities that survive the squeeze of the last decade and the first half of this decade, I think, will still be in a strong position to keep reproducing those two classes. Even with the move toward training, it looks to me as if cultural capital will continue to be valuable, needed, and that students whose parents have money will continue to want to go to places like this, and many students who don't have money will continue to want to try to get financial aid to go to places like this.

**Williams:** It seems to me that there is a greater hierarchization of universities now. You don't hear the rhetoric that you used to, that the state universities, say a Stony Brook, compete with places like Harvard or Yale . . .

**Ohmann:** I think that polarization is going on, though one must remember that the private institutions, with a few exceptions, are under a lot of duress right now, and have experienced some cutbacks and speedups that I think impair the quality of education, but your point is right.

**Williams:** I wanted to ask you about your work with *Radical Teacher*. You publish fairly frequently there, and I know that you're an active member of the group around it. So, what's your connection with it? What does the group do?

**Ohmann:** *Radical Teacher*, well, we call it a socialist/feminist news journal, and that's accurate except for the inappropriateness of the term "news journal" for a magazine that comes out irregularly. It came out of the Radical Caucus in the Modern Language Association after five or six years when Radical Caucus was quite active inside MLA politics and intellectual activities.

**Williams:** About when was that?

**Ohmann:** That was 1975. I think a particular concern of the people who started the magazine was that there was a risk that the move toward High Theory, including high Marxism, might deny teaching the critical scrutiny that it needed. Somebody needed to be looking at teaching as its own political activity or arena, and that was our particular aim—to think about the politics of teaching itself, pedagogy along with the politics of institutions and professions and the politics of knowledge. The magazine has always had a kind of a pragmatic urgency about it—that you can meet your classes three times a week and things go on there, those things are important, and there are ways to do them more or less effectively.

**Williams:** It seems to me that the focus on teaching distinguishes your work from other well-known Marxist theorists, and it also implicitly answers the question what is to be done. And the style that you write in—maybe we can talk about this in a few minutes—uses more ordinary language, in the way Orwell prescribes in "Politics and the English Language," than most theorists.

**Ohmann:** There have been times in the last thirty-five years when Radical Caucus people have stood in some antagonism to Marxist literary criticism because of these kinds of issues, about how theoretical are they going to be and how practical are they going to be and to what extent are those two things in some sort of jarring relationship to each other. But I don't want to leave the impression that I align myself with "what do we do Monday morning" in opposition to theory, and I have strong theoretical interests of my own.

**Williams:** There's an essay in *The Politics of Letters*—I think it's called "Teaching as a Theoretical Practice"—where you talk about a course and cite a handout that you pass out. You talk very specifically about ideology and Marxist theory, as well as how they bear on the works of literature in the course.

**Ohmann:** Exactly. I've mentioned some theorists today that have been important to me, and I'd certainly add Fred Jameson to that list. Fred said to me once when we were talking about this exact matter, that he had always assumed that there would be a certain division of labor on these matters, and I agreed. I don't want to align myself with the . . .

**Williams:** The antitheory crowd?

**Ohmann:** Right, or the pragmatic get-out-in-the-streets-and-put-up-the-barricades kind of people over against the theorists. That antagonism is sometimes real enough and worth sharpening, but I don't believe that we all have to be one sort or the other.

**Williams:** That's sometimes the knee-jerk response. How do you find Jameson useful?

**Ohmann:** Well, in so many ways. I want and need the drive toward both master narratives and utopian visions. When I read him, I often find that I labor pretty hard and I've read two or three pages without much payoff, and then the lightbulb comes on. You know, I think that if you get one idea every three pages, that's a reward for the effort. The first chapter of *The Political Unconscious* is very important in thinking about some of the things we've talked of earlier today, as well as some of the writing I'm doing myself. The article that Fred did on third world literature as allegory is a valuable provocation, probably 80 percent wrong, as Aijaz Ahmad and others have argued, but still, he has to say those things in order for those debates to take place. Or, of course, "The Cultural Logic of Late Capitalism," which I had a serious criticism of, but he put those things out and initiated debates. He's done that time and again over the years, and he is willing to be wrong. I think that's great.

What I get from him are fresh and productive ideas. If you look back on something that you read or were fond of that you wrote fifteen years ago, you wouldn't want to say, "Well, I really settled that argument," so much as to say, "Well, I can see I was wrong in a lot of ways, but you know, I joined in and intervened in the process of critique, and that article or that book can now be thrown in the dustbin of history and I won't feel sorry about it at all." One of the little conventions of our profession that is personally irritating to me, though I probably do it to others, is the use of the present tense—"Ohmann says," "Jameson says"—and it's something that you wrote in 1975. Well, I don't say that now, you know. I said that, and it was sort of right and sort of wrong, and we've moved way beyond that.

**Williams:** To take up the question of style, it seems to me that criticism has circled back from High Theory—Jameson, for instance—to more publicly accessible criticism—as in Michael Bérubé's work. I see this change in writing as salutary in some ways, although I'm skeptical of it, too. Anyway, what do you think of it as far as your writing is concerned, and also about it as a general trend?

**Ohmann:** Well, you have to think very seriously about a bunch of issues when you raise this question. One is about who reads, and that sounds obvious, but there are contradictory forces here, too. The entire professional managerial class and many other working-class people are now positioned to read and be interested in serious but accessible and energetic writings about a variety of subjects, and that's a huge audience. On the other hand, it's an audience that doesn't, in fact, read a whole lot. Probably less in the U.S. than any of the other advanced countries. And although the *Voice* plays a dynamic part in the intellectual life of our metropolis, it's important to remember that just writing reader-friendly prose will not mean that your work gets read in McDonald's or at factories at lunchtime, and so on. And if anybody's serious about that, then they've got to turn to other media; even to reach some of the more general print channels for us is not all that easy.

One of the essays in *Politics of Letters*—the one on television and the sterilization of politics—came out of an effort on my part to try to push through the professional borders. I gave that, initially, as an improvised lecture the morning after election day, 1976. I had a class then, and I watched the evening news the night before, and I got some notes together and talked about it with a class of people who would have watched it, and then I gave it as a talk someplace later. I tried it out on the *Atlantic*. Then I sent it to *Mother Jones*, but they didn't want it either. They wanted more journalistic writing. They didn't want to hear about hegemony. It's not a great piece, but I'm telling this story just to suggest that writing in a lucid and lively way is not necessarily going to get you into *TV Guide*, though Barbara Ehrenreich has been in *TV Guide*.

**Williams:** Jameson certainly doesn't write that way.

**Ohmann:** No, I wish that he wrote a little more accessibly. Anyway, what I would insist on is that questions of writing never be detached from questions of social relations. You won't get very far about public voices and broad audiences and accessible writing without thinking very precisely about who writes, who reads, at what sites, under what circumstances, when there are times that perhaps intellectuals can answer a need beyond our own circle. It's more a question of being able and ready to write in such a way or to talk or make videos in such a way when circumstances present themselves.

**Williams:** I see what you mean. Even a hero like Orwell was speaking to a limited public. In the *College English* piece that I mentioned before, you talk about how critical thought spills over from the university. How does that spilling go on?

**Ohmann:** Well, many people in universities are involved in organizations and activities that are not university-based, so they carry ideas with them and come into some kind of contact with people who are not university members—that's obvious, but of course the spilling does go in both directions, like a tidal flow.

**Williams:** I like the analogy. One question I wanted to ask you, apropos your *minnesota review* essay on PC, where you say that, "we're feminists; we're socialists; some of us are Leninists, not all of us; some of us. . . ." That's a line I try to remember when people ask me what exactly I am. It seems to me that you have a sense of coalition on the Left, and you're certainly not doctrinaire, so how do you see the Left?

**Ohmann:** Um, coalitions . . . they can be very important to rebuilding Left politics in the U.S. The self-conception of the Left needs to be flexible, and I think we need to be open to thrusts and ventures in various directions, all the way from the New Party to whatever vanguard party starts up next, but you won't find me joining the vanguard party. In some ways, it's rather grand to be talking about the Left as if it were a capital "L" and to be agonizing over which strategic turn would be just the right one for this moment. And it's clearly a moment of disarray, of regrouping, I hope, rethinking, reflecting on what did happen, the end of socialism and why, trying to understand what is salvageable from that historical project, if anything. I think we ought to have more of an open-mindedness and candor and admission of ignorance of a lot of these things. The world is not in great shape; certainly the Left is not in great shape. I've seen some good theory about the things we discussed earlier—the movement past Fordism—but I don't think I've seen very many political practices out there that respond to that. I don't have very much to suggest of my own here. I wouldn't mind if we all said, "All right, let's stop talking about socialism, and let's talk about democracy and equality."

**Williams:** Kind of what Rorty would do?

**Ohmann:** I wouldn't do it that way, but I would say, if it would somehow make a difference to fly the banners of equality, including gender equality, racial equality, equality of persons of all sorts, and the banner of democracy, which, needless to say, has never been tried anyplace in the world, then sure, I would say let's do it. I don't think it's going to work that way. I think we have to continue a critique of the bourgeois ideals, the Enlightenment ideals of equality and democracy, even while defending them. Half of the world's population, a billion and a half, earn one dollar a day or less now, and that is comparable to situations in Europe two hundred years ago, but of course far, far, far worse because at that time, so much was outside the market economy. In other words, the world's people are worse off now than they have been probably any time in the history of the whole human race, and a lot of people like you and me are better off than anybody but kings and princes two hundred years ago. There always is crisis, but it seems to me, toward the end of the twentieth century, the crisis is pretty grave and it's global, and it not only covers starvation and epidemics, but the destruction of species and the threats to air and water and earth. And without being too dramatic or apocalyptic about this, these questions should always be somewhere in the margins of political arguments of all sorts, even arguments about how we teach in our classrooms. We shouldn't be carrying on arguments about organizing or pedagogies of composition without keeping in mind that we are in a very strange and very threatening historical time.

**Williams:** As a closing question, I wanted to ask what you're working on. You had mentioned that you're finishing up a book. And I'm also curious to find out which books you haven't finished or had wished you had done, that you mentioned before.

**Ohmann:** Well, I never wrote the one on stylistics. I was going to settle for good the question of form and content, but unfortunately the world will have to wait for my reincarnation to solve the problem of form and content. And then I was going to do a book on the culture industries, which was going to take off from some of the things that are in *Politics of Letters*, and I was going to theorize mass culture, or popular culture, which are basically the same, in the Gramscian mode. That book will never get written either, thank heaven. That would have been a terrible book! What I am doing now is something that I intended to be just one chapter of or essay in that never-to-be-written book, on the genesis of the mass-circulation magazine and the advertising industry. That carried me away and turned me in a different direction. Once the institutions and practices of a national mass culture are established, the situation is quite different from the moment when they are being created. Just for example, there are thousands of studies that say advertising in general doesn't make very much difference—that you have to do it if your company is efficient and have to do it to sell your product, but that it doesn't really make very much difference in total demand or in the demand for particular products. But at one time there was no image-filled, complexly interpellating, nationally circulated advertising, and when that all happened within a decade or so, it made a hell of a difference. Dozens of products like Ivory Soap built major corporations at the time when advertising became a major force. So I'm trying to understand how, in a moment of rapid change in the U.S. in the 1890s, processes that later have become routine were inaugurated. What were the conditions of possibility for those processes then? Who were the multiple agents who, seeking aims of their own, managed an unintentional collaboration with themselves and the culture industry and with the bourgeoisie so that the hegemonic process was redrawn and redirected on a different plane from where it had been before? I hope to make a contribution to thinking about hegemony, as well as about culture and cultural process.

**Williams:** Where are you at with it?

**Ohmann:** Well, it's close to the end. When I had to stop writing last summer, I was in the middle of a penultimate chapter, so probably another summer's work to do or more. It's probably about 550 pages of manuscript. This has gotten to be a kind of fascination and maybe an obsession—I never thought that I would be writing thirty pages on changes in the conception and use of the parlor in the late nineteenth century. There's all kinds of little byways that I've been carried into, and I've learned a lot. We'll see if I can put it together as part of a master narrative or not.

Is that work important enough to be done? Yes, I do think that cultural studies—the kind I like—is important, and its potential for reorganizing some of the intellectual work in the academy—making it more political as well as seriously interdisciplinary—is great. The chances of that not happening are also great because of the imperatives and dynamics we all know about professionalism and many of the eccentricities of university finances now, the things that we talked about earlier today—so I consider the question of cultural studies an open question. In the past, the question of pedagogy has been woefully underconsidered in cultural studies, but when something new comes along, most of the payoff is in the teaching.

# 5

# Between Generations

## *An Interview with Morris Dickstein*

The New York Intellectuals, such as Lionel Trilling and Irving Howe, are often taken as exemplars of the public intellectual, in their own day featured in a cover story of *Time* magazine (1956) and now accorded almost legendary status in accounts such as Russell Jacoby's *The Last Intellectuals* (1987). Clustered around the journal *Partisan Review*, they brought to center stage the then-new art and literature of modernism alongside the thought of Freud, Marx, and other social thinkers. They also criticized mass culture, or "masscult" in the phrase of Dwight Macdonald, which they saw as a degraded form of art and a vehicle of social control. Whether or not one agrees with this position, they represent a significant vein of American criticism, one that stressed, in contrast to the New Critical emphasis on internal form, the connection of art and culture with society.

A lifelong New Yorker, onetime student of Trilling, and sometime contributor to *Partisan Review*, Morris Dickstein is an heir of the New York Intellectuals. But, as he recounts here, he stands between generations, of those New York Intellectuals who came of age in the 1930s and of those critics who came of age in the 1960s and 1970s. While he steps away form his forebears' disdain for popular culture and for the foment of the sixties, he also diverges from the postsixties absorption in theory that sometimes promised a "politics by other means." Like Gerald Graff (interviewed in chapter 3), Dickstein has consistently advocated—and practiced—a socially relevant and publicly accessible criticism.

Born on the Lower East Side of New York in 1940, Dickstein attended college at Columbia University, where he studied with Trilling and received his B.A. in 1961. He went to graduate school a train ride away, at Yale (M.A., 1963; Ph.D. 1967), studying with Harold Bloom, among others, and taking a year off to travel to Cambridge University on a Columbia University Kellett Fellowship (1963–64). In 1966 he returned to Columbia to teach, where he found himself amid growing campus unrest and joined antiwar protests, including the 1967 march on the Pentagon. In 1971 he moved to Queens College and the Graduate Center of CUNY, where he became a Distinguished Professor of English and founded its Center for the Humanities, serving as its director from 1993 to 2000.

Trained as a Romanticist, Dickstein wrote his first book on *Keats and His Poetry: A Study in Development* (U of Chicago P, 1971), which drew from his dissertation. He launched onto the larger literary scene with his second book, *Gates of Eden: American Culture in the Sixties* (Basic, 1977), which was nominated for a National Book Critics Circle Award. Combining literary readings, cultural history, and personal reminiscence, it is an important, early assessment of the sixties. His next book, *Double Agent: The Critic and Society* (Oxford UP, 1992), turns to examine the state of contemporary criticism, criticizing its overprofessionalization and calling for renewed connection with social concerns. His most recent book, *Leopards in the Temple: The Transfomation of American Fiction, 1945–1970* (Harvard UP, 2002), returns to some of the ground of *Gates of Eden* and expands his entry, "Fiction and Society, 1930–1970" in *The Cambridge History of American Literature*, Vol. 7 (1999). It surveys the flourishing of midcentrury writers from Mailer, Kerouac, and Ellison to Updike and Roth. In addition, Dickstein has edited *Great Film Directors: A Critical Anthology* (with Leo Braudy; Oxford UP, 1978) and *The Revival of Pragmatism: New Essays on Social Thought, Law, and Culture* (Duke UP, 1998). Keeping one foot in the academic realm and one foot in the public, Dickstein has also regularly written journalism for venues such as the *New York Times Book Review*, *TLS*, *Dissent*, and the *Nation*.

This interview took place in Morris Dickstein's office at CUNY's Graduate Center on 12 June 2002. It was conducted and transcribed by Robert S. Boynton, a literary journalist and a professor in NYU's School of Journalism. It originally appeared in an issue of the *minnesota review* on "Fifties Culture."

**Boynton:** In *Gates of Eden* you write about coming to consciousness between the fifties and the sixties and claim that you never felt wholly comfortable in either world, "though both were passionately important to me in their turn." What do you mean by this?

**Dickstein:** One of the most exciting things about the fifties was its exploding intellectual culture, and in many ways I felt that I was a child of that culture. At the same time, during the period I was a student at Columbia, which was between 1957 and 1961, my friends and I felt we were in rebellion against that culture. The books that we adopted as special for us were by writers like Norman O. Brown, Herbert Marcuse, Paul Goodman, Norman Mailer. In fact, in my last semester at Columbia we had a lecture series and invited all of them to come. Only Goodman actually came. A few years ago, when I was introducing Mailer at a reading, I was looking over some of his early novels, and a letter from March 1961 dropped out of one of them in which he explained why he couldn't make it.

**Boynton:** What was the goal behind assembling these figures?

**Dickstein:** We had fallen in love with the idea of the "guru," the wise mentor. A friend of mine once ran into Lionel Trilling on the Columbia campus, and Trilling had never heard the word before. He said, "Oh, I *love* that idea. I should use it sometime." And of course he did.

Some of the figures who came to interest me later, like the social critics of the fifties—David Riesman, William Whyte—they were too tepid and liberal for us at the time, and too popular. What fascinated us were the more *apocalyptic* figures who came on the scene in the mid-fifties, roughly around the time of Marcuse's *Eros and Civilization*, although I hadn't read it at the time. I was especially taken with Mailer's "The White Negro" and most of *Advertisements for Myself*. Norman O. Brown's *Life against Death* was practically a sacred text to us when it came out in 1960. I seemed to be out to confirm its message in the papers I was writing for my English courses. I was twenty years old. I sought out writers who would tell me that repression was bad for you, sex was redemptive, a revolution in consciousness was possible. We were looking for daring iconoclastic role models, outlaw intellectuals.

Of course, we were also getting a mainstream education in the Western tradition. We were the products of the Great Books curriculum at Columbia, which was not just a literary curriculum, but also involved contemporary civilization—the history of social thought, philosophy, economics, politics. Unlike the University of Chicago's

Great Books curriculum, Columbia's was organized chronologically. It had a very strong historical dimension. So although we were formed by the Great Books culture of the fifties, we had a kind of historicist take on it that really foreshadowed some of the political interests we developed in the sixties.

At the time I felt like a rebel. I loved Blake and D. H. Lawrence. But in retrospect I realized that I had been on the cusp between two periods. The curious thing is that many years later, when I came to work on *Leopards in the Temple*, I realized that the two periods were not as sharply distinct as I had thought, and much that I associated with the late fifties and the sixties had really begun right after the war. It was a long time before I understood that a harmless-looking book like, say, *The Catcher in the Rye* anticipated the counterculture of the sixties.

**Boynton:** I have to say that I'm a little surprised that you were so enamored of these apocalyptic figures. I've always thought of your criticism as being so tempered and judicious. At one point in *Gates of Eden* you quote Trilling as saying that "all criticism is autobiographical." Do you think this is true for you?

**Dickstein:** In retrospect, I came to see the extent to which things I had taken for granted, like the postwar prosperity, were really decisive. The social forces that determined the sixties explosion, both intellectually and in the streets, were a product of the tremendous economic advances that took place after the war. Writers who seemed like rebels against affluence, like Kerouac, were actually playing off the economic expansion: they had an expansive, Whitmanesque mood that, in a curious way, reflected the expansiveness of the life of the middle class.

I've been working on a book about the 1930s along the lines of *Gates of Eden* and *Leopards in the Temple*. One of the themes in the book is the contrast between stasis and mobility. A key to the culture of the thirties was the dream of flow and movement, that can be seen in things as different as art deco and Fred Astaire. But of course the only real *movement* you got socially during this period was the movement of people like drifters and homeless people, people riding freight cars, not exactly voluntary movement. There was no movement between generations because the birthrate was low. And even the great black migration from the South really slowed down in the thirties because there were no jobs to be had.

It all comes to a head at the 1939 World's Fair in the General Motors "Futurama," where you had these predictions about a car culture that seemed like a pipe dream at the time. The "Futurama" was set in the year 1960, and it anticipated that there would be thirty-eight million cars on the road by the time. That was considered sheer fantasy. But when the year 1960 *did* roll around, there were *sixty-one million cars* on the road! The postwar period enacted and lived out the dream of mobility that had been part of the fantasy culture of the 1930s.

The mobility began with the war, because it pulled people out of their small towns, cities, and ghettos. There was a tremendous migration of rural folk to places where there were jobs in war industries. People who had never left home were now sent off to Europe and Asia. It gave a tremendous impetus to the Civil Rights movement, because even soldiers who had fought in the segregated army were not willing to go back to a racist, segregated country after having fought for it—especially having fought against the racism of the Germans and the Japanese. Even though much of the Civil Rights movement was sub rosa in the forties and fifties, historians now understand that there was an almost perfect continuity between the agitation of Philip Randolph, who got Roosevelt to issue an order desegregating the defense industry in the early forties, and the work of someone like Ralph Ellison. Ellison began work on *Invisible Man* toward the end of the war with the idea of writing a novel about the leadership problem, and although there is very little in the novel directly about the Civil Rights movement (except the activities of the Brotherhood), the book is part of that same restless rethinking of race after the war.

Once you've seen this, the ostensible "quiescence" and conservatism of the postwar period really has to be strongly qualified. This includes women, who were the people who did worst, and were indeed the victims of the reactionary social vision of the forties and fifties. But the myth of "Rosie the Riveter" being forced out of her job and back to the suburbs when the boys came back from the war is simply that: a myth. It isn't borne out by historical research. Instead, there was a very brief downturn of women working outside the home at the end of the war, numbers which very quickly turned upward again, and the percentage of women working outside of the home actually *doubled* between 1940 and 1960. And that was probably because the social mobility of young couples after the war had to be funded by two incomes. So the movement to the suburbs, where veterans bought their own homes, was partly funded by the wife working outside the home. Of course they didn't have many professional jobs. But on the other hand it was a momentous change.

**Boynton:** Tell me about your background.

**Dickstein:** I grew up in the Americanized end of an immigrant family. Both my mother and father were the next-youngest siblings of very large families. Their oldest brothers and sisters, who were very domineering, had come here in their twenties, and their culture was formed in Europe. They spoke Yiddish primarily. My parents came when they were much younger and had a high school education like my mother, or had a high school education from reading the *New York Times* every day, like my father. They were much more Americanized and spoke Yiddish only when they had something to say that the children weren't supposed to understand.

**Boynton:** Where did you grow up?

**Dickstein:** On New York's Lower East Side, on Henry Street, which was around the corner from the old Jewish *Daily Forward* and the famous Garden Cafeteria where I. B. Singer hung out. This was supposedly the Lower East Side way past its heyday, but when I later read Irving Howe's *World of Our Fathers* and Ronald Sanders's *Downtown Jews,* I could still recognize the Lower East Side culture that they were describing from the tens and twenties.

**Boynton:** But unlike the famous New York intellectuals you didn't go on to City College, you went to Columbia, which was practically unthinkable for them.

**Dickstein:** I was different in another way, too. I went to a yeshiva for twelve years, so I had a very strong, somewhat sequestered religious education. It wasn't only that I knew more about Judaism than they did, but it meant a lot more to me. Their religion had been socialism, whereas my religion, at least initially, had been Orthodox Judaism.

The other difference was that by the time I was in college, ethnicity was beginning to be *in*. It wasn't yet the time of "identity politics," but ethnicity was no longer something you hid from. One of my beefs with the older intellectuals was their unwillingness to grapple with the fact that they were Jewish. Kazin was a major exception, as was Howe when he began to work on Yiddish literature in the 1950s. But the people I encountered most closely, like Trilling, seemed to be imitation Anglo-Saxons, utterly alienated from their Jewish backgrounds. The whole Columbia scene had a Waspy air, though it was honeycombed with Jews.

**Boynton:** Was it difficult going from a yeshiva to Columbia? Wasn't that what Norman Podhoretz did when he went to Columbia ten years before you did?

**Dickstein:** I don't think Podhoretz went to a yeshiva high school before Columbia, but he did attend the same program at the JTS, the Jewish Theological Seminary, that people like Robert Alter and I later did.

**Boynton:** What was the purpose of attending both Columbia and JTS?

**Dickstein:** JTS was primarily to train rabbis and cantors. But they also had a full program that was built around the schedule of a student who was attending another school. So going to classes there one afternoon and two evenings a week, you could do a degree program in Hebrew studies, including Bible, Jewish history, and Hebrew language.

The seminary was a very secular, scholarly institution at the time. The idea that Gershom Scholem twenty years earlier had given his lectures on Jewish mysticism at the seminary is an astounding thing, though his approach is detached and completely analytical. Except for Abraham Joshua Heschel, the theologian, who has a Hasidic background, they were severe rationalists who had no truck with that side of Jewish culture. It is only recently that they have professorships in such old-world subjects as Yiddish literature. The seminary was an offshoot of the Haskalah, or Hebrew enlightenment, a part of the revival of Hebraic and Zionist culture that preceded the establishment of Israel.

**Boynton:** Did you go there intending to be a rabbi or cantor?

**Dickstein:** No, my intention was really to modernize the Hebrew education I had already had at the yeshiva. I wanted to update the rather old-fashioned education I'd had by learning more about modern Hebrew, biblical scholarship, and Jewish philosophy.

**Boynton:** In *Gates of Eden* you describe attending a reading of Ginsberg's *Kaddish* on a Friday night on the Lower East Side. You write, "For the first time I knew that poetry meant more to me than faith or ritual." Was this your religious crisis?

**Dickstein:** Oddly enough, being at JTS didn't involve any religious commitment. I was still keeping kosher, and did so for many years after that. I didn't *strictly* observe the Sabbath. I was gradually moving away from Orthodox Judaism. It's probably significant that I was taking the secular option by allying myself with someone who in many ways had Hebraic and messianic roots: Ginsberg. It used to drive him crazy when I wrote pieces about him that kept bringing him back to his Jewish origins. He once told me, "You have to come out to Naropa and study Buddhism. I'll show you what my real background is."

I did the Seminary program for three and a half years, but dropped out during my final semester at Columbia, when I wasn't doing any work there either! But while I was at JTS I studied with all the greats on their faculty. I studied with Heschel, Halkin, Muffs, and others. But I avoided any study of the Talmud, to which I'd already been overexposed.

**Boynton:** Why is it that you write so much about Trilling and others at Columbia, but so little about your teachers from JTS?

**Dickstein:** Because that was where I was *going*. These secular intellectuals had the most impact on me. The people I studied with at JTS were world-class scholars but not cutting-edge intellectuals in the ways that mattered to me at the time. They represented an updating of my past rather than the future I wanted to pursue. Besides, I didn't work that hard at it. It's only recently that I've picked up some of the threads from that period, by teaching courses on the literature of the Bible, for example, or lecturing on Jewish writers.

**Boynton:** How did Columbia fit into that future?

**Dickstein:** I had loved reading since grade school, but I had never heard of anything like a literary critic, and couldn't imagine that someone would actually pay you for doing that. So well into college I thought I'd become a journalist or perhaps a lawyer. It was only in my sophomore year in college that it dawned on me that I could continue doing what I had been doing as a student, reading and writing.

**Boynton:** Did any books in particular help move you toward this epiphany?

**Dickstein:** At the end of my sophomore year I read Jacques Barzun's *Teacher in America*, which explained the profession to me, and Trilling's *The Liberal Imagination*, which introduced me to literary criticism as an art and a calling.

**Boynton:** In your essays you often mention the impact that reading *The Liberal Imagination* had on you. What so drew you to it?

**Dickstein:** As much as anything it was the *style* of the book. Those essays were so seductive and beautifully written. Trilling found a way to write a critical essay that was itself a work of literature, but also a piece of writing that enabled you to track what seemed like Trilling's actual process of mind, the way a critic really thought about a book and worked those ideas through. Whether the essays actually followed

Trilling's sequence of thinking, or whether this was a carefully crafted illusion, I didn't know.

The other feature that attracted me was its political dimension. I had always been fascinated by politics and social history. I remember sitting up with my father to listen to the election returns in 1948. The fact that Trilling was able to pull together literature and politics appealed to me a great deal.

**Boynton:** I can see how it must have been inspirational to have a model like Trilling, but it must also have been quite daunting.

**Dickstein:** Yes, especially because he was a rather elevated figure. Almost the only classes he taught were graduate courses, which he didn't like, or large lecture courses, in which he was very remote.

One exception was a very interesting experimental seminar he taught jointly with Daniel Bell and Steven Marcus on the Victorian era in my last semester. As a class it didn't really jell or come off well. The instructors were on different wavelengths. But the theory behind the seminar was that by studying a period using documents, historical and cultural material, and literature especially, you could get between the lines of an era to what they called the "moral temper" of the times. I thought this was somewhat interesting. It wasn't until twenty or thirty years later that I understood what an enormous impact the seminar had on me. After writing *Gates of Eden*, I realized I was attempting to capture the moral temper of the sixties in much the same way Trilling, Bell, and Marcus had tried to do with Victorian England in that seminar.

**Boynton:** Did you go directly from Columbia to graduate school?

**Dickstein:** I went from Columbia to Yale, where I stayed for two years. I had no idea what I was doing when I went to Yale. I had been warned that those who went to Columbia as undergraduates should not go on to graduate school there, for it was large and impersonal. I applied to Harvard, Yale, and Berkeley, but I had no idea who was teaching at any of them. I wasn't au courant with academic scholarship.

Most of my papers in college had been close readings in the style of the New Criticism. I had found I was good at that. I loved taking texts apart, seeing what made them tick. At some point I had discovered Cleanth Brooks's *The Well Wrought Urn*, and it became an alternative model of literary criticism for me. It was the kind of thing Trilling seldom did. On my first day at Yale there was an orientation session for new students; it had a program that featured Cleanth

Brooks. But unfortunately, it was the Christian side of Brooks that was on display. He said, "I have read and I have known some of the great writers of our time, and as a *Christian*, I can say that they give me no reason for doubt." But since doubt had been the basis of my entire undergraduate education, my intention of studying with Brooks ended that very moment.

I was at Yale on a Danforth Fellowship, which was from a religiously oriented foundation. I got it in part because one of my seminary professors had written me a strong recommendation. For many decades, they had given one hundred fellowships a year to Protestant gentlemen. But starting in 1957 they varied it to give ninety-seven to Protestants, two to Catholics, and one to a Jew. (Robert Alter had been that first Jew.) So even though I was there on a vaguely religious fellowship, my own approach by this point was resolutely secular.

**Boynton:** So I guess you didn't study with Cleanth Brooks.

**Dickstein:** No. At a Danforth Fellows orientation in the Midwest, just before school started, some older Yale English grad students told me that I shouldn't study with anyone I'd ever heard of, like Brooks, but should instead study with professors I'd *never* heard of, like R. W. B. Lewis, Martin Price, Charles Feidelson, and a couple of others. This excellent advice made me far less unhappy than my fellow graduate students.

**Boynton:** How did you end up writing your dissertation on Keats?

**Dickstein:** After my second year at Yale I got a Kellett Research Fellowship from Columbia to study at Clare College, Cambridge. During my year there I gravitated to the people who were most like American intellectuals, and in fact most like Trilling. My supervisor was Raymond Williams, whom Trilling introduced to America when he got Columbia University Press to publish *Culture and Society* and *The Long Revolution*. And, even though he had retired a year or two earlier, F. R. Leavis was giving an undergraduate tutorial in my residential college, which he gave me permission to audit. It was essentially a course on how to read. This was easily the highlight of my year there.

That year I planned a thesis with Williams about Victorian cultural criticism. It was going to be about Carlyle and his influence on Ruskin and Arnold and William Morris, how the very idea of culture led to a different kind of criticism from, say, utilitarian social criticism or purely aesthetic criticism. It was a study in the origins of cultural criticism, the prehistory of the kind of thing that Trilling did in his essay on the Kinsey Report, or in his book on Matthew Arnold, which meshed criticism with biography and social history. When I got back to Yale I was told that this was much too ambitious, and that the English faculty would never countenance a joint dissertation on Carlyle, Ruskin, and Arnold. So I gave up on that and had to look around for a new topic.

Two of the favorite papers I had written as a student were an essay on Keats for Steven Marcus at Columbia, and another Keats paper I had written for Fred Pottle's Romantics course at Yale. Harold Bloom had gotten tenure the year I was at Cambridge, and I showed him the Keats essays. He told me that if I reworked the papers and focused on Keats's early work, which critics tended to ignore, I'd have a thesis. It was a great subject and I never regretted it for a moment. I never got tired of Keats. I'll be teaching Wordsworth and Keats again this fall, so the wheel comes full circle. With their emotional weight and high moral intensity, the Romantics probably speak to something left of the religious sensibility in me.

**Boynton:** While in graduate school, did you feel you were preparing to become a literary critic in the mold of Trilling?

**Dickstein:** No, like most young writers, I wanted to give birth to myself, to shake off all influence, period. The only direct link was the desire to write for an audience broader than an academic audience, and a set of interests that were fairly wide-ranging. I had published a piece on Chekhov in an early issue of *Salmagundi.* I had published a few reviews in *Partisan Review.* One was a review of Geoffrey Hartman's book on Wordsworth; another was a wicked little piece on Saul Bellow. Although I didn't know it at the time, the Bellow article caused a split at *Partisan Review* and led him to break with the magazine, which had published all his early work. The essay was a rejoinder to a cranky talk Bellow had given at PEN. It sounded like one of Herzog's slightly demented, complaining letters. I had loved the novel and I used it against him, and some of the *Partisan Review* editors used *me* to take him down a peg or two.

**Boynton:** How did such a young academic get into *Partisan Review*?

**Dickstein:** I wasn't even an academic yet. I published my first piece there in my first year in graduate school. I had taken two courses with Steven Marcus, and he had recently become an editor at *Partisan Review.* It was he who wrote to me at Yale to invite me to review a book for them. I had published a senior paper I had done on Rousseau in

*Yale French Studies*, and I must have sent a copy to Steven. So he saw that I could not only write course papers but could write intelligibly for publication.

**Boynton:** What was it like returning to Columbia for your first teaching job?

**Dickstein:** It was very exciting. The students were terrific. We were entering a period of turmoil at Columbia that distilled what was happening in the country at large. Perhaps not yet 1968, but it was 1966, and we were getting there. Politics was our daily bread. It was also thrilling to teach the humanities curriculum that had meant so much to me when I was a student. I hadn't understood that much of it as a seventeen-year-old freshman, so it was as if I were reading the basic works, the landmarks of Western culture, for the first time. This was a tremendous adventure.

One of the disabling things about the Columbia curriculum was that it encouraged an affinity only for the *greatest* texts. Later on, when I gravitated toward American literature–where there is very little that is up there in the pantheon with Cervantes and Rabelais—it went against those earlier instincts, which told me—wrongly!—that America had produced only a minor, provincial literature, in short, that you don't waste your time on anything but the greatest, most seminal works.

**Boynton:** But other than Keats, you've spent your whole career writing about literature—American or otherwise—that would not be judged as great according to this criterion. How did you make the transition?

**Dickstein:** In part because I soon came to see literature as part of an ongoing social or cultural history. Also, around the same time, I started reviewing books, for the most part contemporary books, which were by definition hit-or-miss. The second book I reviewed for *Partisan Review* was a collection of stories by Ivan Gold, who had also been a student of Trilling's. I felt that no matter what your area of scholarly expertise, you should also keep up with contemporary literature, because that was *your* culture, part of the experience of your own age. Decades earlier, while Trilling was teaching Victorian literature, he was writing about James Agee! Although I wasn't conscious of it, that must have been some kind of model for me. And the fact that I was writing about modern literature but was also strongly drawn to the Romantic writers also had to be influenced by Trilling and Marcus, who had both done the same.

**Boynton:** Still, it's a long way from reviewing books for *Partisan Review* to becoming the kind of cultural critic you've fashioned yourself into. How did that happen?

**Dickstein:** In 1968, ten years after I heard Ginsberg read *Kaddish,* he came back to Columbia to read poems that would eventually be published in *Planet News,* which collected his work from the 1960s. I was very taken with them. I had an idea of doing a piece about Ginsberg for *Commentary,* but I didn't want to do it strictly as a literary essay. Instead, I saw all the currents of the sixties flowing through Ginsberg. So I used the poetry as an occasion to talk about the differences between the fifties and the sixties: how the new young novelists, like Pynchon and Heller, were different from the fifties novelists, such as Bellow and Malamud. There was an implied history, a great deal about cultural rather than literary matters. I showed the piece to a book editor I had known at Columbia (Erwin Glikes, who was then at Basic Books), and he thought it could be expanded into a book on the sixties. As an editor Erwin was a great midwife, wonderful at conceiving how a book could be done. I did an outline of nine chapters. And that was *Gates of Eden.*

**Boynton:** You've told me that you are reluctant to write autobiographically, but there is a fairly strong sense of autobiography throughout that book.

**Dickstein:** I felt that I had not just textual but personal experience to bring to bear, not just experiences with protest demonstrations, rock concerts, and pot-smoking sessions but with the elusive inner life of the period. So it ended up being a kind of hybrid that was part criticism, part cultural history, with some autobiography. I wrote about the mentors who had attracted me in college, the prophets of liberation who later presided over the decade. The book took me a couple of years longer than I thought it would. Part of this was because I had trouble sitting down to write the last chapter, which was the most autobiographical. A friend of mine later told me that it was Trilling's death in 1975 that enabled me to write the final chapter. It must have freed me from the surveillance of an intellectual superego.

**Boynton:** You seem to be one of many critics and students who have been haunted by Trilling.

**Dickstein:** Yes, while he had a powerful, and in many ways positive, impact on younger writers—including fiction writers—he also was a great burden to them. He had very exacting standards and he was *never* pleased. I know writers who were paralyzed by this.

**Boynton:** How did interacting with so many "great" critics—Trilling, Williams, Leavis, Bell, Marcus, Dupee, Bloom—influence your own expectations for what criticism could be?

**Dickstein:** It gave me an unlikely affinity for the critics of that generation and made it harder for me to connect with critics of the generation after mine, the "theory generation," whose style I found difficult to get down. Those "great" critics offered an appealing model of the generalist, but a rather special kind of a generalist. Not the generalist who becomes a talking head on McNeil-Lehrer, but the generalist who writes for the quarterlies or for the *TLS*. More like the Victorian men of letters, with a sense of tradition and a strong intellectual conscience, sometimes grappling with difficult philosophical issues. There is a widespread misconception that the New York Intellectuals were the popular, accessible intellectuals of their period, when in fact they had a small audience. *Partisan Review* had a circulation of six or eight thousand at most. It was only in their last years, when they were perhaps not doing their best work—and especially after their deaths—that they were retrospectively canonized as the "last" American intellectuals, and perhaps the most impressive critics of their time. This was nostalgic, inaccurate, and unfair to those who followed them.

**Boynton:** Yes, it has always struck me that many of the people who most often praise the New York Intellectuals clearly haven't read them. They are in love with the idea of this group, but haven't taken the time to grapple with the reality, which is that their texts were often quite demanding and specialized. Their serious work, like Phillip Rahv on Henry James or Trilling on Matthew Arnold, was anything but the work of a "generalist." Or rather, they were very different from the way we conceive of generalists today. Someone like Trilling was a "generalist" only in the sense that he brought many different interests to bear on particular texts, such as when he wrote about Freud or the Kinsey Report.

**Dickstein:** Right. They were writing for a small but not strictly academic audience. There were plenty of hip, intelligent readers who weren't at universities, who had intellectual aspirations and cultural interests, who read *Partisan Review* because it was the thing you read in order to keep up, to be cultured. It was almost the definition of seriousness for a certain class of people. For decades it was synonymous with highbrow, always good for a laugh.

From a later perspective, their so-called generalism was quite narrow. It rarely included anything to do with popular culture, which was one of my quarrels with them. I also had trouble with their strong anti-Communist position during the Cold War. It went back to experiences in the thirties that meant little or nothing to me. They were classic cold war liberals, and I was not. Coming of age during the sixties—an age of great music and great new films—I felt a strong affinity for popular culture, and for blurring the lines between different branches of the old cultural hierarchy. And that put me very much at odds with that older generation, though it didn't quite give me the pop sensibility of the cultural studies generation that followed mine. I found the notion of "textuality" undiscriminating, since the arts had developed special ways of making their effect. I held on to differences between art and entertainment, literature and pulp writing, though I enjoyed both and could see where they overlapped.

**Boynton:** In *Double Agent* you asked whether meaningful criticism is still possible, or whether the professionalization of criticism has turned it into just another academic field where the "criticism of criticism" occupies a comfortable niche. How would you answer that question today?

**Dickstein:** I'm afraid both are true. The kind of criticism that responds vitally to art with strong literary judgment and a keen interpretive eye will always be available, but the canons of the profession discourage it. Literary commentary has been hemmed in by institutional pressures. As universities and their English departments have increased in size, literature and literary studies have been marginalized in the general culture, along with reading itself. This has increased the pressure on critics to be less intuitive and more "professional." This began long ago, as literary scholarship became more technical: philological criticism a hundred years ago and New Criticism fifty years ago were trying to be more scientific than the old belletristic criticism. Now, from our perspective, the New Critics look belletristic, but from their point of view, they were much more rigorous than the gentleman "men of letters" they detested.

Jeff Williams once sent me a very good piece he wrote about the new fascination with the public critic and the public intellectual in the nineties; he described it as a turn toward the "belletristic." But I think he doesn't quite understand the invidious connotation of belletristic for the generation of public intellectuals I grew up reading. They thought it meant someone *totally* unserious, like some late Victorian gentleman essayist.

So academic criticism became highly specialized and quite separate from literary journalism. Theory was simply another step in this direction, with the old empirical constraints tossed overboard. But some theory went too far toward the politically correct, toward a more jargon-ridden specialization, and toward a criticism that not only had very little relation to literature, but was actually *hostile* to literature and to real authors. The "hermeneutics of suspicion" meant that your initial reaction to writers you'd been drawn to, partly out of admiration, was to find out what was wrong with them, what was flawed about them. Ideological critique took the place of interpretive reading.

But there was also a reaction against the "theory wave," and much of what we've seen in the nineties—autobiographical criticism, public intellectual writing, more accessible forms of social criticism—have been reactions against the *private* quality of so much academic scholarship in the seventies and the eighties, against work that sometimes raised interesting questions but seemed addressed to a coterie of the like-minded. Now many former theorists have been reaching out to a wide audience in more personal ways. Theory reached a deadend, and it's only human for a writer to want to be read. Besides, the post-Communist era hasn't been kind to the politically correct.

**Boynton:** One aspect of *Double Agent* I liked when I first read it was that you rejected the Spenglerian pessimism about contemporary criticism. You wrote, "The notion of the critic as generalist is very much alive today among younger writers in magazines as different as the *Village Voice*, the *New Criterion*, the *New Yorker*, *Threepenny Review*, *Salmagundi* and *Vanity Fair*. I could list two dozen superb young critics still in their thirties and forties who write for such general magazines." But then you left me feeling cheated because you don't name any of them!

**Dickstein:** I got into a lot of trouble because of that. Some otherwise favorable reviews gave me grief because I didn't name names. I probably wounded some egos. The names I had in mind were critics like Luke Menand, Bruce Bawer, Paul Berman, Jed Perl, Mary Gordon, Andrew Delbanco, Sven Birkerts, Katha Pollitt, and Adam Gopnik. If I were making a list today I'd add Joan Acocella, James Wood, Geoffrey O'Brien, and Martin Amis.

**Boynton:** But there probably isn't anyone on that list, except perhaps James Wood, who is under thirty-five.

**Dickstein:** Well, the names I first mentioned were all in their thirties or early forties when I wrote that.

**Boynton:** Do you see a similarly gifted generation coming up behind them?

**Dickstein:** They are probably there, but I'm not necessarily the one to spot them. There are some first-rate critics writing for online magazines like *Slate* and *Salon*, which are more open to young writers than most print journals. The *Times* has a couple of superb young movie critics, including A. O. Scott and Elvis Mitchell. They bring to bear a new style, a different set of interests. So does the fine young music critic of the *New Yorker*, Alex Ross.

**Boynton:** So what contemporary critics do you admire?

**Dickstein:** I tremendously admire people who, though they began with some form of academic specialization, work their way through to the broad, general interests that underlie their field. They still call upon the strengths of their scholarship, but bring it to bear on a much wider area.

The sociologist Alan Wolfe, for example, is almost the ideal public intellectual. He can beautifully summarize almost any large social issue and bring both wide reading and plain common sense to bear on it. He and I taught courses together at Queens College, where we loved poaching on each other's fields. I know that when he went up to Boston he developed a personal relationship with some of the surviving social scientists of what he calls "the golden age of sociology"—people like David Riesman and Daniel Bell—because he felt more of an identification with them than he did with the more specialized sociologists of the next generation.

Skip Gates did the same thing. At the height of the theory period he was making his reputation by writing some very recondite things, earning the respect of his academic peers. But by the early nineties he was successfully addressing a much larger audience on a slew of literary and social issues.

**Boynton:** There is a passage in *Double Agent* where you question whether the academic star system has an adverse influence on the work itself. You write, "If the object of criticism is to gain attention, then our star academics certainly have the public's ear. Why, then, do I feel that this splendid uproar, though sometimes good for professors' salaries, has been less than ideal for criticism itself, especially the kind of cultural criticism to which this book is largely devoted?"

**Dickstein:** What I object to about the academic star system isn't the ego involved, or the lemming-like movement of people at the MLA to the "star" sessions, or the vapidity of those sessions. It is the fact that during the theory years, not only theory itself, but various subsets of theory, developed a high degree of academic insularity. Marxist criticism and psychoanalytic criticism, reader-response criticism and postcolonial criticism led to the domination of *methodology* over what the subject of criticism might have been, which is literature, literary history, or the cultural object. The star system is very closely related to the marketing techniques by which each of these "stars" developed a recognizable method, one that could be imitated and reproduced. It's that processing of literature through an advanced set of categories—through a strict methodological paradigm, that then becomes your "corporate signature" or "brand"—that I find difficult to take. The only thing that troubled me more were the critics who were so trendy that they shifted quickly from one brand to another, presenting a moving target. As soon as their latest tricks were exposed, they were on to something else! Criticism fell victim to the shifting tides of intellectual fashion.

**Boynton:** So I guess you don't like the star system?

**Dickstein:** Well, it's not an entirely dark picture. Some of the smartest, most energetic, most wide-ranging people in the profession became stars and became known for particular methodologies. And some of the most brilliant graduate students were attracted to them because these approaches could be intellectually very challenging.

There is an institutional basis for this. The academic job market collapsed, so that branding became a convenient way of creating a niche for yourself, to compensate for the fact that the broad range of jobs that once existed no longer did. For young scholars it became a device to compensate for the failures of the job market and the academic recession, but it was a device that worked against the power of literary criticism itself. There was very little of what I would consider criticism in the work done according to these theoretical methodologies.

**Boynton:** Are there any movements in contemporary criticism that intrigue you?

**Dickstein:** I was fascinated in the early nineties when critics wrote more personally and autobiographically. It was something I had done intuitively twenty years earlier. But since I believe that the basis of *all* criticism is autobiographical, that genuine criticism is ineluctably personal, I hope this doesn't turn into the flavor-of-the-moment. One astute observer of this trend told me that a publisher had already asked him—barely a year after it started!—to edit an anthology of autobiographical criticism.

A further problem is that not all autobiography is equally interesting. Soon after this criticism became fashionable, a number of writers brought in details that were boring, irrelevant, tasteless—not everyone has something worthwhile to say autobiographically. It made me long for the older, more detached kind of criticism.

**Boynton:** How would you describe the critical stance which has come to fruition in a book like *Leopards in the Temple*?

**Dickstein:** Criticism—unlike literature, but like translation—dates rapidly. We very quickly perceive the stylistic presuppositions of the translation, and just as quickly see the intellectual suppositions of a critical essay. Criticism tends to survive not because of its ideas, which are soon either assimilated or forgotten, but because of its style. Very few people would read T. S. Eliot's criticism today except as a moment in the evolution in modernism or an illumination of his own poetry, but for the fact that some of those essays are very well-turned: gnarled, crabby, wonderfully eccentric pieces of writing. That's why some of the Victorian critics remain readable, and why modern critics like Trilling remain readable—because of the elegance of their attack. Their idiosyncratic sensibility still engages us.

Criticism must spring from a personal engagement with a writer or text. Like all good writing, it should flow from something deep inside you. It turns intuition into discourse. It's an interrogation of the gut response you had in the moment of reading, the moment when something you've read before seems suddenly different, or connected to things in a new way. The role of the critic is to unpack those fugitive intuitions, to open up the text to new and larger contexts, to see the way the language functions.

Great critics often write aphoristically, with bold leaps of metaphor and association. They're invariably masters of the rhetoric of persuasion. Look at Hazlitt, Coleridge, or Arnold. The best critics have always been remarkable writers.

**Boynton:** In Irving Howe's essay on the New York Intellectuals he underscores the sense of "belatedness" that they felt. He writes, "One shorthand way of describing their situation, a cause of both their feverish intensity and their recurrent instability, is to say that *they came late*." I sometimes get the feeling from your books that you share this sense of belatedness.

**Dickstein:** *Everybody* in the modern period feels that he's come late. T. S. Eliot felt he had come late to the Middle Ages, or the seventeenth century. That's why we have so many "post's," whether it is post-modernism or poststructuralism.

I felt a particular sense of belatedness because of my strong identification with the critics and intellectuals of a slightly earlier generation. I also felt a belatedness because I had come late to the works that most inspired them, which were the great modernist classics of the 20s. I don't think Trilling and his contemporaries understood that we who read Eliot and Joyce and Pound and Proust and Kafka and Mann in the late fifties and early sixties were just as excited and transformed by them as his generation, reading them in 1920–30.

**Boynton:** Why was Trilling so reluctant to recognize this?

**Dickstein:** Trilling was enormously cranky, and he thought about things by being discontented with them. After several decades of teaching he was extremely disaffected with his students—something that comes out in his essay on the teaching of modern literature, in which he essentially writes them off. Perhaps it was a rhetorical ploy, but since I was one of his students at the time, I was quite insulted by it. I felt that our generation at Columbia was one of the best student generations there, that we were right up there with the earlier generation of Norman Podhoretz, Richard Howard, and John Hollander in the late forties. I know this sounds grandiose, but, hell, it was an exciting time. We felt the whole culture was opening up, and we were part of it.

**Boynton:** Why are you writing your next book on the thirties?

**Dickstein:** I hesitated to write about the thirties because I worried that it would be too much like the sixties—another period of radicalism when culture and politics converged. I worked on it for a couple of years before I realized how different it was. The sixties were a product of the postwar culture of affluence, while the thirties were a product of the Depression. And how different the issues were: because of the centrality of the Communist Party, because I so loved the movies of the thirties, and because the economic situation created a whole other set of concerns.

It is a book like *Gates of Eden* in the sense that it uses literature and film and music as a way of reading the larger social text. I want to get at something elusive in the temper of the thirties that a historian working with more directly documentary material would have a hard time pinning down, the whole tenor of life, you might say.

**Boynton:** So you're back to that Columbia seminar with Bell, Trilling, and Marcus.

**Dickstein:** Yes, in a way, my work still bears the mark of what they were trying to do with Victorian culture in that course. I guess I understood something after all.

# 6

# New New York Intellectual

## *An Interview with Louis Menand*

Reports of the demise of the public intellectual have been greatly exaggerated, at least in the case of Louis Menand. In one sense, Menand has taken up the mantle of the New York Intellectuals, regularly writing literary journalism and intellectual history for the *New Yorker*, the *New York Review of Books*, and other prominent forums. In another sense, Menand represents the new incarnation of the crossover academic, as he has maintained a firm foot in the university, teaching for over twenty-five years at Columbia, Princeton, and City University of New York, and writing academic scholarship on T. S. Eliot, modern criticism, the history of pragmatism, and the state of the university, while also stepping over to write in more public venues.

In an essay on Edmund Wilson, Menand characteristically turns a clarifying eye on some of the idealized views of Wilson as a public intellectual, noting that "Wilson's relation in his own lifetime to this abstraction, 'the public intellectual,' was much more ambivalent than the way it is usually represented." The interview that follows discusses some of the complications of what it means to be a public intellectual, as well as providing an account of how Menand came to occupy both academic and journalistic camps.

Born in 1952 in Syracuse, New York, where his father was a graduate student in political science, Louis Menand attended prep school in Massachusetts and spent his undergraduate years on the other coast at Pomona College (B.A., 1973). After a year at Harvard Law School, he changed career paths (as he discusses here) to do graduate work in English at Columbia University (Ph.D., 1980). In 1980 he landed a teaching job at Princeton, but, facing the infamous hurdle of Ivy League tenure, in 1986 he turned to journalism, working as an associate editor of the *New Republic* in Washington, D.C. In 1987 he returned to New York to take a position at Queens College of CUNY, and in 1993 he moved over to the CUNY–Graduate Center, where he is currently a Distinguished Professor of English. He also continued to write journalism, for *Harper's*, the *New York Times Magazine*, the *New York Review of Books*, for which he was contributing editor from 1993 to 2000; and probably most familiarly for the *New Yorker*, for which he was literary editor for a short stint in 1993 and since 2000 has been a staff writer.

Menand's first book, *Discovering Modernism: T. S. Eliot and His Context* (Oxford UP, 1987; new ed., 2002), placing Eliot in the context of professionalism and other currents, draws upon his dissertation "The Nineteenth Century in Modernist Criticism: T. S. Eliot, Edmund Wilson, and F. R. Leavis" (1980). Though the late eighties and nineties, Menand wrote many pages of journalism as well as academic essays and edited several volumes, including *America in Theory* (with Leslie Berlowitz and Denis Donoghue; Oxford UP, 1988), on the Constitution as a dynamic document; *The Future of Academic Freedom* (U of Chicago P, 1996), commissioned by the AAUP, which includes a typically lucid essay by Menand, "The Limits of Academic Freedom"; *Pragmatism: A Reader* (Vintage, 1997), a now-standard collection; and, with A. Walton Litz and Lawrence Rainey, *Modernism and the New Criticism*, volume 7 of *The Cambridge History of Literary Criticism* (Cambridge, 2000), to which Menand contributed a chapter on T. S. Eliot and, with Rainey, the introduction. Menand's interest in pragmatism culminated in *The Metaphysical Club* (Farrar, Straus and Giroux, 2001), a best-seller and winner of the Heartland Prize for nonfiction that intertwines pragmatism's genesis from the context of the Civil War and Darwinian theory with biographies of Holmes, James, Peirce, and Dewey. *American Studies* (Farrar, Straus and Giroux, 2002) collects fifteen of his longer journalistic pieces.

Some of his more influential essays include "What Are Universities For?" (*Harper's* [Dec. 1991]); "How to Make a Ph.D. Matter" (*New York Times Magazine* [22 Sept. 1996]), a provocative proposal to streamline the humanities Ph.D.; "The Demise of

Disciplinary Authority" (in *What's Happened to the Humanities*, ed. Alvin Kernan [Princeton UP, 1997]), a masterful survey of the changes in literary studies over the past half century; and "The Marketplace of Ideas" (ACLS Occasional Paper no. 49, 2002). Related to this interview, see also "Edmund Wilson in His Times" (in *Edmund Wilson: Centennial Reflections*, ed. Louis Dabney [Princeton UP, 1997]); "Pragmatists and Poets: A Response to Richard Posner" (in *The Revival of Pragmatism: New Essays on Social Thought, Law, and Culture*, ed. Morris Dickstein [Duke UP, 1998]); and "Sporting Chances" (rev. of *The Game of Life*, by Shulman and Bowen, *New Yorker*, 22 Jan. 2001).

This interview took place 1 June 2001 in Louis Menand's office at the CUNY–Graduate Center in New York. It was conducted by Jeffrey Williams—an erstwhile freshman composition student of Menand's when Menand was a graduate student at Columbia—and transcribed by Laura Rotunno, managing editor of the *minnesota review* while a doctoral student at the University of Missouri. It originally appeared in an issue of the review on "Academostars."

**Williams:** It seems as if you effortlessly bridge the two spheres of literature and criticism, or journalism and scholarship. I'd like to ask about your background and how you came to do this. But I'd also like to ask how you see the two spheres fitting together; on the one hand, you make it seem like a natural mix, but on the other hand, you have a somewhat anomalous position. You could easily be identified as part of the new breed of public intellectuals, but still most professors don't usually do both journalism and academic work.

**Menand:** The answer to the first part of your question is that I went to Pomona College, whose English department in those days was very eclectic. Some of the people there wrote poetry, some directed theater, some did scholarly editions, literary history, criticism, and so on. The big thing that we English majors did was follow contemporary poetry in little magazines. This seemed a very natural way to have an English department, with a lot of different approaches to literature and to literary culture, and with connections to the bigger world of contemporary literature and the arts. So it doesn't feel anomalous to me at all to be someone who has an identity that embraces both scholarly and nonscholarly kinds of writing. I'm also fortunate to be at

CUNY, because we have a relatively eclectic faculty. We all do different things, but we don't make any invidious distinctions among them.

I think that because I am a professor and because I write for magazines like the *New Yorker*, people make the assumption that I wear two different hats. I don't think of myself that way. I just think of myself as a writer. I write about things that interest me. If it's for a scholarly audience, obviously you make certain assumptions about your audience that are different from the assumptions you make if you're writing for the *New Yorker*. But as far as the writing goes, I don't think of myself as doing anything differently. I pretty much write the same way and strive for the same virtues in my prose.

**Williams:** What are the virtues you strive for?

**Menand:** I just try, like any writer, to be entertaining and interesting. I want people to get some pleasure and to learn something. It doesn't really matter whether it's about T. S. Eliot or about Tom Clancy. I don't think of myself as someone who has a scholarly motive and a political motive. I think the term "public intellectual" tends to imply that distinction. When people talk about public intellectuals, they seem to be talking about people who have an academic career that's based on work in a professional discipline or with a small group of peers, who then step outside of that discipline to address a larger audience on issues of public interest that they feel strongly about. I certainly don't identify myself with that model. So I don't think of myself as a public intellectual; I just think of myself as a writer.

Another thing about public intellectuals that's confusing is that there are two models, and they're quite different. One model is the New York Intellectuals of the fifties—Trilling, Howe, Kazin. They played the role of purveying intellectual culture to a wider audience, and spoke to people outside their own fields. People who get called public intellectuals today are different. Now it's thought of as citizen-scholars, people who want to engage with issues about globalization or affirmative action or U.S. policy or whatever it might be, which drives them to find some kind of public space to let their views be known. They're engaged, which I think is great, but I wouldn't put myself in that category.

**Williams:** I want to come back to the question of politics, but first I want to ask more about your trajectory. After Pomona, you went to Columbia for grad school. Why literary studies?

**Menand:** Why did I get into literature? I don't know. I went to law school first, for a year when I got out of college. But I just wasn't interested enough in it, I think partly because I was a creative writing major in college. I wrote poetry and didn't really do much else, so I didn't have enough of a social science background to get what was going on in law school. Now I regret it because I'm much more interested in those things. I didn't know what to do, and I applied to the journalism school at Columbia and to the English department, because one of my college teachers had a Ph.D. from Columbia. I had never really been to New York, but I went to see the dean of the journalism school for advice, and he asked me, "What kind of writing do you want to do?" I said, "I want to write for the *New Yorker*." And he said, "Don't bother with the school of journalism," which was good advice.

I was way too insecure and unformed and hadn't really written anything, so I didn't look for a job but decided to go to graduate school. It was a little bit of an accident, in other words; it was just where I ended up. When I was in graduate school, I thought I would probably not continue in the profession when I got my degree. But I started teaching—which is where we met—and I was amazed that I enjoyed it (even teaching you, a very contrary student). I got a job fairly easily out of graduate school, really liked being a college teacher, and I stayed in it.

**Williams:** That's not the first time I've been called contrary. After Columbia, you taught at Princeton, you worked for the *New Republic* in the late eighties, and then for the *New Yorker* in 1992 or so . . .

**Menand:** I worked for the *New Republic* from 1986 to 1987, and the *New Yorker* from 1992 to 1993.

**Williams:** Not many people walk away from jobs like that.

**Menand:** Well, I walked away from law school, so I'm big at walking away. That's one of my specialties. I've had chances to get out of academic work, but it just seems like a good place to go back to, not only for job security and tenure, but because you're your own boss. There's not many places where you feel that.

In terms of the literary angle, most of my work has actually been on criticism, not on literature. My book on Eliot is almost entirely about his criticism and his dissertation on Bradley. Even the stuff that's on his poetry is not so much a reading of it as it is a historicizing of what he was doing and an examination of the context of ideas about literature that people had in that period. In other words, I've been interested in the history of ideas probably more than in the history of literature. And that's how the new book, *The Metaphysical Club*, which has nothing about literature in it at all, seemed a very natural thing for me to do.

**Williams:** I'm curious about how you see yourself in relation to contemporary literary theory, to New Historicism and the like. In *The Metaphysical Club* you talk about how the pragmatists were very much formed by the Civil War, and you allude to the fact that the sixties generation was similarly formed by Vietnam. One of the effects typically attributed to that generation is the establishment of literary theory. Whether that's true or not is debatable, but it seems that you are not entirely in step with normal academic literary criticism or theory, as people like Fish or Michaels or others who might be identified as neopragmatists.

**Menand:** One thing that I can say is that those people are important, and wrote more important essays, and I'm not and haven't. But I don't feel at all out of sync with what they do. I feel completely in sync; I just do it in my own way. I'm not a theorist, I don't write theoretical essays, but I think that I'm as much a postmodernist as anybody. I think one of the things that gets attached to the reputation of being a writer for the *New Yorker* or the *New York Review of Books* is the assumption that you have traditional, conventional ideas about the value of literature. I don't have those views, but because of the way I write it seems antitheory or pretheory. I wouldn't set myself up as a deep theoretical thinker, but I don't feel at all out of step with what's going on.

As far as New Historicism is concerned, I think, again, that that is my mode as a writer. I try to historicize everything I write about and to see what's going on in a deep cultural sense. I don't feel as though I'm fighting a battle to rescue high culture.

**Williams:** What do you think is especially interesting on the current scene in literary studies?

**Menand:** I don't think I'm up to date enough to answer that. Naturally I've been following the pragmatist revival, so I'm interested in people who are associated with it, like Richard Bernstein, Michaels, Fish, or Rorty. That's been my main academic interest for the last four or five years working on the book. But I don't really know what's going on in, for instance, queer theory.

**Williams:** Your first book, *Discovering Modernism*, focuses mostly on Eliot, but, if I remember correctly, your dissertation was on Edmund Wilson, as well as F. R. Leavis and Eliot. Was Wilson a model for you, as a journalist as well as a literary critic?

**Menand:** No. The dissertation was about the reception of modernist literature, arguing that it involved a certain characterization of nineteenth-century literature, Romantic literature and Victorian literature. It tried to show that, in an effort to repudiate nineteenth-century literary values, those values were transposed into modernist language, which clicked for various reasons having to do with both the literary and the extraliterary contexts. Wilson's *Axel's Castle* was an instance of that kind of performance, as was *New Bearings in English Poetry* by Leavis and Eliot's early criticism. I didn't write about Wilson because he was an important figure for me, but because he was part of that phenomenon. Actually, Eliot was the most interesting of the critics I wrote about, and that's why, when I came to write a book amplifying what I had done in the dissertation, I picked Eliot. I disagree with Eliot about almost everything, but I think he was very canny and intelligent, and I thought it was fascinating to try to figure him out.

The writers who influenced me the most were Joan Didion, Janet Malcolm, Norman Mailer, and Pauline Kael. It wasn't Edmund Wilson and it wasn't Lionel Trilling, even though I certainly read them. When I was a graduate student I thought about them as possible models, but when I look at what I have done since, they have not been particularly influential. The reason I like the writers I named is because they seem very sophisticated in seeing through issues about culture and ideas that actually is very like contemporary academic thinking. The thing about Wilson—that in the end is frustrating about him—is that he had no ability to think theoretically. In the few cases where he does, it is his least satisfactory work.

**Williams:** I'm surprised by Mailer, but they have in common a kind of American style, that's spare, Hemingwayesque, colloquial.

**Menand:** I don't try to *write* like any of those writers. I certainly don't write like Pauline Kael or Norman Mailer, and couldn't do it if I tried. But it's not the style, it's the intellectual component of what they do that I think is inspiring and what good writing is. And they are also very clear, entertaining writers, which is good.

**Williams:** So how did you go the pragmatist route?

**Menand:** That happened when I was at Princeton, where I started in 1980. I had been in the Columbia department, which was very literary-historical, and that was what I was, a literary historian. And the Princeton department was literary-historical too, which was why they hired me. But most of the other assistant professors who came in with me were very interested in theory. There really hadn't been much theory at Columbia, except for Edward Said. So I was suddenly confronted with issues raised by deconstruction and all the stuff surrounding it then. I was very confused for a long time about what theoretical paradigm I should adopt, what I should read, what was useful, and what was not important. I wasn't really sure how I was going to fit into the discipline, which suddenly was showing a different face to me.

**Williams:** I think first jobs are underestimated as part of our formation, as a kind of second graduate education in the profession. One usually thinks it all happens in grad school, but it's also where we end up institutionally.

**Menand:** I wasn't completely sure I wanted to stay in the field, but then I read *Consequences of Pragmatism*, Rorty's collection of essays. They're still my favorite things in all his work. There's an essay on Derrida called "Philosophy as a Kind of Writing," and it was incredibly clarifying. If there's one thing I ever read that changed my life, it was that essay. And the thing that was clarifying about it was that he explained what Derrida was doing by essentially saying, "Don't pay any attention to the theoretical plane that Derrida works on and you'll get it." It was really an eye-opener. I became a lifelong fan of Rorty's work. He is, for me, the Man. My field was the history of ideas, and Rorty had a way of talking about ideas that made it possible for me to do my work. It made it possible by allowing me to take a step back from having to champion or critique a set of ideas, but simply to look at them as instruments that people use to cope with the world they find themselves in.

On the other hand, I don't think of myself as a pragmatist in the sense that I have a philosophy. I'm not a philosopher, and one thing I try to do in the book is not make it seem like a referendum on the philosophical merits of pragmatism. I just wanted to present a kind of balanced historical account of it. But there's no question that I felt that, in their time, the pragmatists had the better argument. And I think that's true today.

**Williams:** *The Metaphysical Club* refers to—just to fill in some background—a group that Oliver Wendell Holmes, William James, and Charles Peirce formed in 1872, for a short time when they were young, and the book interweaves a history of ideas with their biographies and the various people that they run across. You also make a point of situating their trajectory in the wake of the Civil War, which spurred a new set of ideas for its time.

**Menand:** The Civil War was very important in creating a set of conditions out of which pragmatism emerged, but another factor was *On the Origin of Species*, which was published in 1859. Pragmatism is as much influenced by Darwin as it is by the reaction against the Civil War. One thing that happened to pragmatism is that after 1945 it went into eclipse. The heroic figures of pragmatism—Holmes, James, and Dewey (Peirce was much less well known)—were rarely taught and were generally condescended to during the Cold War. Rorty and a couple of people like Richard Bernstein were the lone academic defenders of Dewey and James.

**Williams:** Why? I would have thought it would have been an apt fit with American imperatives, at least as an indigenous American school of thought.

**Menand:** I think it had to do with the moral imperatives of the Cold War era: people felt it was very important to have a set of political principles that could be treated in a more or less absolute way. The entire intellectual culture of the Cold War period was very antipragmatic. For example, Martin Luther King Jr. preached continually against relativism and pragmatism, and Reinhold Niebuhr was a big antagonist of Dewey. I even think that the first wave of theory in the seventies and eighties was antipragmatic in the sense that it was kind of foundational. That's what I felt at Princeton. I felt these people always have a place to stand, and I didn't.

So it was liberating to encounter Rorty. You know, in the beginning, for example, in *Philosophy as the Mirror of Nature*, which was published in 1979, Rorty barely mentions pragmatism; he ends up suggesting hermeneutics might be a way of doing things. It wasn't really until *Consequences of Pragmatism* that Rorty became identified with pragmatism, and it wasn't until *Contingency, Irony, and Solidarity* that he started having a bigger influence, which was toward the end of the eighties.

I conceived of and started *The Metaphysical Club* right at the end of the Cold War, around 1989. And, in the ten or twelve years it took me to write it, more biographies came out about Holmes, James, Peirce, and Dewey, more collected letters, and more editions, plus a huge amount of secondary work, than had appeared in the fifty years before.

**Williams:** One of my frustrations with pragmatism is its account of change. For instance, with Fish, interpretive communities explain a lot about literary practices, but it's been pointed out that they do not explain how you change from one community to another, or that you might straddle multiple communities. You provide one account of change at the end of a response to Richard Poirier in the thick Duke volume, *The Revival of Pragmatism*. Sorry to spring a quote on you, but there you say, "Theories are just one of the ways we make sense of choices. We wake up one morning and find ourselves in a new place, and then we build a ladder to explain how we got there." Now, I'm with you on the first part, but not on the second, about how we just magically wake up to find ourselves in a new place. It doesn't explain the institutional conditions that bring us to particular places and give us particular choices, and it elides any sense of politics.

**Menand:** Toward the end of *The Metaphysical Club*, I talk about pragmatism's limitation as a philosophy: that it takes interests for granted and doesn't explain where they come from. It's something that Weber and Freud and Veblen and other contemporaries of the pragmatists were interested in—where we get our desires and why we choose to do one thing rather than another thing. The pragmatists have a kind of Whiggish view: as organisms we need to adapt to the world and make it a better place. It's unproblematized by things like mediated desire and charismatic or institutional authority, and I think that's a great weakness. One of the places that we do get our desires and our needs is through the mediation of the institutions that we are enmeshed in.

On the other hand, the greatness of pragmatism in its time, in the first generation, was that almost every large-scale nineteenth-century philosophy was determinist in one way or another, either as a kind of absolute idealism or providentialism or as materialism. Pragmatism gave people credit for agency. It said that people can make choices and those choices can have an effect on the world. That was very liberating. If it leaves out some of the determining influences on behavior and choice that we recognize, in its time it had the effect of allowing reformers and progressives and liberals some kind of philosophical breathing room in which they could feel they could make a difference in the world.

**Williams:** To segue to some political issues, I want to ask you about what you think of the current university. You have fairly regularly commented on the state of the university, from the well-known *New York Times* piece about reforming the Ph.D. to the book you edited on tenure. And more recently you had a piece in the *New Yorker* on *The Game of Life*, about the imbalance of the stress on sports in universities.

**Menand:** Well, there's a lot of different areas that I've written about. I did review a lot of the big "culture war" works, like Bloom's and Kimball's and Jacoby's, so I was part of that conversation when it was happening in the late eighties and early nineties. Some of the stuff I've written attempts to address what I think are institutional problems which everyone experiences, and one of them is graduate education. I felt, from my own experience but also from the statistics of the job crisis, that people now spend eight, ten, twelve years in graduate school, and that it is destructive of their lives, especially because a lot of people ultimately don't get tenure-track jobs but are relatively old before they realize that they are not going to have the careers they hoped to have. So I proposed in the *Times* piece restricting graduate school to three or possibly four years, on the model of law school, so that, if you don't get a job, you aren't thirty-five or forty years old. No one seems interested in doing that; I think that they think it would devalue the degree.

**Williams:** Part of it is the labor problem—universities need the bodies to staff courses, that are essentially disposable and replaceable. It's attractive to administrators who keep the books.

**Menand:** There's no question that it's attractive, especially in a place like CUNY where there's a huge amount of graduate student teaching, and it's a very big system. But that's a poor reason to defend the practice of keeping people in school that long. I also think shortening the degree would add focus to the disciplines. I'm not just talking about English; it's a problem in math, it's a problem in chemistry, it's a problem in history. I think that's the main area for reform in higher education, because graduate education is where the academic profession reproduces itself. The values and the assumptions that graduate students acquire when they're in doctoral programs become the values and assumptions that they have when they teach. That's their idea of what the discipline of literature is.

Graduate programs are the most backward, it seems to me, of the whole system of higher education. If you go to small liberal arts colleges that don't have graduate programs, like Trinity College or Wesleyan or Swarthmore or Antioch, and you look at the curriculum, what you see has very little relation to what goes on in graduate schools. It's much more interdisciplinary, much less tied to the traditional paradigm of scholarly inquiry, and a lot more on the model of study centers. But you still have to get your degree in a field, in a discipline, and it's a very traditional kind of writing that you have to do when you write your dissertation.

**Williams:** One thing that strikes me is that there's a disjunction in teacher training, between elite schools, where people might have only taught or co-taught one course, and state schools, where they might have taught, without exaggeration, fifteen or twenty courses as a graduate student. I always think it a somewhat bitter irony that the people we hire at Missouri from elite schools—Harvard, Chicago—have taught very little, but our own grad students have taught more than they will at tenure time. The other thing that strikes me is that there seems to have been a split circa 1970 between the teaching and the research rationales of the university. In my story of the field, "theory" provided a research rationale for literary studies in the university, whereas the New Criticism was consistent and coherent with a teaching rationale.

**Menand:** Christopher Jencks and David Riesman wrote a book, *The Academic Revolution*, in 1968, in which they said that for the first time in the history of American higher education, research became the dominant paradigm. That's what professors were expected to do for professional advancement, as opposed to teaching or service. The effect was to make the research university professor the type of the professor generally, so that even in liberal arts colleges where people taught three or four courses a term, they were expected to produce scholarship. Research universities are a fraction of the higher education world, but they tend to set the standard for everybody.

There's also an assumption when you get into the profession that you want to be mobile, and the only way to be mobile is to have publications because nothing else is transferable as a value. I think that

that has had an unfortunate effect because it has tended to overprofessionalize undergraduate teaching.

**Williams:** Other than the question of graduate education, what other changes do you see in literary studies over the past decade? You talk about some of these changes in your essay "The Demise of Disciplinary Authority."

**Menand:** I've thought for the last couple of years that there's been a breakdown of disciplinary boundaries in the humanities that would have some effect ultimately on the way in which departments were organized. For instance, I just spent a long time writing a book that had nothing to do with literature, and most of my colleagues don't actually write about literature in a traditional sense anymore. Given that's where scholarship is going, and given what new study centers represent, the credentialing process ought to move in that direction instead of staying with disciplines that no one really takes seriously anymore. But I don't actually see that happening. I don't see any moves to change the organization of the disciplines or departments. I think there is a postdisciplinary mind-set that's accepted now, but I don't really see an institutional response to it.

The important thing about departments is that they protect academic freedom. They are self-governing, whereas programs are not. Programs don't hire, they don't fire, they don't credential. So you don't really want departments to wither away. And obviously a big problem is part-timers and adjuncts. It's bad for morale. It often weakens the caliber of education because it's divisive in a class way within the profession.

**Williams:** At CUNY the union has been very active, especially with Barbara Bowen as the new president, and I keep crossing the paths of grad students who have come through the CUNY system and who have been active in the Grad Student Caucus of MLA, like Marc Bousquet, now at Louisville. What do you think of the CUNY union, or do you prefer to keep some distance from it? I guess I want to press on the question of what it means to be a writer as opposed to a public intellectual.

**Menand:** I'm a member of the union—everybody on the professional staff is. But it's a complicated story. The thing you have to remember about CUNY is that it is very much a political football—not just in the city because, in fact, most funding for CUNY and all the funding for the senior colleges comes from the state. So the governor has an enormous effect on the budget. The budget is set every year, and it's a continual tug-of-war between the governor and the Democratic leadership of the assembly in Albany. We have to compete with SUNY, and SUNY has much stronger representation because there is a SUNY campus in every legislative district in the state of New York. CUNY is just represented in the city, so we have a much smaller impact, and it's a big problem.

One of the things that happened over the years, with the former leadership of the union, was that faculty salaries began to deteriorate relative to other areas and institutions of comparable size, and now they're quite low. It's a problem for retention, it's a problem for recruitment, and it's a problem for morale. I'm relatively well-off because I'm in the Graduate Center, but if I were in a college, I would have a huge teaching load. So I'm very much in favor of the union taking aggressive action.

The reason I've qualified my answer a little has to do with the fact that two years ago the mayor got Benno Schmidt to head a commission to write a report on what we should do with the City University. I thought that there was a lot of very divisive and unfortunate rhetoric coming from the mayor and the others like Herman Badillo, so, like a lot of people, I was suspicious of Schmidt's motives and not very optimistic about what he would find. But, unlike a lot of people, I actually thought he wrote an excellent report. He basically concluded, against what I thought were all the odds, that CUNY should retain its historical mission, which is to educate by and large first-generation college students, and that it should receive adequate political and financial support to perform that mission.

Some of the proposals that were made in the Schmidt report did have the effect of changing the remediation procedures at the university, which were a bone of contention and which led to a situation in which remediation is being shipped out to the community colleges. And I can see why people have problems with that, because remediation in writing, for example, often just has to do with the fact that English is the student's second or third language, and hasn't much to do with anything else. But it's not that they're ending remediation; they're simply trying to provide it in a more efficient way. So I think it's worth trying.

I think that the union and others here unfortunately have taken a very antagonistic posture toward the Schmidt report and toward the board of trustees. I think that our posture as faculty should be: put your money where your mouth is. This is what you say we should be doing, and the report says you should be helping us to do it by giving us better budgets to work with. We should be asking for the money, not carping about the politics of the report.

**Williams:** Though you don't usually take up many political mantles, you did come down fairly strongly about sports and the university in your recent *New Yorker* review of *The Game of Life*.

**Menand:** I thought *The Game of Life* was one of the most revealing books I've read about higher education, even though it's a narrowly focused book. The fact is that universities don't make money off of sports: they're a racket. They're there to satisfy legislators. It will be interesting to see what kind of impact *The Game of Life* has, if any. That's a culture that is very hard to change, but I thought that the implicit analogy to affirmative action was extremely powerful.

**Williams:** I want to come back to the question of the public intellectual, and perhaps talk about the academic star system. One thing I especially like about your essay on Edmund Wilson, in the *Centennial Reflections* volume, is that you debunk received ideas about Wilson as a quintessential public intellectual, as well as the frequently made claim that there are no more public intellectuals. And you also correct notions that he was a New York Intellectual, and point out that he had two phases of his career, the second phase when he largely withdrew and became a "private intellectual."

I have an essay on "name recognition," where I try to debunk typical assumptions about the star system, for one thing that it only applies to the great theory stars. I think it applies across the board, and goes all the way down. And in general I argue against the idea that it's frivolous, to be dismissed, or for that matter to be praised; instead, it's the primary code of our present system of distinction. We don't get paid much in this business, or so everyone seems to complain, but, if we have one reward, I think it's the same reward that other writers have, of name recognition.

**Menand:** It's not why I write. The most enjoyable writing I ever did was for the *New Yorker* when they had a section called "Comment," which used to be part of the "Talk of the Town."

**Williams:** They're signed now.

**Menand:** Right, but that was before they were signed. I used to write a lot of them and I loved doing it, because the people you really care about are the people at the magazine, and they all know you wrote it. There's pleasure in it. The truth is you don't really care what the rest of the readership thinks, because people read in crazy ways. You'd go crazy yourself if you worried too much about pleasing everyone out there.

The attractive thing about magazine work is that it's a group activity: you are trying to work with other people to get a product out. I'm not saying that writers are selfless, because they're not, but there are times when you share the pleasure that everyone shares in a finished product. You take pleasure in your colleagues' good work. That's not the case, most of the time, in academic disciplines, as David Damrosch says in *We Scholars,* where people are trained to work as atoms, according to an individualized notion of scholarship. Academics outside the sciences generally don't work collaboratively and are even suspicious of that kind of work. It's basically a very competitive individual enterprise. Magazines are not like that. That's what I like about them.

**Williams:** Tell me more about your magazine work. How did you get into it?

**Menand:** It was just a lucky break. I was at Princeton, and I had written a couple of pieces for the *New Republic.*

**Williams:** You just sent them in over the transom?

**Menand:** No, they called and asked for them. Everything I've written has been assigned, except for the very first piece, which was about Woody Allen. Someone had referred them to me to do a review of a book, they called me, and I wrote the piece. I wrote a couple more pieces for them, and I got to know them because I went down to Washington to meet with the editor and look around. One of the editors was taking a leave to write a book, and she called and asked if I would take her place for a year as an editor. It was my last year at Princeton, and I didn't have tenure and really didn't want to hang around, so I said yes. I had never been in that position before, except for college papers.

I really liked the *New Republic* in those days. Michael Kinsley was the editor, and Leon Wieseltier was the literary editor. I spent a year in Washington and had a fabulous time. I expected I would stay in magazines because I was enjoying it and didn't see the point of going back into the academy. But I was lucky enough to get a job at Queens College, and my wife wanted to come back to New York. Then the *New Yorker* changed editors in 1992. I had started writing for the *New Yorker* a couple of years before, and when they changed editors, I was invited to be the literary editor. But I didn't really enjoy it, so I left and came back to teach.

**Williams:** Why didn't you enjoy it?

**Menand:** I felt that there was a lot of confusion about the editorial mission of the magazine, and I didn't feel I was in the loop. I edited the book review section (and theater and art), but there wasn't a lot of editing that went into it because there were regular reviewers who had a beat and would just do what they do. I only did it for two or three months, and then I felt I wanted to write. I stopped editing and became a staff writer for about ten months, and then I decided that I had the same problem as a writer that I had as an editor. When I left I was asked to become contributing editor of the *New York Review of Books*, which I've done for the last seven years. It's more writing than editing, but I do consult with them on some of their articles, although I don't have an office there and I don't actually edit things. I write a certain number of pieces for them. I've enjoyed it a lot, and it's been a good place for me. Then last year I became a staff writer at the *New Yorker*.

**Williams:** How does that link with your academic work? I take your point that it's not all that different from other kinds of writing that you do, but most people would see it as two different kinds of tasks that would be hard to mesh.

**Menand:** It just seems natural to me. Like most academics, I write what I write because I'm interested in it. I like writing book reviews, I like writing "Comment" and "Talk of the Town," I like writing about the history of ideas. To me, it's all part of what I'm interested in. I'm lucky to have good places to do those things.

That's one advantage of being in New York—the opportunities to do what you want to do. I have a love-hate relationship with New York, but part of the love thing is that you can be anonymous in the city, as opposed to a small town or college town, like Princeton, where you are constantly running into your colleagues. No one knows who you are when you are out of the building in New York. It's an extinction of personality. I like being in a crowd because nobody knows you. I don't like to see my name in the paper. Not that I don't have a sort of vain satisfaction when people enjoy what I write, but it's not that I want my name to be on a billboard.

**Williams:** Now that you've finished *The Metaphysical Club*, obviously a hefty project, what are you working on? Once you mentioned you were going to write a book on the sixties.

**Menand:** Well, a funny thing happened, which was that I taught a class on the sixties. It was a graduate class that was a kind of interdisciplinary look at art and political thought and philosophy and literature and movies of the sixties, and it was one of the best classes I've had here. The students were great, and they were very interested in the material. Some of them were old enough to have had memories of the period, and there was great chemistry in the classroom. At the end of the course, I explained to the class that I might write a book about the sixties based on the material that we covered, and asked if they thought it was a good idea. They all said no! It took me a while to figure out why, but the reason was that they were interested in the breakdown between high culture and low culture; they were interested in the introduction of gender into literary criticism and sexual politics; they were interested in *The Golden Notebook* and Betty Friedan; they were interested in Malcolm X and Martin Luther King Jr. But they thought that those things were primitive versions of ideas that they were extremely familiar with.

We read *The Structure of Scientific Revolutions*. When I first read *The Structure of Scientific Revolutions*, which was probably around 1972, it blew me away. For them, it wasn't a big deal; it was sort of old hat. They read that stuff in the newspaper. It no longer has a provocative air to it. I was in despair for a while, but I decided the only way to do a book about the sixties was to write a book about the whole Cold War period. In order to explain the sixties, you have to explain the fifties, and you have to explain the seventies and eighties where the fallout happened and these ideas became part of a general way of thinking. So I decided to write an intellectual history of the Cold War period that I'm sure is way too big.

**Williams:** What will it cover?

**Menand:** It will be mostly American. It will be a book about how many of the things that happened from 1945 through 1989 that seemed to have nothing to do with the Cold War were in fact shaped by the circumstances of the Cold War. We talked earlier about the Civil Rights movement and the general eclipse of pragmatism: that's an example of something that is distinctive about that period. You wouldn't think that the reputation of Dewey would have much correlation with the fact that the U.S. was in the Cold War, but I think that is a very important part of what happened. It's going to be an effort to look at the history of literary criticism and the history of ideas about art and the history of moviemaking and so on as kinds of Cold War phenomena, not in the sense of allegorizing Cold War tensions, but more in the sense that those things were shaped by larger forces somewhere behind them.

To give you an example, one of the things that happened because of Sputnik and the arms race was the use of the federal government as a source of funding for university research, something that hadn't happened before 1945, when the government got its research by contract with independent laboratories. But after 1945 a system was put into place that allowed government money from the Defense Department and National Institutes of Health and other big agencies to go to universities, so that pumped up the research university. It had a huge overflow effect in the humanities, just because of the overhead, which provided all this extra cash. Also, a lot of federal money went into the teaching of foreign languages. One of the reasons that foreign language departments are shutting down is because there is no Cold War imperative for learning Russian and Chinese. The effect of pumping up the research university had an effect on literary criticism to the extent that it superprofessionalized the job of the English professor, which you describe as the rise of theory, and which justifies a scientific model of inquiry in teaching and studying literature. So I'm trying to tell a story in that way. In between, I have a collection of essays coming out.

**Williams:** I was going to ask you about that, because you must have a pretty sizable collection of reviews and disparate essays, and you haven't yet gone the Edmund Wilson route and collected them into a *Classics and Commercials* or *Shores of Light*. Are they more academic pieces or more your journalism?

**Menand:** I'm not going to call it *Shores of Light*, I can tell you that. I have a collection of longer pieces, mostly from the *New York Review* and some from the *New Republic* and the *New Yorker*. The first is on William James, and the last one's on Maya Lin, and it's called *American Studies*.

# 7

# Canon and Curriculum

## *An Interview with Paul Lauter*

By some professional markers—a Yale Ph.D., now Smith Professor of Literature and American Studies at Trinity College in Connecticut, and billed as "A Star of American Studies" in a feature in the *Chronicle of Higher Education* (June 2001)—Paul Lauter could easily be thought to have fulfilled a quintessential academic career. But, to borrow from an ad slogan, he's not your father's idea of a professor. After his training at Indiana, where he studied with the New Critic Cleanth Brooks, then at Yale, where he wrote a dissertation on Emerson, he became progressively more radicalized through engagement in the peace, Civil Rights, and women's movements of the sixties. His activism carried over to a career-long effort of canon reform, working to recover women, ethnic, and other minority writers. This led to his co-founding, with Florence Howe, the Feminist Press in 1971, and many curricular initiatives, culminating in *The Heath Anthology of American Literature,* perhaps the most important contemporary revision of the canon of American literature, which he discusses here.

Lauter represents some of the significant changes in literary studies since the foment of the sixties, not only in opening the canon but in foregrounding its social contexts and fusing it into the more compendious American Studies. Though not a member of the sixties generation, like Richard Ohmann (interviewed in chapter 4) he came to look at the university and its practices as part and parcel of the social inequality that the sixties exposed. In an era of high theory, he maintained a focus on the less prestigious but perhaps more consequential realm of curriculum; against the specialization and research focus of the Cold War university, he adopted a generalist's attitude in both the research and teaching of American culture.

Born in 1932, Lauter attended NYU (B.A., 1953), Indiana University (M.A., 1955), and Yale (Ph.D., 1958). Launched from there to teach at Dartmouth, University of Massachusetts at Amherst, and elsewhere, he stepped off the standard academic track during the 1960s to teach in the Mississippi Freedom Schools and to become involved in the pacifist American Friends Service Committee in Chicago, Students for a Democratic Society, Resist, and the U.S. Serviceman's Fund. In the academic realm, he was a founding member of the Radical Caucus of the MLA, participating in the famous activism at the 1968 MLA convention (resulting in the election of Louis Kampf as president). Putting his money where his politics were, he was fired from the University of Maryland–Baltimore County for supposedly subverting the grading system by offering a communal final exam. In 1967 he became director of the first community school in the nation, Adams-Morgan in Washington, D.C., and was later active in the faculty and staff union at SUNY–Old Westbury, where he taught for seventeen years, before moving to Trinity College in 1990. Testifying to changes in the profession, he was elected president of the American Studies Association in 1995.

Lauter's first publications were a bibliography of e. e. cummings (Swallow, 1955) and an anthology, *Theories of Comedy* (Anchor, 1964). Departing from staid scholarship, thereafter he published *Teaching about Peace Issues* (American Friends Service Committee, 1965); *The Conspiracy of the Young* (with Florence Howe; World, 1970), an account of student activism; *The Politics of Literature: Dissenting Essays on the Teaching of English* (with Louis Kampf; Pantheon, 1972), a major collection resulting from sixties activism advocating black, feminist, and other studies; and *The Impact of Women's Studies on the Campus and the Disciplines* (Assoc. for Higher Ed., 1980). For the Feminist Press he directed a project, originating in 1978, called Reconstructing American Literature. It resulted in a volume of actual syllabi showing how minority writers might be incorporated, *Reconstructing American Literature: Courses, Syllabi, Issues* (Feminist P, 1983), and fed into *The Heath Anthology of American Literature* (1990; 4th ed., 2002), for which he serves as general editor. Recently, he coedited an introductory text, *Literature, Class, and Culture: An Anthology* (with Ann Fitzgerald; Longman, 2001); he also serves as series editor of the revamped Riverside Editions, for which he edited Thoreau's *Walden* (Houghton Mifflin, 2000). Perhaps his most well-known book, *Canons and Contexts* (Oxford UP, 1991), collects essays on the canon, the profession, and the university. *From Walden Pond to Jurassic Park: Activism, Culture, and American Studies* (Duke UP, 2001) collects his recent essays and includes "Reflecting on *The Heath Anthology of American Literature*." See also "On Revising *The Heath Anthology of American Lit (American Literature* 65 [1993]).

This interview took place on 10 October 1997 in New York and was conducted by Mike Hill, associate editor of the *minnesota review* then teaching at Marymount Manhattan College and now at SUNY-Albany, and transcribed by Rachel Gabara, an intern for the journal while a student at Marymount. It originally appeared in an issue of the review on "The Academics of Publishing."

**Hill:** I thought we could begin with some discussion about the origins of *The Heath Anthology of American Literature*. In what context did *The Heath Anthology* emerge, and what specific objectives did you have?

**Lauter:** We started working on the book, at least conceptually, in 1968. There was an uprising of sorts within the Modern Language Association at that time, and part of this was to get the MLA to take political stands on a number of issues—the Vietnam War, civil rights, and so forth. It was a time of restlessness in the profession in general, but one thing that we were concerned with specifically was to redirect the MLA's support away from the Center for American Authors, which was then and is still, as far as I know, an organization that services the publishing of definitive editions of the standard American authors. At that point those authors were all white and male, and it just seemed a strange kind of allocation of resources, in view of the questions being raised by the Civil Rights movement and the very early women's movement, to go on reproducing those texts.

**Hill:** How in particular was MLA supporting this?

**Lauter:** It was really just that the MLA's imprimatur allowed money to flow from foundations, the National Endowment for the Humanities, for example, toward the publication of elaborate critical and scholarly editions of books that everyone already knew. There's nothing wrong with that in principle, of course. But it meant the money wasn't going into finding and publishing many significant minority and women writers, who hadn't been recently published and so were not available. In 1968, we were fighting to change the directional flow of funding toward certain kinds of publication. It was really in 1969 that the great burst of publishing of African American writers took place. That was in part born out of this earlier struggle.

**Hill:** So was this politics of publication based on inclusivity, or one intended to change the standards of literary value?

**Lauter:** It was a politics of inclusion—essentially what the Civil Rights movement was about. Of course, the thinking behind it was that if you begin to include and include and include, then at some point the hierarchies change. You can't just include a lot of writers that you haven't had in your curriculum before and leave the curriculum the same. That at least was the way people were thinking at the time. Frankly, a lot of us didn't know who the writers were who were not included. We knew that they were out there. We knew a little bit about someone like Frederick Douglass, whose work was in print. We might have known a little bit about Claude McKay, say, but not much. Nineteenth-century African American writers and many nineteenth-century women writers were just simply not in print. A couple of Wharton novels were being read, but that was about it. So we began to speculate: What would happen if? And the "if" was making the texts available. How would that change the teaching of what was called American literature? And beyond that, since what is considered significant culturally is one of the ways in which things become considered significant socially and politically, how would the publication of marginalized authors change the politics, if at all, of the United States?

**Hill:** In a talk you gave in 1990 to the SUNY union of faculty and professional staff, the UUP [United University Professions], you used a couple of interesting terms: "literary archaeology" and "institutional establishment." Would you explain them, and how they relate to one another?

**Lauter:** The process of literary archaeology is going back, looking at the magazines, looking at the books that were published, beginning to read and teach them in some critical relation to what one was reading and teaching before.

**Hill:** It was simply archival work, then?

**Lauter:** It was archival work—and, by the way, it is still going on. Paula Bennett, for example, has over the last four or five years gone through virtually every periodical that you could name in the nineteenth century, looking for poems by nineteenth-century women poets, and she has brought out a major anthology with Blackwell called *Nineteenth-Century American Women Poets*. It will bring back into view lots of stuff that people don't even know exists. And when you do that, it allows you then to begin to use that material in classes. Getting it published, and using it in classes, begins to institutionalize these texts, and this changes the nature of the curriculum. The questions we were asking in 1968—the impetus behind what would become *The Heath Anthology*—were directed primarily toward curriculum change. One of the best ways of doing that is through the mechanism of an anthology. Anthologies tend to be like museums. They contain those works that are culturally considered to be significant. But every museum, after all, has many, many times more work than they can possibly hang in the space that they have available. So what they choose to hang is what is currently fashionable or what is of interest to the curators, or what is of interest to a significant donor or something like that, and that allows a lot of other stuff to stay buried. That buried stuff, or rather, its relation to what is traditionally seen, is what an anthology like the *Heath* is designed to exhibit.

**Hill:** Let me press a little bit on the question of the institution. Does what you are describing happen at the practical expense of more canonical authors? Is this about the replacement, or the recontextualization, of tradition? In other words, does publishing and the way it gets institutionalized change, or just the names and faces?

**Lauter:** Well, in fact both replacement and recontextualization happen. One of the complaints that traditionalists had was that we were getting rid of the writers that they felt were of a universal (and certainly of personal) value. The tendency is to read changes in the canon as an attack on traditional writers, which was the function of some of those early books, like Kate Millet's *Sexual Politics*, among others. But if there was a tendency to attack or to put the white male canon into question, it was also a process by which the criteria for selection could be more openly addressed, and the tough choices about what to include and what not to could be made. As I discovered once teaching at Old Westbury, doing a course that I called "American Voices," if I was going to do Charles Chesnutt then I really would not have room for Henry James. I just had to bite the bullet.

**Hill:** No James? Was that seen as scandalous?

**Lauter:** Well, not at Old Westbury, but I'm sure it would have been scandalous elsewhere. Probably such a choice would not have been accepted at other institutions. Westbury had a predominantly minority and female student body, and one of our mandates was to construct a different kind of curriculum, precisely because the students there were nontraditional.

**Hill:** Can you talk more concretely about the issue of how publication changes the curriculum? What kinds of presses were willing to enable the archival work you had in mind in the sixties and seventies? I know you were involved with the Feminist Press. Could you talk a little bit about that?

**Lauter:** The Feminist Press started on a model drawn from the Third Press in Detroit, an African American Press. Florence Howe, its president, and I were interested in starting a press that would serve the needs of the developing academic women's movement. This was about 1969, 1970, somewhere in there. We thought we would be able to publish various kinds of alternative books: children's books that were nonsexist, biographies of women, and reprints of lost or forgotten works. It's been the reprints that have been the staff of life at the Feminist Press and many of the other independent presses that came along at the same time. There were quite a number. And there were also some reasonably mainstream presses that published substantial works—Arno Press and the NYTimes, for example, in 1969 put out an enormous series of African American texts. The problem with them was that they were photo-offset. And although they put them out in paperback for a while, they didn't remain in print for very long. So by the mid-seventies most of them were gone, and all the work had to be done all over again. That was one of the problems that we were facing at the Feminist Press, having to bring something back into print, to go through all of that rigmarole to get it out there and then keep it in print. How, in other words, do you institutionalize this forgotten writing such that its transformative value is maximized and maintained? By and large that usually meant how you make this work part of a curriculum.

**Hill:** So there was a kind of indie-press movement in the sixties that served as the testing ground for the institutional changes we're experiencing more widely now. What, if anything, did this movement lose in the process of its eventual institutionalization? Some would say that it's rather a stark contradiction that marginality has lately become such a central feature of academic work. *The Heath Anthology* has helped set and now maintains that arrangement. But is its institutionalization altogether appropriate to the indie spirit? In other words, are you a victim of your own success?

**Lauter:** That's a reasonable question, particularly in relation to the *Heath*. Initially, it was a project which we called Reconstructing American Literature, and it was started on the basis of grants to the Feminist Press. But it became clear that the Feminist Press did not have the resources to publish a major two-volume anthology of American literature. So we had to look around for a traditional, commercial publisher.

**Hill:** I know the anthology is now being published by Houghton Mifflin. But was economics the primary reason to go to D. C. Heath originally?

**Lauter:** Yes, but we didn't go to Heath. We were just in the process of beginning to query a number of publishers about the possibilities when, fortuitously, the editor at Heath came upon what we were doing. They were looking for an American literature anthology for their list, and we were looking for a publisher. Over the course of the next two or three years, as we developed the work on the anthology, they did a lot of market research to see if it would actually fly from a commercial standpoint. And the response was very positive. Which is ironic, I suppose. Heath was owned at that time by Raytheon, and, whatever else is true about Raytheon, its general attitude toward its subsidiaries was that, as long as they brought in the bottom line in black, they'd leave them alone. They really did not interfere with us one bit, certainly not ideologically. Heath was also good because, unlike many of the other textbook houses, they did not take the position that we could deviate from the norm by only a certain percentage. The general view of other textbook houses, which I have heard from the editors of *The Harper Anthology of American Literature*, for example, is that they could not deviate more than about 20 percent from the standard texts.

**Hill:** Really? There are actually quantifiable numbers assigned by publishing houses to what the combinations of traditional and nontraditional texts might be?

**Lauter:** Yes. But the only restraints we had at Heath were the very limited restraints that grew out of what the market research said. And it said, simply, that people want to have a full and complete novel in each of the volumes, and they want *The Scarlet Letter* in volume 1 and *Huckleberry Finn* in volume 2. So we would give them *The Scarlet Letter* in volume 1 and *Huckleberry Finn* in volume 2. But aside from that, we had no real constraint. We did not put anything in that we felt mandated to include by any outside pressure.

**Hill:** How, then, did you make your decisions on what to include? I know from looking at the masthead that you amassed a veritable army of contributing editors. Were your selections hashed out by consensus?

**Lauter:** Yes. I selected the editorial board, and we were fortunate to have some foundation money in order to meet. We met five or six times over the course of about three years at various places across the country. I would haul along five big trans-files filled with the proposals for inclusion by people from all over the nation and at many different kinds of schools. Instead of starting with other anthologies and what we knew, we wrote to everybody we could in the profession and said, "Send us whoever and whatever you think should be in this anthology."

**Hill:** It was a blank slate, then, more or less?

**Lauter:** In principle. And then we read. There were three of us, basically, who read everything, which was a labor of love. And then we began to try to pare it down and make decisions. There's no single set of criteria on the basis of which you can make decisions. But it became fairly clear that we really wanted to challenge the profession's general marginalization and often omission of minority and women writers. That was clearly a priority. And probably that had more effect on the contemporary section, where there are relatively few white male poets. People were rather shocked by that, I remember, when the book came out. But it was a healthy shock.

**Hill:** What was your sense of the immediate effect of publishing what was at the time an unprecedented anthology? And has the *Heath* produced the results you originally had in mind?

**Lauter:** Well, what happened was that the *Heath* became a part of a movement toward change within the framework of the literary profession. In a way, it has become a kind of banner, with some cachet. People would go into a Fulbright interview and say, "You know, I'm really doing things here on the cutting edge. I'm using the *Heath*." And it has also become a kind of tool for people to teach things they might have wanted to, but were restricted from doing so by the unavailability of the texts, or because of internal pressures to conform to a particular curriculum. Somebody can now lay this massive book on the desk of the department chair or dean and say, "Here, this is why I'm doing this course this way." Here is a recognized and legitimate publisher putting out this book. So we provided people with something they wanted and could use in all sorts of ways. But doing the book changed us, the editors, too. We had this institute at Yale, which really marked the beginning point for physically assembling the book, in 1982. The *Heath* itself did not appear until 1989, with a 1990 copyright as I recall, for the first edition, so we're talking about eight years. A huge amount of work, because you're sorting through a lot of ideas that other people are presenting to you, and you've got to take them seriously. That and you're dealing with a lot of writers that you've literally never heard of.

And we had to seek advice on who not to include. That was not from D. C. Heath, that was coming from experts who, for example, uniformly said that we should drop Frances Harper. I was very resistant, and a couple of other people were very resistant, and we included Frances Harper, who, again, in the interim now has become a fairly well-known and significant figure in nineteenth-century American literature, but was not so ten years ago. You had to stay with your principles, such as they became articulated throughout the editorial process. It forced the editorial board to try to articulate what those principles were, which we did both in the preface to the *Heath* and then I did so in a more developed way in my book, *Canons and Contexts*. A lot of our criteria were developed ex post facto. You came to recognize the basis on which you were making selections, but again, only in the process of actually doing all that reading. It isn't as if one starts with a theory and then proceeds to apply it. That's not the way theory and practice are integrated, in this case.

**Hill:** Maybe this is a good moment to move to some conceptual questions about publishing and canons. Do we have the canon right today? How to separate canonical from contextual work?

**Lauter:** As you well know, a canon is always in formation, always changing, and always contextual. I've mentioned before that Paula Bennett and others have been looking at nineteenth-century women's poetry. This work has been about as marginal as you can get. The way in which we typically understand it is the way in which Twain presents it in *Huckleberry Finn*, as this sentimental drivel. But in fact a great deal of nineteenth-century poetry by women and probably by men as well is rather interesting. It is interesting in ways that are different from the way in which we as modernists tend to regard poetry. So that's a whole area in which there's a reworking of an understanding about an enormous body of work. And that's going to go on for a while. It's also the case that early black writers are really coming into view, late eighteenth-century and early nineteenth-century people, in ways that I would not have anticipated four or five years ago. And then there's the whole question of modernism and what constitutes modernism, and what the role of very marginalized figures are, such as Amy Lowell, who I'm looking at myself right now. So I think canon formation is eternally in process.

**Hill:** Canons are also performances, then, or negotiations?

**Lauter:** They certainly are, always. For an anthology like the *Heath*, it's always a matter of interchange and exchange between the editorial board, the contributing editors, the teachers, and, ultimately, the students. And even though the form gets fixed for four years between the covers of two huge volumes, the next time down the line it may have a somewhat different appearance, like the fourth edition, which has just come out. It doesn't have major changes, but it has some substantial additions. And this is born out of a lot of feedback from users, a certain amount of lobbying. We didn't include Malamud, for example, in the first edition. Then there were a couple of people who lobbied like mad and insisted we include him in the second edition. There were already more writers of Jewish origin in the *Heath* than in any other anthology, but still we got static from people who were interested in Jewish writers. When I looked into it, I found that there was almost nothing in the anthology that really deals with the Holocaust, and so, rather self-consciously, we looked around and then included, among other things, a story by Cynthia Ozick and a wonderful, wonderful poem by Charles Reznikoff. A guy from San Francisco, Craig Kleinman, proposed that in the third edition we use a play from 1819 by Mordecai Manuel Noah, and we decided that was an interesting idea because it would give us a sense of what was on the stage in the United States in that period.

One of the issues that came up when first putting the anthology together was what we meant by the term "America." Were we talking about North America, or about a part of North America? Well, I thought to myself, that's a very good question, but let's face it, given the nature of the market, given what people think about when they talk about American literature, this question is what Feiffer called premature morality. Now, of course, the question of nationhood is on the agenda in a different and more pressing way. The question of borders, the question of national borders and national literatures, those are much more permeable than they were fifteen or eighteen years ago when we began the idea of reconstituting the canon. And they are likely to be even more so. We are going to see a lot of writing on the Spanish-American War, the struggle for Philippine independence, and so forth. And this will raise a lot of questions about American imperialism, and a lot of questions about what constitutes America. Where these questions will lead exactly is hard to tell. In American Studies in general, I think it leads into a lot of consideration of America as a transnational or international idea, as an international culture.

In terms of an anthology and the traditional structure of the curriculum, that's a somewhat different question. I think there are going to be restraints that are built into the nature of institutions which are more limiting than what is actually going on in the work being done in American Studies. One really does need to differentiate between what people do when they talk about American literature and what people do when they talk about American Studies. I think American Studies is going to be much more affected by and interested in border questions, much more influenced by people like Gloria Anzaldúa and José Saldívar and other work of that sort. But whether that's going to affect literary study as such is still not clear to me.

**Hill:** What I'm hearing you say is that the boundaries being explored in the national sense—say, the way American culture is being globalized—and the border work going on between genres—the straining of the category of literature as such—have a great deal in common. Is this correct?

**Lauter:** Yes. If you take a look at the work of Gomez Peña, for example, he and Sifuentes put out this book connected with a kind of performance piece. It was based on an art installation, and the book itself is a hybrid form of media. It has a CD attached to the back of it. If you look through the cover, which has a cutout, you look at these two women dressed sort of like nuns in a very passionate embrace, and when you open it up it turns out to be a postcard. The book itself is printed on different kinds of paper, in different kinds of fonts, with all sorts of different kinds of things happening, pictures, photographs of the installation, and so on. The book itself is a sort of performance. I mean, it is a kind of exemplary border text.

**Hill:** But under what disciplinary heading does one presume to study such a text, let alone produce it?

**Lauter:** My answer to that is that you study it under the disciplinary heading of American Studies. But once you've said that, then you're also saying that American Studies now necessarily encompasses both sides of the border, and the borderland in between them. And if you begin to use that model in relationship to Mexico—Gomez Peña is Mexican by origin and insists upon being a border inhabitant—you've adopted a model that is interestingly applicable in other contexts.

**Hill:** I'm going to pick up on this term that you used, a "border text," and try to push a little bit on that. How, to use an awkward phrase, does the borderization of the canon as manifest in publishing projects like the *Heath*, or more dramatically in the Gomez Peña text you mentioned, relate to identity politics? There are people, and many of them progressive people, some of whom I know you're familiar with, like Todd Gitlin, who are now decrying the effects of identity politics as inadvertently fragmenting class politics. I suppose this is another way of questioning the relative ease with which the *Heath* has entered the institutional domain, especially when compared to writing that is expressly about class and class consciousness.

**Lauter:** Well, I would want to differentiate, first of all, between the whole concept of a borderland and the issue of what you are calling identity politics in the United States. I think the kind of argument that Todd makes really comes down to saying that the downside of identity politics—its tendency to provoke division—outweighs the positive parts of it—that is, its tendency to inspire a sense of internal unity and the need for groups of people to get themselves together and resist the status quo. And I think he's just wrong about that. I don't think any significant movement for social change in this country is going to come about without attention being paid to the particularistic needs of different communities and to the persistence of forms of discrimination and forms of isolation that are based upon and lived out as identity.

As far as border texts within institutions are concerned, I'm not sure any of them necessarily fosters a revived sense of class consciousness. I think what does do that are social movements, events like the UPS strike, which put on the agenda the question of differentiation between part-time workers and full-time workers in a way that is far-reaching because it had resonance in the lives of a lot of different groups of people. A strike like that bears on the academy, too, because now more than ever one sees an increasingly sharp class differentiation between people in the administration and senior professors, like myself, and people who are hanging on by their fingernails as part-timers, in two or three different jobs, with no benefits. It seems to me that it is through the material conditions of people's lives that the idea of class in the United States begins to have some purchase. The relationship of class to questions of ethnic, racial, or gender identity seems to me as obscure as ever in this country, and I do not see anybody coming forward with any useful formulation of that up to this point. It's something we are trying to work on. And I think one of the ways in which you work on it is to begin to recover certain texts and teach them.

**Hill:** Isn't there already a canon for class analysis, if one that's almost wholly neglected?

**Lauter:** I don't think there is a canon as such. I think there is a bit of a canon for studying working-class experience at particular historical moments. But the various conceptual frameworks which we use to talk about class are not very well developed, and they're certainly not very well looked at in the normal classroom in the United States, certainly not in the literary classroom. And I think that's a considerable problem which is complicated by the whole border phenomenon. One could argue that, to the extent that American Studies turns its attention to this question of borderlands and the relationship of exploited people in Vietnam, or Indonesia, or Mexico, then one is also turning a critical eye on the relative comfort of people in the United States. But in doing so it also potentially distracts our attention from the kind of class struggle that is going on within, and is quite particular to, the United States. That's a constant problem. How does one, without being utterly sectarian about it, see the relationship among incommensurate political struggles?

**Hill:** It would seem that such a question would be particularly difficult to ask in an institutional setting. But doesn't this relate to the publishing objectives you had in the late sixties with regard to MLA and its support of more traditional books? You had to go through fairly unorthodox channels to adequately formulate your political goals, at least initially. Given the downsizing both within academe and without it, is it too optimistic to suggest that the independent thinking of the kind you were engaged in during the sixties might be on the horizon today? With so many who want academic and other middle-class jobs being turned away, how do you think this will affect intellectual work?

**Lauter:** Well this is already happening, just to give an example, in the MLA right now. The Graduate Student Caucus is running two people for the MLA council. They are putting on the agenda a motion that has to do with a more proportional representation of the growing underclass within literary studies. Now, somebody might say, "Well, you know, when you talk about class structure, you're talking about people who are in the university, so what are you talking about, underclass or working class?" But the fact of the matter is that process that we casually talked about twenty or twenty-five years ago, the proletarianization of work within the university, has in fact taken place. And you have large numbers of workers, both intellectual workers and manual workers, in colleges and universities, who are by any definition working class. And the division between them, these people who have very little control over the status of their work and who don't make a lot of money, and the senior faculty and the administrators with whom they are assumed to identify, is an increasingly difficult problem.

**Hill:** There was a conference of university press publishers in D.C. last year called "The Scholarly Monographic Crisis/If You Won't Publish My Manuscript How Can I Get Tenure?" People talk all the time today about the demise of the specialized scholarly monograph and the advent of the better-selling crossover or midlist academic book. And lately I hear that fairly prestigious presses are increasingly asking for an author's institution to provide a subvention to publish their books. Any speculations about the politics of publishing, American Studies, and the rising hurdles younger scholars especially now face?

**Lauter:** Well, I actually think that's got to do much more with technological questions than with ideological ones. I think that the scholarly monograph is going to survive, but in the form of electronic publication. And houses or individuals or universities will figure out ways in which scholarly monographs will be made available and, if you want to use it, you will have to pay some marginal fee to download the materials. So instead of buying a book you're going to buy access to an on-line database. This deals at least with what the principal problem with book publishing is today, which is economics. Everybody knows that if you sell 700 or 750 copies of a scholarly monograph you're doing very well as a scholar. But most presses can't break even on that. The problem within digital publishing, though, is how to credit and referee what gets produced. That'll get straightened out in time, I assume. But to answer your question, I really don't see any necessary relationship between the so-called demise of the scholarly monograph and the processes which are driving the increasing division of labor within colleges and universities and elsewhere in the economy. That process of differentiation between the well-to-do and the relatively well-to-do and, of course, the super well-to-do is going to continue regardless of what to me seems more of a technological glitch. This view doesn't make me terribly popular among people who are trying unsuccessfully to get their monographs published, however.

**Hill:** Does this technological glitch stand in a complementary or antagonistic relation to the market, or is that a fair question?

**Lauter:** Well, *The Heath Anthology* was in part a capitalist investment, originally for Raytheon, and now for Houghton Mifflin, and for us it was an investment in cultural change. They turned out to be very much related, which is part of life's little ironies. It's not surprising, is it? After all, in the sixties, the *New York Review* published an issue which had a long essay by Tom Hayden on the Newark Rebellion. And on the cover of that issue was a diagram of how to make a Molotov cocktail.

**Hill:** You don't plan on including that in the *Heath* anytime soon, do you?

**Lauter:** No, but it was an interesting example of how you can commodify anything, even a Molotov cocktail or a semirevolutionary upsurge in Newark. So it's not altogether surprising, this proximity between political change and the market. You know someone will make a buck. It's a funny thing, but in the world of theory, the category of canon studies is not a subject that has much visibility. If you look at texts on theory, it's often not even in the index, which is an interesting phenomenon from my point of view anyway. The translation of ideas about the canon into an actual practice takes, well, as long as it takes to produce a syllabus for your next course. And that's really where the politics of publishing, so far as canons are concerned, are likely to be found.

# 8

# Instituting Cultural Studies

## *An Interview with E. Ann Kaplan*

What can we learn from the pop singer Madonna? In *Rocking around the Clock: Music Television, Postmodernism, and Consumer Culture*, a pioneering study of MTV, E. Ann Kaplan explores just such a question. Though bemoaned as a harbinger of "Madonna studies" in antiacademic diatribes such as Roger Kimball's *Tenured Radicals* (1990), Kaplan's work has turned the critical tools of literary theory, especially feminism and psychoanalysis, to analyze popular culture such as television and film, especially how they produce cultural conceptions of women.

Kaplan's work represents one of the more dramatic changes in literary studies over the past three decades: the shift to cultural studies. She has been part of the wave, along with Andrew Ross (interviewed in chapter 15), and others, that brought the concerns of British cultural studies, most famously associated with the Birmingham Centre and figures like Raymond Williams, Richard Hoggart, E. P. Thompson, and Stuart Hall and with the group of film theorists clustered around the journal *Screen*, to American literary studies. As she discusses in the interview that follows, one of the more pressing tasks of cultural studies is not just in writing but in building new institutional structures to bridge disciplines and to make innovative cultural study possible.

Born in 1936 in Newcastle, Staffordshire, England, Kaplan attended the University of Birmingham, receiving a B.A. in English in 1958. After earning a postgraduate diploma at the University of London, she was a lecturer at the British Film Institute (1960–62) and at Kingsway Day College, London (1960–63). She then emigrated to the United States to do graduate work at Rutgers (Ph.D., 1970), where she wrote a dissertation on the relatively traditional topic of Hawthorne in the context of American and European Romanticism. After teaching at Monmouth College, she returned to Rutgers in 1974, organizing and chairing the new Interdisciplinary Film Program, among other administrative positions. Since 1987, she has been founding director of the Humanities Institute at SUNY–Stony Brook, where she has sponsored myriad programs, as well as lectured over the globe.

Kaplan's many books include *Talking about the Cinema: Film Studies for Young People* (with Jim Kitses; British Film Institute, 1963); *Women and Film: Both Sides of the Camera* (Methuen, 1983); *Rocking around the Clock* (Methuen, 1987); *Motherhood and Representation: The Mother in Popular Culture and Melodrama* (Routledge, 1992); and *Looking for the Other: Feminism, Film, and the Imperial Gaze* (Routledge, 1997). She has also edited many related collections, including *Women in Film Noir: An Anthology* (British Film Institute, 1978); *Fritz Lang: A Guide to References and Resources* (G. K. Hall, 1981); *Regarding Television: Critical Approaches—An Anthology* (American Film Institute, 1983); *Generations: Academic Feminists in Dialogue*, coedited with Devoney Looser (U of Minnesota P, 1997); *Psychoanalysis and Cinema* (Routledge, 1990); and *Feminism and Film* (Oxford UP, 2000). Additional edited collections arising from Kaplan's programs at the Humanities Institute at Stony Brook include *Postmodernism and Its Discontents: Theories, Practices* (Verso, 1988); *The Althusserian Legacy*, coedited with Michael Sprinker (Verso, 1993); *Late Imperial Culture*, with Sprinker and Román de la Campa (Verso, 1995); *The Politics of Research*, with George Levine (Rutgers UP, 1997); and *Playing Dolly: Technocultural Formations, Fantasies, and Fictions of Assisted Reproduction*, with Susan Squier (Rutgers UP, 1999).

This interview took place on 11 May 1994 at Ann Kaplan's apartment in New York City. It was conducted by Mike Hill, an associate editor of the *minnesota review*, then teaching at Marymount Manhattan College and now at SUNY–Albany, and transcribed by Jan Forehand, an assistant for the review while a graduate student at East Carolina University. It originally appeared in an issue of the review on "From Literature to Culture."

**Hill:** Most folks have an idea about cultural studies' past, its relation to the Birmingham Centre, and its association with Hoggart and Hall. It began in the sixties as a marginalized academic practice, if one can say it was an academic practice at all. What about your own work with cultural studies in the past, as opposed to how it exists now?

**Kaplan:** My own experience began in London, working with Stuart Hall and Norman Fruchter, and some people around *New Left Review* before the Centre at Birmingham even got started. What was very important about our work then was its taking place completely outside higher institutions of education. We were a group of people from the universities, trained largely in English studies. But we were young adults not particularly thinking of going on to graduate school. I was teaching in a further education college; Stuart was in a teacher training college; other people were in adult colleges of various kinds. Norm and I wanted to find a way to connect with our working-class students. Our interest in teaching popular culture began in this way. Let me shorten this and say that the work was political: we were trying to enlighten our students about the oppressive structures within which they lived, and in particular about the oppressive mechanisms of popular culture.

Leavis had begun the notion of a need for moral education, and that literature and the canon could lift people to a higher level. I guess we were employing a sort of Leavisite or Frankfurt School idea of popular culture. But we thought that we could take that idea of lifting people to a higher level by working where people were, which was with popular culture. In one class, for example, we took different versions of "Mack the Knife," from Kurt Weill to Bobby Darin, trying to show our students why and how the Kurt Weill version was better. So there was this moment when we were moving from the notion of aesthetics and moral education to something that of course has become very different.

**Hill:** When and how did film studies enter into it?

**Kaplan:** My experience of London in the sixties was already split between the group that formed the cultural studies Centre at Birmingham, many of whom had a sociological and Marxist approach and who were influenced by Richard Hoggart and Raymond Williams, and the people coming out of Oxford, people like Laura Mulvey, Ben Brewster, and Colin McCabe, who were trained, many of them, in linguistics, and who were philosophically oriented and very much in touch with French developments. They then congealed around film studies and began *Screen*. Between the *Screen* group and the Birmingham group was the British Film Institute, which was promoting film education in high schools, in further education colleges, and in teacher-training colleges. Film studies got a tremendous push from the British Film Institute, which promoted courses; I taught many weekend courses for youth leaders and high school teachers while I was still in London in 1961 and 1962, training them how to use film in the classroom with the methods we were using at the time.

**Hill:** You mentioned that there were explicitly pedagogical origins to the cultural studies movement in Great Britain. A lot has happened since then. With its immigration to the United States, for example, there is a highly professional component, one that didn't exist in the earlier period. Could you talk about that?

**Kaplan:** Well, the emergence of cultural studies in the United States in the early nineties has been an odd experience. The United States did not pick up cultural studies all those years while Stuart Hall and Richard Hoggart were giving master's degrees in cultural studies. So what is this about? Why now? It seems to me the forms of interdisciplinary studies in the United States in the seventies and eighties—film studies, women's studies, black studies—were already doing some kind of cultural studies. The people studying film were very much influenced by *Screen*'s methods—psychoanalysis, semiotics, linguistic issues, and eventually deconstruction. Althusser of course was a key figure in *Screen* work. I don't want to make too rigid a polarization; we're talking about a very complicated set of ongoing confluences. There was a strong input from Paris-the *Cinémathèque française* and Jacques Lacan. Meanwhile, women's studies was much more activist and involved with issues of class, belatedly in issues of race.

**Hill:** Is it fair to say that a significant part of what cultural studies lost, or at least got reoriented in the United States, revolves around issues of class? The focus on discursive issues or symbolic practices rather than explicit material effects seems to rule the day. Is that accurate?

**Kaplan:** Let's try to remember what was going on in 1990. My take on things is that theory clearly had overdone itself, overwrought itself; it had gotten to an incredibly refined, inaccessible, and overcomplex, rarefied space, and there was a reaction against this overrefinement. And rightly so. There was an attempt to return to the historical and to a sense of a political constituency out there. Now, exactly why cultural studies as a term came in is unclear. Some American scholars were turning to Stuart Hall, and it just may have been a moment when they said, "Oh, yes. This makes sense to us; this brings us back to some political focus." Don't forget that by the nineties the achievements of the sixties were in disarray. Socialism as a politics and a set of practices could no longer hold sway, particularly with the situation in Eastern Europe. So it seemed to me a sort of reaching for how we could become political again. Now, having said that, you're right to mention the way American institutions take up intellectual concerns: we tend to take up concepts and area studies that could be political, but immediately professionalize them because we're very much about professional training. We believe we have to train students for a job market or for an institution.

**Hill:** That's a good place to make a transition to some specific institutional stories. I know that you've been involved on a number of fronts in, for lack of a better term, instituting cultural studies—your involvement with the new MLA section, developing the Consortium of Humanities Centers and Institutes, directing the Humanities Institute at Stony Brook. And you've also started the cultural studies certificate that you're in the process of developing at Stony Brook. Would you talk about how cultural studies plays out in any of these particular institutional domains?

**Kaplan:** Well, I think an interesting thing that happened in the late eighties and nineties was the formation of humanities institutes. They were part of the dissatisfaction with the limitations of disciplinary borders. They began on the tail of the rarefication and oversophistication of theory I was talking about before; they too turned toward cultural studies and have, I think, been quite powerful in running conferences, bringing in speakers, addressing major issues in cultural studies, and in beginning to open up for students the kinds of interdisciplinary studies that have something at stake in them, to use Stuart Hall's phrase. The conference at the University of Illinois, called "Cultural Studies," followed by the *Cultural Studies* volume, was very influential—it marked the first return to that term, putting out something that was packaged as cultural studies. In the conference at Illinois, Stuart Hall argued that, while we agree that cultural studies is open and doesn't have its own set of objects, it *does* have a stake in the choices it makes.

**Hill:** Is it then possible to have a cultural studies curriculum, or a cultural studies certificate for that matter?

**Kaplan:** That's what we wrestled with at Stony Brook. I brought together representatives from all of the humanities and some of the social science departments to try to ask ourselves, "What would our curriculum be? Do we want to have a core?" And it was a very interesting and often quite heated process as we tried to decide what we should do. I had said to the group, agreeing with Stuart Hall, that there is no predetermined object, that CS can't be anything specific. I had said, however, "Let's start from who we are, from our research specialties." And we came up with a list that was a mixture of critical theory—Adorno, Habermas, Gramsci, Marx, Foucault, Lyotard, and so on—and more cultural studies scholars, ranging from James Clifford and Clifford Geertz, and of course Stuart Hall himself, Raymond Williams, Richard Hoggart, and people from the British school. And we decided we would call ourselves critical theory and cultural studies.

What's very important to remember about the American scene is that the disciplines are well entrenched, partly because our institutions are enormous compared to European institutions. We have English departments that have one hundred members; we have enormous universities with thousands and thousands of people, and there are many, many institutional organizations focused on literary figures and journals—societies centered around individual authors like Herman Melville. You're not going to easily dismantle this highly structured set of institutions, which is why in the United States we needed humanities institutes and new programs like the ones in cultural studies, or ones like University of California at Santa Cruz's History of Consciousness Program. So when we began to think of the certificate, we initiated a program students would take in addition to their disciplinary degree. I think these programs will proliferate and that each one will have to be figured according to who's sitting around the table, who the faculty are, rather than being a series of programs that have some predetermined shape or form.

**Hill:** I'm hearing two different points here. One is that there is a cultural studies canon, more or less a list of authors and texts who would be understood by the majority of workers in CS to be seminal. On the other hand, you're telling me that you envision retaining some kind of specificity, depending upon institutional resources, interests, etcetera. Would you then agree or disagree with folks out there who are saying that above all cultural studies should not become a discipline?

**Kaplan:** It can't become a discipline in the sense that it would have a fixed body of knowledge. Although even disciplines that supposedly have a fixed body of knowledge, the more you look at them, the less body there is. One would have to start by asking students to study theories of culture, but basically the focus would be on a notion of institutions that surround any textual cultural productions, on institutions *of* cultural production, institutions of mass culture versus high culture, theories of gender and subjectivity—these would be the concepts that one would want to insist on being part of such an interdisciplinary program. Sometimes language professors say to me, "We've also been doing cultural studies. Since we study language, our programs have been training our students in cultural studies for years." Clearly we need to distinguish the kind of studies of culture that we are doing from this; it's not simply an historical account. For instance, in cultural studies we're going to look at power hierarchies and imbalances, as well as issues of race, class, and gender.

**Hill:** I'm going to press a little bit more on the problem of cultural studies as an engaged practice, dealing with power and resistance, and as a professional practice, one in which it is possible to be degreed and tenured and get a certificate in. This brings up a whole series of questions, not the least of which is the charge of tenured radicalism, which I know you're aware of. Would you care to comment on that?

**Kaplan:** Yes. I'd very much like to comment on that because I've long been trying to understand these charges as they grew from *Tenured Radicals* to stating that the academy was rife with political correctness. Look, the problem with the American academy is that, because of McCarthyist legacies, everyone agrees there is something wrong with scholars being associated with politics. In England and much of Europe, it is absolutely taken for granted that intellectuals and scholars will be liberal if not belong to some leftist party. In America, the charge of tenured radical immediately provokes guilt: "No, I'm not a radical. No, I don't do politics in the classroom." As if to admit that, as a citizen, one has a political life is somehow scandalous in the university! I absolutely agree that the classroom is not a place for a soapbox or for political advertising or initiation of any kind, but asking students questions that have political relevance seems to me absolutely vital.

Many of us in the academy by our very generational matrix are sixties people who were involved in one way or another with sixties liberation movements. I think we're enormously useful in the academy; I think we have revitalized the academy, and that some of the most important developments over the last twenty years have come from post-sixties groups—feminists, gays, African Americans, and other minority groups.

**Hill:** You mentioned that elsewhere intellectuals seem to have managed to forge a relationship to the public that we in the U.S. have had a hard time doing. Let's talk about the issue of cultural studies and its "publics." There is a characterization floating around that cultural studies is a new form of cultural populism, almost a kind of celebration of commercial cultures. This obviously pertains to your work on Madonna and MTV. Could you talk a little bit about that?

**Kaplan:** Yes. This is a large question and an important one, and it gets to debates that have been set up between so-called cultural studies proper and what is called cultural populism or culturalism, the one being associated with actual study of dispossessed or marginalized groups, the other, as you were saying, with discursive practices and commercial entertainment. I've often been put in the category of culturalism because of my work on Madonna and postmodernism; this is also a debate between cultural studies and postmodernism. Postmodernism is accused of not being political and not dealing with power relations. The other day I gave a talk, however, and somebody picked out the Leavisite and British Marxist moment underneath my work. These are important dialogues that are going on, and I think in my own work I'm wrestling with them. I don't just celebrate commercial culture; I think commercial culture is incredibly ambiguous and that its functions are diverse and multiple and that much of it simply repeats the status quo uncritically. Much of it has subversive moments and so it can't be generalized. I mean, we'd have to go genre by genre or mode by mode to argue this out.

**Hill:** Or moment by moment in its consumption too, right? This notion probably isn't particularly Marxist, but would you say that it's possible for resistance to occur at the level of consumption and not production?

**Kaplan:** Absolutely, and that's a whole other issue. I think we have underestimated consumers and what they can do and the resistances that people can make. bell hooks has talked very lucidly about this. You know, groups can be empowered by looking at the construction of their own subjectivities and by objecting to and rejecting representations, as bell hooks has described with *Amos and Andy*. But for every such group of receivers there will be another group who will be completely overwhelmed by it, or accept the strategies.

But we were also working toward the question of the intellectual and the public. Someone like myself, having produced work on Madonna, got all this attention from media producers who themselves were kind of puzzled and fascinated—but very dubious—about an academic who would write about the "junk" (in their cynical view) that they produce. Most of the producers of popular culture are more elitist and more high-culture freaks than professors are.

**Hill:** Did it feel strange to become a bit of popular culture yourself? I know you've been on a couple of TV shows, *Sally Jessy Raphael* for one. It must have been interesting to move from the Humanities Institute to daytime TV. Do you think someday we'll have ITV for intellectuals?

**Kaplan:** It's a really interesting question at this intellectual moment in America because there is a group of intellectuals—Michael Bérubé is one, and Gerald Graff another—who have promoted intellectuals "going public" and told us that this is what we ought to be doing. We ought to be countering the conservative intellectuals who have got the ear of the public, people like Allan Bloom, Roger Kimball, Dinesh D'Souza, and others, who wrote best-sellers. As Graff has been telling us, "You from the middle wing have to get out there and do it."

**Hill:** Do you think some of us on the Left are afraid to become popular?

**Kaplan:** Well, I think so. I remember when Sally Jessy Raphael invited me, I actually consulted with people at the institute, and I decided I would try it. It was an amazing experience, the topic really of another interview, but in brief, I am not sure that my voice came through. I was so constructed by that medium and format. . . . The show was called "Madonna Mania," and I was constructed as the "expert" who had been claiming that Madonna was good for young women, and they were determined that that construction would be severely critiqued. I was quite shouted down.

**Hill:** It's interesting to hear you measure your effect in terms of applause. You have a certain ambivalence about being popular?

**Kaplan:** Yes. There's a lot of ambivalence and there's a lot of dubiousness about whether we can be allowed to speak as who we are. Perhaps it's possible on Charlie Rose or Bill Moyers and isolated spots which are not mainstream television. I'm waiting to see whether our voices will in fact make a difference.

**Hill:** You mentioned that you were situated on *Sally* as an expert. I wonder if the alternative is being a fan. Would you make that claim in any context? That is, are you a consumer of Madonna as well as somebody who studies her?

**Kaplan:** Yes, I can't imagine doing a study of, say, MTV or Madonna, if I weren't a fan because I've had to watch MTV for many hours. From 1981 to 1987, when I published the book, I consumed MTV daily for hours. I'd be at my computer with it on, constantly watching for certain videos to be run, trying to see what was going on. And I loved it, of course. It was and still is tremendously pleasurable for me. I'm a total victim of all media strategies, which I think enables me to decode them. I stand back from the product and think about how it's worked on me; I couldn't get those insights if I weren't totally hooked. So I think you've got to be a fan to study popular culture.

**Hill:** A couple of the terms that you used, "being a victim of their strategies" and "being hooked," put you in a more passive role than scholars are used to. These tie into the old notion of belletrism, that one does what one loves—one is a professional amateur. And, in a certain sense, those are the pleasures that hide power and that hide politics, but your response involves a twist, in that it involves a certain amount of victimage or surrender.

**Kaplan:** Yes, that's right, but it's a surrender later recalled and analyzed. That makes a big difference. Those of us studying popular culture don't feel that mastery; we really do get wrapped up in the event, and that's very different from the belletrist pleasures. It's pleasureful as well, but not that kind of mastering pleasure. It's for understanding a *process* more than displaying expertise or power *over* a text.

**Hill:** Let me go back to something we were talking about before. There's a concern that, as cultural studies gets increasingly institutionalized and centers begin to pop up, they'll replace full-blown departments as the hotbed of work in the institution—in other words, performing a convenient corporate trimming of disciplines into less numerous groups of folks that are going to these institutes and touring their stuff. Could you comment on that scenario?

**Kaplan:** Well, there are a couple of very important things there. One thing is the agenda of the administrations vis-à-vis institutionalizing cultural studies and interdisciplinary studies. Let me just say a word or two about that before coming to the second part of the question. In a sense this happened with the women's movement and feminist studies; one could argue that capitalism needed more bodies in the workforce, and feminism came along at that time. In other words, capitalistic states opened up space for women to say, "I'm tired of being at home and I want to go out to work." I'm simplifying terribly, but you get the point. Administrations want to save money, and it's better to have a department of languages and literatures than it is to have a French department, an Italian department, a German department, and a classics department. So, they're thinking interdisciplinarity for their own agendas, as we could say capitalism did with feminist movements. I think the danger of attending to this argument and stopping what we're doing is that, as with feminism, we have to make and retain our own agendas, while recognizing that we are also serving their agendas. Now this is a tricky operation—so-called stars "touring their stuff" through institutes can be productive. Don't forget, in each case, different bodies are listening, different mixtures of students coming out of their disciplines. In this context, new ideas pop out. People go back and rethink research because a speaker has come through. So it's a matter of seeing that a phenomenon has some undesirable aspects to it while it serves a certain kind of need. It's double-edged.

**Hill:** I know that you've just recently returned from a trip abroad, and a couple of conferences, like the Pacific Rim Conference at UC–Santa Barbara. Cultural studies seems to be inter-everything, and I know that recently it's become international. How does cultural studies play out between nations? Are there continuities and discontinuities from place to place that you could comment on?

**Kaplan:** Yes, but let me say first that I think cultural studies has to be seen as a set of research tools and methods that develop differently according to which discipline brings about the relationship. We could have cultural studies in the eighteenth century in English literature that will take a certain kind of form. However, I do think we need to be in dialogue with the social sciences and that any cultural studies program should have anthropology and sociology, history, and political science, if one can find a department that's congenial with one's methods or theoretical underpinnings. But we shouldn't all rush out to do social science kinds of projects either; those of us in the humanities who are very skilled at analyzing texts need to work with people in these other fields. We don't all have to become ethnographers or social scientists. I do want to make that very clear.

Now, back to the larger question that you raised about the globalization of cultural studies and what that means. In Japan, where I was most recently, one of the professors was working on the traffic in women, which I consider very much a cultural studies project. She's looking at gender and the remaining patriarchal legacies in modern Japan and how these have produced the practices of bringing in women from Thailand or Korea to be sex workers. So, many people in different countries are certainly doing cultural studies projects. International conferences, like the Pacific Rim, are very good loci for sharing this research. The methods or actual questions you will ask will depend on your local, national, geographic, and racial specificity, and I think cultural studies can lead us to look at institutions and practices that are quite specific to rather narrow terrain. Cultural studies in India, say, will obviously be asking a whole range of different questions, but projects may arise out of similar concerns, to find out what the power relations are, how gender is constructed, what impact new technologies are having, how consumer markets are working, etcetera.

**Hill:** In closing, would you care to pass on some idle predictions? What prospects, or prescriptions, or warnings do you have for cultural studies? What remains for it to do?

**Kaplan:** I think we're just at the beginning of an enormous development. I think we're going to see a lot of new interdisciplinary programs in the humanities that will in one way or another be involved in cultural studies, whatever term they are given. Students are telling us that this is what they want to study; it's what they see as important. I think it will take different shapes, as we said. We have to raise questions about the politics of research, about what it is and what shape it takes, as we did at the [October 1993] "Disorderly Disciplines" conference at Stony Brook. I think there will be more attempts in some programs to do ethnographies, as is happening with the CUNY group, of Latin American or other immigrant groups, and this is going to be extremely important. As we bring in—and I hope we can bring in—

African American studies and Latin American studies into cultural studies, along with anthropology and sociology, the shapes of projects will change. Faculty equipped and knowledgeable in these areas will enrich the cultural critical theory project and make interventions that have not been able to happen so far.

# 9

# Theory into Practice

## *An Interview with Barbara Foley*

For Barbara Foley, literature is inseparable from class politics. Through scholarship such as *Radical Representations: Politics and Form in U.S. Proletarian Fiction, 1929–1941*, she, like Alan Wald (interviewed in chapter 10), has worked to reinstate the largely forgotten tradition of radical and proletarian writing into the canon of American literature. Foley has also, like Richard Ohmann (interviewed in chapter 4), persistently turned a critical eye on the politics of the academy; as she writes in "Subversion and Oppositionality in the Academy," despite "the tone of radical panache" of much contemporary criticism, "it falls short of its emancipatory rhetoric and frequently ends up reconfirming those very structures of authority it purports to oppose."

Foley, like many of those interviewed in this volume, speaks to the influence of sixties social movements on contemporary criticism. Hers is a generation that ushered in theory over New Critical "close reading," which obscured political context and conceptual depth. And hers is a generation that carried out some of the impetus of the sixties in revising the canon and changing the academy. However, Foley not only has engaged in "politics by other means" but has consistently worked with political groups inside and outside the academy to combat inequality. Though many academics have recently been celebrated for their crossover writing as public intellectuals, Foley provides a more pointed definition of what it might mean to be a public intellectual.

Born in 1948, Foley was a member of the class of '69 at Radcliffe-Harvard. She went on to do graduate work at the University of Chicago, where she earned her Ph.D. in 1976 with her dissertation, "John Dos Passos' 'U.S.A.' and the Depiction of History in Fiction." After a stint at the University of Wisconsin, in the 1980s Foley taught at Northwestern University until 1987, when she was embroiled in a controversial tenure case. With a well-regarded first book, *Telling the Truth: The Theory and Practice of Documentary Fiction*, she was recommended for tenure by her department and dean, but that decision was overturned by the upper administration because of her political activism, notably because she helped to lead a protest against a lecture by Adolfo Calero, a Nicaraguan Contra leader, at the university. In 1988 she took a position at Rutgers University at Newark, where she continues to teach and where she is active in the New Jersey chapter of the National Organization for Women, in particular its Combating Racism Task Force, and where she has hosted a local public access cable television show. Currently, she is on the steering committee of the MLA Radical Caucus and was one of the 117 professors designated by Lynne Cheney and Joseph Lieberman as "unpatriotic" for their response to 9-11.

*Telling the Truth* (Cornell UP, 1986) unearthed the marginalized genre of the documentary novel from Defoe to Dos Passos and Ernest Gaines, and Foley's second book, *Radical Representations* (Duke UP, 1993), uncovers the mostly forgotten but active tradition of working-class fiction. On the politics of contemporary criticism, one might also consult her essays "The Politics of Deconstruction," in *Rhetoric and Form: Deconstruction at Yale*, ed. Davis, Robert Con and Ronald Schliefer (U of Oklahoma P, 1985); "Subversion and Oppositionality in the Academy," in *Pedagogy Is Politics: Literary Theory and Critical Thinking*, ed. Maria-Regina Kecht (U of Illinois P, 1992); and "'Lepers in the Acropolis': Liberalism, Capitalism, and the Crisis in Academic Labor," *Contemporary Literature* 39 (1998). For Alan Wald's Radical Novel Reconsidered series, Foley edited (with introduction) Myra Page's *Moscow Yankee* (U of Illinois P, 1995). She is currently working on projects on Jean Toomer and Ralph Ellison that examine the relationship between African American writers and the Left, and her next book, *Spectres of 1919: Class and Nation in the Making of the*

*New Negro*, will be published by the University of Illinois Press in 2003.

This interview began in December 1998 at the Radical Caucus reception at the MLA Convention in San Francisco and was completed by e-mail during the spring of 1999. It was conducted by Noreen O'Connor and Rich Hancuff, both Ph.D. candidates in the Human Sciences Program at George Washington University. It originally appeared in an issue of the *minnesota review* on "Activism and the Academy."

**O'Connor and Hancuff:** It appears that many people in the academy are committed to teaching and scholarship on theories of race, multiculturalism, feminism, Marxism, and postcolonialism. But as Cynthia Young points out in her *minnesota review* piece "On Strike at Yale" [45-6 (1996)], scholars are often reluctant to investigate the praxis of these ideas. For example, while feminist theory courses and women's studies programs proliferate on many campuses, the status of the largely female faculty who instruct introductory undergraduate courses grows steadily more exploitative. How do we understand the schism between academic thinking and the reality of academic institutions?

**Foley:** Yes, I remember it well: Sara Suleri and other presumably radical Yale faculty playing such a reprehensible role during the Yale strike. How do we understand this? On the one hand, it is important to bear in mind the incredibly elitist setup of academic departments. Graduate students and adjuncts—leaving aside the gender question for the moment—are invisible to full-time faculty (adjuncts especially so). At institutions with graduate programs, faculty at least get to know some grad students in their classes. I meet the adjuncts in my department only at the copy machine. I get to know them only if I introduce myself or they introduce themselves. They are never invited to department meetings. They don't even get their own keys to the john. So no matter what the content of what one teaches, the institutional arrangements in the capitalist university militate mightily against the kind of collegiality needed to form the sort of united movement of teaching staff that is needed in turn to confront the currently disastrous state of affairs facing all but tenured faculty. (And who knows how long their/our exemption will last?)

On the other hand, if we think carefully about what it is that most academics on the "cutting edge" of current literary and cultural study are actually up to, the disjunction between "academic thinking" and "the reality of academic institutions" should not be all that surprising. For, if I may be blunt about it, much of the most progressive-sounding (and presumably paradigm-shattering) current theory lacks the anti-capitalist framework that is necessary for understanding—and addressing—that reality. For instance, in order to grapple with the predominance of women among the most exploited sectors of the academic proletariat, we need to understand the material basis for the universal devaluation of labor coded as primarily female. This material basis rests firmly in the need of capital to exploit—hence the unpaid labor performed mainly by women in the home, central to the daily and generational reproduction of labor power; the huge amount of work undertaken by women in the informal economy, which permits capitalists to pay proletarians, male and female, sub-subsistence wages; and the dramatic sexist differentials in pay between male and female proletarians. I don't mean to preach to the choir here. But I don't think that such issues take center stage nearly often enough in feminist theory and women's studies courses. And the lack of such a class approach to sexism has far-reaching effects—including, in the issue before us here, the relative ease with which feminist professors can work cheek by jowl, as it were, with female adjuncts whose conditions of labor remain invisible and uncontested.

I won't make the arguments here, but a similar critique can be made of much that passes for progressive in postcolonial studies, critical race theory, queer theory, and cultural studies.

**O'Connor and Hancuff:** In *Radical Representations*, you see cultural recovery of neglected leftist writers as an important component in analyzing contemporary cultural problems. Yet you have also argued that teaching radical writers doesn't really accomplish revolutionary goals, because the university institution is malleable enough to co-opt that teaching as part of its "multiculturalism" or "diversity," essentially minimizing the threat such teaching might have to the institution. How does the teacher push a revolutionary activist pedagogy within the confines of the institution?

**Foley:** I can argue this one out of both sides of my mouth! It is absolutely necessary that Left faculty teach Left books. Proletarian literature, at its best, not only sets forth a class analysis of racism, sexism, alienation, etcetera, but also puts the question of working-class revolution on the agenda. Myra Page's *Moscow Yankee*—which describes an unemployed Detroit autoworker's embrace of Soviet socialism during the First Five-Year Plan—has an incredible impact upon U.S. students, particularly those from working-class backgrounds. William Attaway's *Blood on the Forge* and Richard Wright's *Uncle Tom's Children* provide valuable, if wrenching, opportunities for talking about the economics of lynching, the use of racism to break the back of the labor movement, and the politics of gendered race and raced gender under Jim Crow. John Dos Passos's *U.S.A.* trilogy gives students a radical take on modernity and a grasp of early twentieth-century U.S. history that they will get in few other places. I could go on and on. Those of us who consider ourselves leftist pedagogues have a responsibility to teach books like these, for they greatly enlarge students' sense of the range of human potentiality.

Yet we can't have illusions about the nature and extent of the radicalization of students that we'll accomplish in the classroom, no matter how good a job we do. Again, the arrangements of the capitalist university play a defining role. Students are, often without knowing it, profoundly cynical about what it takes to get by. As Jerry Graff has observed in a different context, they'll argue the unknowability of reality for one professor and the certainty of knowledge for another without batting an eye. While they may indeed be persuaded by much of what Marxist academics have to say, they also see us giving exams, assigning grades, and receiving a salary for doing so. Indeed, those who are most moved by us will often conclude that it is a virtue of the university that we do what we do: that the function of the university really is what the university says it is, to provide a "free marketplace of ideas." I feel this contradiction most sharply when I am being the most Left. When I sketch out the fundamentals of the base-superstructure paradigm, for instance, and under the rubric of ideological state apparatuses discuss the role of the university, I feel pretty weird. Universities are, after all, principally ideology factories; under capitalism, they cannot simply be appropriated by would-be subversive academic radicals engaged in Gramscian wars of maneuver. If we think we are accomplishing something really "oppositional" by burrowing from within through our classroom activity, we are, I think, sadly mistaken. We take advantage of what opportunities are open to us at this moment, of course. But these opportunities come not without cost, especially, perhaps, when we feel ourselves being most effective.

At a juncture of history like the present, when the ruling class has little to gain and something to lose by being too openly repressive of leftist faculty, we operate in a highly contradictory context. At other moments (or now in other countries), such conditions have not existed and/or do not exist: witness the fate of the Herbert Housing Apthekers and Philip Foners in the U.S., the more tragic stories of Marxist intellectuals in openly fascist countries right now. Our principal responsibility is to do all we can, on and off campus, to build the kind of movement that will make the ruling elite scared enough of us to fire us. That's another contradiction; but, then, everything's a contradiction.

**O'Connor and Hancuff:** That brings home the problem of the multicultural "marketplace of ideas"; Marx's theories come to occupy the same position as the latest business management techniques—content to be mastered by midterm, rather than tools to raise class-consciousness and transform the current system. It reminds us of Paulo Freire's distinction between "banking" and "problem-posing," or liberating education, because for Freire the most radical content means nothing if it's presented within traditional education frameworks. Could you comment on the role of the revolutionary educator in challenging the ways in which students receive the course's content?

**Foley:** That's a difficult one; I am not sure how much control any teacher has over how students "receive the course's content," since students, particularly working-class students with jobs and families to support, come to our classrooms with so much baggage. But some pedagogical techniques work well to help students see what is at stake in both reading and interpreting literary texts. It sounds a bit hackneyed, but drawing attention to plain-old "relevance" usually gets students going, particularly if we are teaching a text with explicit radical content. I'm currently teaching *Uncle Tom's Children*; Wright's portrayal of lynch terror has an eerie applicability to the police murder of Amadou Diallo in the Bronx, and many students appreciate the opportunity to draw the connection. (Most of our colleagues don't deign to discuss mimetic referentiality in such mundane, and reflectionist, terms!) Sometimes, too, I set students up in a debate over the validity or workability of some aspect of a text. A few weeks ago my class on minorities in American literature debated the ending of Gold's *Jews without Money* and got, I think, some insight into the politics embedded in what looks like a merely literary debate.

The main way to challenge how students view the contents of a course, in my view, is to get to know them outside of the classroom. This can be tricky while they are still in the course; the opportunities for opportunism, either by student or by teacher, are rife. But it is very important to let students know we take them seriously by inviting them to our homes. Some might want to join a discussion group on Marxism or just have informal sessions where they examine politics and culture from a variety of perspectives. I've conducted such groups for years and years; we read everything from Engels to Ernest Mandel to the *Nation* to the *Economist*. Also, some action-oriented students like to conjoin theory with practice and join some activist campus or off-campus organization. In my case, some former students from my American literature classes have ended up working with the Combating Racism Task Force of NOW that I'm involved in. It's also fun to march on May Day with one's students.

**O'Connor and Hancuff:** You mention that the "ruling class has little to gain and something to lose by being too openly repressive of Leftist faculty." The market seems to be triumphant everywhere—in television and other media advertising, young children, truck drivers, and New Agers share in the glory of capitalism's successes, while a mild-mannered, dapper Peter Lynch pops up to offer the "common investor" even-voiced advice so they too can join in the victory. But the persistent existence of the Left seems to speak to the capitalist democracies' magnanimous nature. Could you speak further on building a Left movement, under these contradictory conditions, that would "make the ruling class scared enough to fire us"?

**Foley:** On the one hand, there is no mass movement in the streets, and the lack thereof does significantly constrain what we can do. It is important that, hungering for such a movement, we do not overestimate the significance of whatever oppositional events do take place. The LA rebellion responding to the Rodney King affair, while antiracist and possessing an inchoate class politics, was almost completely spontaneous (in the full Leninist sense). Conversely, the current manifestations of outrage over the Diallo murder are almost completely controlled by the NYC ruling class, with hack politicians like Charles

Rangel getting symbolically arrested and proclaiming the integrity of "the great majority of the women and men in blue." We need to be clear-eyed in our understanding of where things are. There is a lot of passivity, of going along with the program, among the U.S. proletariat and allied class sectors. On the other hand, it is vital that radical academics not overestimate the extent of the bourgeoisie's ideological hegemony. Many working-class people are deeply, deeply cynical about their rulers and believe virtually nothing they get through the media, or at least believe it and not believe it at the same time. There's a mass base for fascist ideas and practice in the U.S. population, no doubt about it; but there's also a mass base for Red ideas and, in the not too distant future, practice.

My view is that, sooner or later, the global crisis in overproduction is going to boomerang back on the U.S., and the Wall Street bubble is going to burst. At this time, if I may pile up a few more widely mixed metaphors, lots of chickens are going to come home to roost, with massive unemployment, homelessness, and hunger. The shredding of the safety net under the Clinton regime will mean desperation for millions, and we can anticipate that the ruling class will be using many more sticks than carrots to keep things under control (their preparation for this development, by the way, is the context in which the Diallo incident should be understood). In this context, which I think we should call fascism, though I know some Left academics eschew the term, lots of people, liberal to Communist, will be roped in. So we might as well be part of a movement that is about the business of attacking the whole system and proposing an alternative.

**O'Connor and Hancuff:** One of the characters in Tess Slesinger's 1934 novel *The Unpossessed* proclaims exasperatedly, after an evening of listening to a group of academics discuss revolution, "You talk and talk but I'd like to know what any of you do." The perception of the university as the "ivory tower" divorced from the "real world" still carries great cultural weight, on both the Left and the Right. You've been an advocate for and practitioner of academics getting involved actively in issues "outside" the university, both in local grassroots campaigns and national questions. However, do you see any way in which the academic functions usefully as academic in these activist situations, or does that positioning lead to division within an activist movement?

**Foley:** I do think it crucial that radical academics be involved in a political praxis that takes them off the campus (as well as in one that commits them to fighting around issues on campus). I can't speak generally about the issue you raise here; perhaps some academics who function "as academics" in such in-the-streets activities may encounter, or indeed create, divisiveness. But it need not happen this way. As a member of the Combating Racism Task Force for about a decade (and for several years the chair), I've certainly not hidden the fact that I earn my living as a professor. The skills I've acquired in this line of work are useful to the collective seminar style, as it were; we begin each meeting with as widely ranging a discussion as possible of what is going on globally and nationally, then zero in on the implications of these insights for our particular campaigns. We get pretty Left and pretty rigorous at times! And I know my pedagogical training comes in handy here.

But we need to recognize that the reason there's such differential access to these skills is that capitalism in fact needs and wants only a very small segment of the population equipped in this way; despite all the guff about "critical thinking," a critical and truly thinking working class is intolerable to the present order. So the Left academic who functions in grassroots organizing is sharing what she/he knows, that's all. As long as we are as willing as the next person to make posters, lead chants, confront policy hacks rationalizing welfare repeal, demonstrate against racist cops, escort women past right-to-lifers at abortion clinics, and generally do whatever jobs need to be done, there need be no contradiction between being an academic and being an activist.

The greater challenge, to me, is bringing pro-Communist politics into struggles around reform issues. Having been involved for three decades now in taking arms against the sea of troubles caused by capitalism, I am wholly convinced that, as a system, it is unreformable. Indeed, for the masses of the world, it grows more vicious by the day. We can win specific reforms, to be sure. But, as witnessed by the recent stripping away of many of the gains won under the New Deal (themselves granted because the capitalist class feared insurrection otherwise), reforms can and will be taken away as long as the capitalists hold state power. Given the derailing of the first wave of workers' movements for egalitarianism that has occurred in the twentieth century, revolution is hardly on the immediate horizon. So lots of people think that winning small reforms represents the outer limit of what is possible right now. But I think otherwise; the system has minimal credibility with millions of people and awaits destruction by a revived and self-critical mass movement for a classless social order. So we have to talk about the alternative, and make it real, even as we inhabit this seemingly unchangeable present. That's the real challenge facing all leftists nowadays, academics or otherwise.

**O'Connor and Hancuff:** In a sense, your work with the Combating Racism Task Force provides a good example of an academic functioning "as academic," that is, bringing the critical thinking skills that, as you say, capitalism wants available only to a small segment of society to a larger population. Do you see a relation between your experience and some implications of Lenin's concept of the vanguard party?

**Foley:** I don't see much of a connection. Not to say I am against Leninism—far from it! But what I am describing is the kind of activity that any leftish academic can and I think should be involved in. Whether we are pink or red or whatever, we need to contest the elitist divisions that divide us from our students on the one hand and plain old nonacademic working people on the other (and of course these groups usually overlap!).

**O'Connor and Hancuff:** You speak to a problem that radical educators face when they get involved in reform struggles, namely, that deep down we feel the system is unreformable. We seem caught between a belief in ultimate unreformability and a desire to get involved in anything that will address the present oppression that people face every day. How do you respond to the possible critique that reform struggles are necessarily complicit with the current ruling order?

**Foley:** The dilemma you raise here is real. On the one hand, people have urgent and immediate needs; it's arrogant (and stupid) to say that these needs should not be fought for because they do not constitute a "revolutionary" demand. On the other hand, if we just call upon capitalism to reform itself, and then in some small ways it does (as is often the case, because its leaders are smart), then we are strengthening the system that gives rise to the crisis and the need in the first place. The key to fighting for reforms in a revolutionary way, to me, is to analyze what sorts of, if you will, Communist ideas emerge from the struggle and the process. Take the Diallo case, for instance. If we join the fray by calling for more black cops, or a civilian review board, or Al Sharpton for Senator, we are only aiding and abetting the loyal opposition and helping the NYC ruling class get its act together. But if we couple the call for indictment and firing of the cops in question with an analysis of the fascist function assigned to the Special Crimes Unit, and then link this analysis to a still broader analysis of the reasons why the ruling elite in NYC is tightening its hold on black, Latin, and immigrant neighborhoods, then the issue of getting rid of the whole damn capitalist system becomes part of the debate. Reds can meaningfully, and honestly, unite with non-Reds around all sorts of reform demands if they keep anticapitalist politics in the forefront and insistently link such seemingly unrelated things as the crisis in overproduction with the military maneuvers in Kosovo with police brutality with welfare repeal. In "What Is to Be Done?" Lenin wrote of the need for revolutionaries to bring the knowledge of totality to the working class. What he said at the beginning of the century is equally true at its end.

**O'Connor and Hancuff:** At the Delegate Assembly of the MLA this year, and in Radical Caucus and Graduate Student Caucus protests held at the MLA, you were a vocal and visible supporter of change within that institution. Can you talk about your activist role in this organization and in others like it?

**Foley:** As a member of the Radical Caucus, I think there needs to be a persistent, multiyear struggle to transform it from a "professional" to an "advocacy" organization. After all, that's what academic workers increasingly need. To those who say that this is a waste of time, I'd cite the effect of the Radical Caucus's most recent (if modest) victory: the passage through the Delegate Assembly of a strong resolution condemning the City University of New York administration for its elimination of remedial education at the four-year colleges. While this resolution has yet to be approved by ballot vote of the MLA membership, it received about a two-to-one margin of support at the December 1998 Delegate Assembly meeting, even though the Executive Council solicited highly derogatory commentaries on the resolution from the CUNY administration, and the CUNY vice chancellor appeared at the open hearing on resolutions and tried to torpedo it. In the hearings and demonstrations in early 1999 in New York City, this MLA move was repeatedly cited by the partisans of affirmative action and open admissions. So it gave crucial support at a crucial time. I think it will also make a difference that the MLA has now, through approval of a series of motions put forth by the Graduate Student Caucus, committed itself to setting standards for the employment of part-time and adjunct labor and for imposing sanctions on campuses that violate these standards.

Above all, we need to reverse the changes in the MLA constitution made about a decade ago so that we can once again pass resolutions on issues beyond the immediate purview of the academy. Every implication of recent trends in literary scholarship suggests the permeability of the membrane between literature and politics, rhetoric and praxis. Yet we have shot ourselves in the foot by simultaneously changing the rules and muzzling ourselves. (Sorry for the mixed metaphors—but they convey my agitation!) The absurdity of all this came out at the December 1998 convention when some of us presented a resolution condemning the language used to rationalize the bombing of Iraq. (You know, "collateral damage," "weapon of mass destruction," "degradation," etcetera.) Although the resolution passed the DA by a two-to-one margin (it needed three-to-one to get to the membership, since it was an emergency resolution), a number of its supporters noted that they'd much prefer to be condemning the bombing itself. I couldn't agree more.

**O'Connor and Hancuff:** This year the Graduate Student Caucus managed to bring the job crisis to the forefront of the MLA's agenda, with employment standards in the works. What power does the MLA have to impose sanctions on offending institutions, and do you believe these punishments will achieve results?

**Foley:** I think the MLA has considerable power to impose sanctions, if only it will do so. It would be a major slap in the face, at least as things are now, for institutions in violation of employment standards to be prohibited from advertising, whether tenure-track jobs or even the "new wave" of untenured temporary heavy course-loaded lectureships, in the *MLA Job List*.

But in order for the MLA to have the nerve to undertake such a course, it will have to reconceive itself as an "advocacy" rather than a "professional" organization. And at this point it's a far cry from doing so. So that's one of the tasks confronting the Radical Caucus. Even as we strive for this admittedly "trade unionist" goal, though, I think that those of us who consider ourselves Marxists should see this also as an opportunity to politicize our coworkers about the capitalist causal context of the employment crisis facing those of us who teach humanities in higher ed. In opposition to those who might think that raising this context will prohibit our colleagues from getting on board, I say that it is precisely this analysis that will give our movement staying power. So let's get busy.

# 10

# From the Left

## *An Interview with Alan Wald*

Against the mainstream of American literary and cultural history, Alan Wald has worked to recover a Left tradition, largely forgotten or erased during the Cold War period. His *New York Intellectuals: The Rise and Decline of the Anti-Stalinist Left from the 1930s to the 1980s* has become a standard history of that lauded group, providing a thick description of its large cast of characters and tracing its course from avowed Communist and Trotskyist politics to its eventual (and less than laudatory) "deradicalization" and drift into neoconservatism. In other scholarship, he has called attention to forgotten Left writers from the 1920s through the 1950s, such as Guy Endore, Sanora Ball, H. T. Tsiang, and John Wheelright, as well as others who wrote in popular forms such as detective fiction, science fiction, and screenplays, usually excluded from the canon.

Like Barbara Foley (interviewed in chapter 9), Wald was radicalized during the sixties, and his work since then represents an effort to combine activism and scholarship, as his comments here make clear. A student member of Students for a Democratic Society, a member of Solidarity and other political groups, and a contributor to Left magazines such as *Against the Current*, Wald does not see politics as a separate sphere from academic work. Rather, his scholarship aims to recover and reappraise Marxist and other radical traditions in modern American cultural history.

Born in 1946, Wald attended Antioch College (B.A., 1969) and the University of California at Berkeley (M.A., 1971; Ph.D., 1974). Educated in the crucible of late sixties politics, he participated in the antiracist and antiwar movements, which have influenced his thinking since, forging an internationalist Marxism that draws on many traditions. After teaching briefly at San Jose State University and Berkeley, since 1975 he has taught at the University of Michigan, affiliated with both the English department and the Program in American Culture while continuing his activist work.

Wald's books include *James T. Farrell: The Revolutionary Socialist Years* (NYU P, 1978), which stemmed from his dissertation; *The Revolutionary Imagination: The Poetry and Politics of John Wheelright and Sherry Mangan* (U of North Carolina P, 1983); *The New York Intellectuals* (U of North Carolina P, 1987); two collections of diverse essays, *The Responsibility of Intellectuals: Selected Essays on Marxist Traditions in Cultural Commitment* (1992) and *Writing from the Left: New Essays on Radicalism and Politics* (Verso, 1994); and, with George Breitman and Paul Le Blanc, *Trotskyism in the United States: Historical Essays and Reconsiderations* (1996). He most recently published *Exile from the Future: The Forging of the Mid-Twentieth-Century Literary Left* (U of North Carolina P, 2002).

Wald also inaugurated and edited an important series, The Radical Novel Reconsidered (U of Illinois P), which republished many "forgotten" radical works. For additional accounts of his work as an activist scholar, the interested reader might also consult his essay "A Pedagogy of Unlearning: Teaching the Specificity of U.S. Marxism," in *Class Issues: Pedagogy, Cultural Studies, and the Public Sphere*, ed. Amitava Kumar (NYU P, 1997), and his introduction to *The Responsibility of Intellectuals.*

This interview took place over several days in late November 1998 at George Washington University on the occasion of Wald's lecturing there, with some additions made by telephone. It was conducted by David Tritelli and Sharon Hanscom, doctoral candidates in English at GWU, and originally appeared in an issue of the *minnesota review* on "Activism and the Academy."

**Tritelli:** In your contribution to a recent forum on teaching Marxism, you claim that an awareness of the full scope of the U.S. Marxist cultural tradition is an urgent necessity for activists today. How have you, as one of the leading scholars of this tradition, learned from the cultural workers who have preceded you?

**Wald:** I try to operate with a consciousness of a long tradition, a legacy of Left activist-scholars that has passed through several major phases.

The conceptual framework of these semiautonomous stages might be regarded as problematics (in the full sense of the term, including absences) derived from the response of Marxist cultural workers to the world situation and the condition of the U.S. Left at certain points. When one examines this tradition throughout the century, there are of course similarities and continuities as well as important differences, and I try to carry out my work with an awareness of that whole background. For example, the problematic of the generation associated with the crisis of the Great Depression—creating a tradition which extends into the forties and early fifties—is shaped by a world situation featuring fascism marching across Europe, the evolution of the Russian Revolution from a liberatory upsurge to a brutal dictatorship, the emergence of the CIO, and new forms of antiracist struggles. This objective situation significantly shaped the consciousness and influenced the practice of cultural workers, and the record of their successes and failures remains an extraordinary legacy. One of the most difficult issues with which to come to grips in grasping this past is the difference between the discourse of anti-Stalinism, a Cold War phenomenon that was reactionary through and through, and the legitimate and honorable critiques of the Stalin regime first generated by revolutionary Marxists during the twenties, despite their failure to build an equivalently powerful and effective political movement.

Then there is the problematic of the generation associated with the sixties, which, again, is a historic moment that started earlier and extends longer. However, the landscape of the era of the sixties poses new kinds of challenges: the industrial unions are not center stage; the Civil Rights movement transforms into the Black Power movement; the student population plays a catalytic role; a new kind of international situation, with the effort of the U.S. to crush a national liberation movement in Vietnam as a centerpiece, is in place; a new kind of cultural revolution, with a strong drug presence, is in progress, and so on. Yet, in my view, these ostensibly discrete moments, as well as the present problematic of the nineties, are profoundly connected. There is much wisdom, including an awareness that there is some near-insoluble conundrum, to be extracted from the entire legacy. Thus I think of my activism and scholarship not as a new paradigm for emulation but much more modestly—as merely a contemporary extension of this troubled but honorable tradition. In other words, I am saying to anyone who might listen: "Don't follow me—learn from and join the tradition of the Paul Robesons, C. L. R. Jameses, Josephine Herbsts, Harvey Swadoses, Carlos Bulosans, and many others whom I admire." Of course, I'm talking about these figures as social activists, crusaders, and organization-builders of the Left, not exclusively as writers or as cultural studies icons to adorn academic work.

**Tritelli:** In saying that your scholarship and activism constitute a contemporary extension of this tradition, how are you distinguishing between activism and scholarship?

**Wald:** Let me emphasize that I don't make a sharp distinction between my activism and scholarship, as if they were isolated spheres necessarily in mortal combat for my waking hours and energy. While it is true that everything significant in life demands time, once one poses the situation in terms of competition—with activism as the alleged reason that one isn't accomplishing as much in other spheres, including personal life—there is the danger of activism becoming the scapegoat. Hence activism becomes the first thing that is sacrificed when one is under pressure. One of the lessons I've learned from the past is that the all-too-common and unfortunate result of defining activism as a competitor can be to take the tack that one's career is actually one's contribution to the movement. However, divorced from the controls provided by involvement in radical organizations and movements, one's career can very well end up taking one in unanticipated directions. When I wrote my book on deradicalization, *The New York Intellectuals*, I used a quotation from Goethe's *Faust*: "You think you are doing the pushing / But it is you who are being pushed."

Of course, it is true that another of the lessons of the past is that one must not judge scholarly or artistic efforts by knee-jerk political criteria, so I'm adamantly against an anti-intellectual ethos for the Left. But this must be balanced by the view that activism in collectivist Left organizations can be a method of testing, correcting, and gauging one's scholarly efforts, and perhaps the course of one's life as a whole. I'm talking about participation in social struggles actually improving the quality of such work in terms of providing empirical evidence, bringing the scholar more in touch with the world outside the library and university, and even offering a vision to drive one to greater accuracy and longer-term productivity. I think that such compatibility might certainly be the case for anyone working in the humanities and social sciences.

It doesn't follow, though, that one should capitulate to any pressures from movement activists when it comes to the question of whether one should abandon one's cultural work for allegedly more practical activity. We have seen, occasionally, especially in the operations of Leninist-type organizations, pressure for cultural workers to put their skills at the service of a party leadership in terms of producing polemical journalism, documents, etcetera. We have also seen how scholars and cultural workers have periodically felt tremendous pressure to abandon their work in favor of what appears to be more urgent forms of organizing, or proletarianization. Naturally one must do what seems most suited to one at different points in one's life, understanding the advantages and costs of various choices. There's no point in abandoning art for the revolution, only to find that one is a terrible union organizer, when one's posters might have become powerful beacons in the struggle. It's also reasonable to experiment with different kinds of activism, depending on one's age, the state of one's cultural and scholarly work, and one's personal situation. For example, up until my mid-forties, I was most comfortable doing Jimmy Higgins work in socialist organizations and groups in solidarity with anti-imperialist struggles. I was the person who attended all the meetings, took minutes, prepared and distributed newsletters, brought signs to and served as a monitor at demonstrations, and even did plant-gate newspaper sales and leaflet distributions. I never held leadership positions, or thought of myself as one who formulated policy beyond tactical suggestions as to where an action might be held or how to deal with police or administrators. Then, in the late eighties and early nineties, circumstances unfolded that encouraged me to become more visible as a person in terms of participation in a very public sister city delegation that went to Nicaragua during the Contra war, and on a fact-finding mission to Haiti to expose domestic repression during the military junta. (The object of these activities was to get as much publicity as possible.) In this same period, for the first time, in my early forties, I realized that I could play a role in helping to guide socialist publications, and so I became active in editing *Against the Current* and later *Science and Society*, as well as contributing where I could to other radical publications such as *Radical Teacher*, *Guardian*, *Z*, *In These Times*, *Monthly Review*, and *International Viewpoint*. So there has been an evolution, obviously in response to aging, the accumulation of experiences, the changing objective political situation, my job situation, and my personal life.

Other people, in their twenties, start out as political leaders of committees and groups, but that was not my trajectory. Probably because I was already involved in so much self-expression in my creative and scholarly writing, I found the Jimmy Higgins work in the mass movements much more appealing. But let me also add that one of my main conclusions from the study of U.S. Left history is the necessity of keeping alive serious socialist organizations, which is especially difficult in a period where they remain tiny and have few resources; so I maintain my membership in Solidarity, a socialist-feminist and antiracist network of Marxist activists on the far Left. I do what I can on behalf of its projects (support to *Labor Notes*, Teamsters for a Democratic Union, the Labor Party), and I also sustain international links with similar organizations and their cultural workers. This is what I consider to be my base; I do not see myself as a university-based activist, even if my physical presence is mostly there. Of course, on the campus I'm involved in the defense of affirmative action through the organization of a rank-and-file faculty group and participation in the student-based group, and I carry out international solidarity and pro-labor activities when I can. What I've described here is just my personal, perhaps idiosyncratic, trajectory of activism, which I try to keep in balance with my scholarship and a relatively stable personal life. (I'm a widowed, single parent of two teenage daughters, one in college.) Other people find that they have the confidence to start editing socialist journals in their twenties, and still others find their talents lie in community activism or in being a spokesperson on public issues like the economy, or being a leader in AAUP or of a radical caucus in their profession, or in running some kind of program or institute on a campus that has a progressive orientation. One's choice of commitment is not ipso facto more valuable than another's; it's very destructive to start insisting that everyone else carry out another's agenda.

**Hanscom:** Some of the work with which you have been involved—both as a scholar and as a member of the faculty at the University of Michigan—has been in the area of countering attacks against affirmative action. Would you discuss your general analysis of antiracist struggles in the present context of anti–affirmative action policies? And in this respect, how have you incorporated Marxism into your own antiracist activism?

**Wald:** In my view, the affirmative action struggle is essentially a continuation of the Civil Rights movement, which in turn grew out of earlier struggles against segregation and inequality. We are still trying to remove barriers to equal access, to level the playing field. However, the terrain has shifted from explicit segregation to institutional racism. That means that the levers of inequality are more deeply hidden in terms of the race bias inherent in criteria for admission, hiring, tenure, and promotion. Due to the mystifications of white supremacism, it is much harder to explain to some people how these institutionalized mechanisms work, and the forces of reaction have unashamedly seized on the demagoguery that our campaign for justice in admissions is really about special privilege in the form of racial preference. At the moment, the nature of the anti–affirmative action attack at the University of Michigan is focused on student admissions to the undergraduate program and the law school, so our fight-back is focused on mobilizing students and faculty, from the bottom up, to explain to the broader public why it is in everyone's interest to maintain affirmative action. One of the most optimistic new developments is an effort to work with community activists statewide to develop a pro–affirmative action proposition for the ballot.

I am much impressed by the clarifying power of the original Leninist distinction between nationalism of oppressed and oppressor groups, as well as the distinctions between national liberation struggles and nationalist ideologies. These offer categories for analysis that can help illuminate issues that I often find confused in contemporary discourses on nationalism. In addition, the strategy that the Communist Party and parts of the Trotskyist Left applied to the antiracist movements in the United States is important as well. In particular, the understanding that oppressed people first need to organize themselves, around their own issues and under their own leadership, as a precondition for unity with whites, remains valuable to this day. There is also the notion that people of color should not subordinate their interests and demands to whites, especially if whites are slow to move, and that people of color can play a vanguard role by setting an example. The old debates about what constitutes an authentic nation, about national and cultural autonomy, and about internal colonialism are a valuable legacy for theorizing cultural as well as political work in the late capitalist era.

**Tritelli:** Barbara Foley's work offers a competing assessment of the legacy of twentieth-century Left movements. She argues that the focus on nationalism is a weakness in that it indicates a reluctance to foreground class contradiction. Is this a different understanding of history than your own?

**Wald:** Yes, that does sound remarkably different from the tradition and perspective that I've been expounding here, and about which I have written, especially in my book *The Responsibility of Intellectuals*. I have to say that I have a very high opinion of Barbara's chapter on "The Negro Question" in *Radical Representations*, which I felt built effectively on the scholarship of Mark Naison and Robin Kelley. My initial reaction is that support of the right of self-determination blends well with an overall project of multiracial working-class unity, according to the model I offered in response to the preceding question: that the precondition to such unity is that people of color can self-organize and choose their own leadership independently, not subject to majority rule by whites; nor should they be pressured to hold off on demands for racial justice until such a time as whites are ready to embrace them. In fact, I don't see the self-organization of working-class women as a threat to ultimate unity between the sexes, even though women as a group don't have features of a nationality. Unity between those with unequal resources is a dubious unity, and different groups have different kinds of access to power in a capitalist society. So, in dealing with race chauvinism as well as male chauvinism, it is understandable that special measures are taken.

**Tritelli:** You have written that your work as an activist scholar is informed by certain kinds of praxis lived and absorbed in the sixties. Would you talk more about your own political formation?

**Wald:** I wrote about this in the recent book from New York University Press edited by Amitava Kumar, *Class Issues*. There I describe how fortunate I was in that I was not one of those people who was first formed as a liberal in the sixties, only to be shaken and traumatized by the turbulence of the decade. I was already alienated from the system before the sixties, at least from the time I was a junior high school student and was drawn to existentialism, the Beats, and the cool jazz scene. All during high school, 1960–64, I was a nonparticipant in the political process, although increasingly aware of the Civil Rights movement. The sixties New Left gave me my first chance to participate on my own terms, and this was through grassroots activism independent of the

Democratic Party or of the liberal establishment. I was emotionally drawn to the Civil Rights movement, and I chose to attend Antioch College partly because I knew it was interracial and had a strong connection to the movement. Moreover, I imagined that its work-study program would enable me to live out the on-the-road fantasies nurtured by the TV show *Route 66* and Jack Kerouac's fiction. My first activities were antiwar and antidraft, but I can't say that my views were exactly pacifist, since I certainly believed in self-defense and was instantly in sympathy with black organizations that promoted it. In fact, I was turned off of pacifism after an experience in 1965 at the Dayton, Ohio, fairgrounds, where the police surrounded our tiny antiwar demonstration and then allowed a motorcycle gang to come in and attack us. Our leaders told us to sit on the ground in concentric circles, with tall men (like me) on the outside with our arms linked; mine were held so tightly on either side that I could not fend off blows, let alone retaliate. The experience proved to me that I was definitely one of those unsuited for a Gandhi-style pacifist movement. On the other hand, I certainly supported nonviolent tactics and never sought out physical confrontations with the police or right-wingers. That personal disposition became clear around the same time a small group of us tried to protest at one of the huge pro–George Wallace racist rallies that were going on in southern Ohio. No doubt it stemmed from my recognition that I had a fear of people with guns, bayonets, and clubs, or of mobs waving Confederate flags, as much as from a political understanding that such confrontations backfire in terms of the Left getting blamed for intolerance.

Possibly the most crucial of my formative moments was my participation in the Cleveland ERAP [Economic Research and Action Project] sponsored by SDS [Students for a Democratic Society] in the winter and spring of 1965–66. There's a good study of the Cleveland project in James Miller's *Democracy Is in the Streets*. However, Miller treats the experience from the perspective of the group of older people, in their mid to late twenties, who had colonized the Near West Side ghetto and lived in an experimental commune situation. They had been criticized for indulging in a kind of "cult of the ghetto," living Spartan-like in the worst neighborhoods. Led by Paul Potter (recently the SDS president) and Sharon Jeffrey, they tried to carry out participatory democracy in their daily lives and decision-making processes, while organizing for jobs, tenants' rights, and welfare rights in this depressed community. Since I was only nineteen and lived in a two-room apartment a few blocks from the main house, I was witness to but not so caught up in their communal experience. The older SDS-ers invited me to a number of their meetings—for example, a firsthand report by Tom Hayden on his recent trip to Vietnam—and they assigned Kathy Boudin, who is now serving a life sentence in prison for her alleged terrorist activity, to be my political mentor.

But my main interests were always literary, so I was primarily assigned to help develop a community theater that adapted Brecht plays to our neighborhood situations. We drew on people from the local Bohemian arts milieu for support and produced our plays in an empty neighborhood storefront with a community discussion held afterward. Simultaneously I worked at a full-time job at the Cleveland Metropolitan General Hospital, as a child care worker with African American kids suffering from sickle-cell anemia. The total experience—an intensive four months—helped me to sort out many things. In regard to the job at the hospital, I could see that social work and personal caregiving were much too demanding for me, emotionally and physically. In regard to the ERAP project, I unquestionably felt an existential attraction to the idea of the endeavor, even though my grasp of the actual political strategy and possibilities of the ERAP effort was rudimentary. Years later I read about the Russian Narodniks and felt there was a similarity. (Here I must confess that there were often personal reasons for making these kinds of ostensibly political choices: I was first inspired about ERAP because of a college girlfriend, just as I was first introduced to the idea of going to Antioch by my high school girlfriend. From the sixties onward, my personal and political life were fused.) To be frank, it did not seem like a sacrifice but was actually bracing to feel the full force of ghetto conditions in my daily living—to live in a freezing-cold, dilapidated apartment in a semiabandoned building with derelicts sleeping on the steps. Many hours were spent in front of my apartment's filthy kitchen window looking into a grim alley, writing poetry and prose fragments to try to objectify my emotions and gain control over them.

Even before Cleveland, I had been drawn to living in the worst available neighborhood of Washington, D.C., and a poor one in Pittsburgh, while holding down jobs for three or four months at a time. This unquestionably upset my parents, although I doubt that that was my main motivation. (Actually, I arranged things so that they never saw my D.C. and Cleveland dwellings, which would certainly have caused a family crisis.) Perhaps this behavior was partly a way of affirming a kind of masculinity, since all the other avenues of conventional masculine affirmation—the military, business, sports—were either repulsive, boring, or unsuitable. Finding SDS-ers who were doing something similar made me feel less of an oddball in my alienation from middle-class and especially upper-class culture (not that I ever experienced much of this), although none of us had the illusion that our temporary situation resembled that of those who would be trapped in these conditions permanently. Still, while I certainly felt a kind of bond with the ERAP cadre, I knew that I didn't want to live in a commune with eighteen-hour-long meetings. I needed a large degree of solitude for my own reading and writing (mostly poetry then), and I was already formed as something of an antisocial personality. In the end, though, I had clarified my position so that my long-standing emotional reactions were partially redeemed: I recognized that I had been a misfit in middle-class society not because I was selfish and ungrateful (although I was certainly both of those things—and still am!) but because by temperament and intellectual bent I was with the poor against the privileged, the have-nots against the haves, and those of color against the whites. Moreover, I came to see that my disgust with middle- and upper-class culture was not, in my case, the snobbish elitism of those who thought that they were the truly educated, but that such disgust was founded on the kind of values I had encountered in SDS documents such as the "Port Huron Statement" and the ERAP manifesto "An Interracial Movement of the Poor."

So I was all set for some sort of definitive moral, cultural, and intellectual break with capitalist society; the problem was that the alternative perspective, liberatory Marxism, had been purged from academic, intellectual, and cultural life at that point, due to McCarthyism. As a result, I suffered considerable depression centered around the idea that I could not visualize a future for myself, occupationally or personally, in the dominant culture. My parents, however, were sure that my depression came from my rebellion, and that a return to a conformist way of life was the cure. So I got into kind of a battlelike situation where I wrote them brutal letters arguing that their efforts in that direction would only make things much worse. Even before then, my family contact was minimal—I walked out of high school in the spring of 1964 to attend a summer session at Antioch, which had a year-round program, and was probably never at home for more than three or four days at a time after that. Now, with the events of the sixties tearing society and culture apart in many other ways, family relations entered a phase of bullheadedness on both sides from which it never fully recovered. As a result, I have lacked confidence in my own ability to parent, and I resist any kind of parental relation to students.

**Tritelli:** Would you talk more about how your experience at Antioch College contributed to your radicalization?

**Wald:** I can't possibly overemphasize all the advantages I gained from this experience, although Antioch was not an academically rigorous place in a conventional sense, and now that I am a professor I realize that most of its faculty were not extraordinary. However, the work-study program enabled me to experience a wide range of jobs and also to see the burgeoning New Left at work in several key locations. For example, I was in Washington, D.C., working as a copy boy on the *Washington Post* during the first SDS anti–Vietnam War protest there. I was in Pittsburgh, working at the Home for Crippled Children, when SDS began to emerge at Case Western Reserve and the University of Pittsburgh. I was in New York City on several occasions, once working for the underground newspaper *East Village Other*. For the fall of 1967, I was in Birmingham, England, and I was active with the London "Stop It" Committee of antiwar U.S. citizens. I traveled with a group of Antioch students, and one professor, to the demonstration at the Democratic National Convention in Chicago in 1968. Since I spent five years at Antioch, I didn't leave until the spring of 1969; then, after traveling across the country for a week, I arrived in Berkeley right in the middle of the People's Park uprising when the city was under siege by the National Guard. It just seems as if I got all the lucky breaks!

Another feature of Antioch was the presence of a large number of Red Diaper Babies, children of the Old Left who grew up with the culture of the Communist Party. For a long time I couldn't figure out why they had these organizational skills and possessed so much knowledge about racism and imperialism. I felt that my boring high school had cheated me out of an education in the real world, and that I would never catch up. I felt ignorant, humble, and tongue-tied in their presence. But I had no doubt that these Red Diaper kids (I didn't use that phrase at the time, and they usually didn't refer to their parents' past) were the most interesting people. They took their ideas seriously in that their studies were aimed at action to change the world. Also, since they were the post-1956 generation of children of Communists, they were culturally and politically more flexible than their parents. They tended to be secular Jews (although they didn't hide their Jewishness) who felt a strong identification with African Americans in regard to cultural issues. I felt that, too, but I didn't have a way of talking about it. Also, to connect the personal and political again, I repeatedly found that the most interesting women that I wanted to date tended to be African American women and Bohemian, "Beat" women (often secular Jews)—and the Red Diaper milieu at that moment brought blacks and Jews, politicos and Beats, together. So the Red Diaper Babies were living in a culture of which I wanted to be a part.

Gradually I began to discard my totally ignorant view that regarded Marxism, socialism, the working class, etcetera, as outdated and irrelevant ideas, and I began to study them for the first time. This was specifically under the tutelage of former SDS president Carl Oglesby, who was brought to Antioch as Activist Scholar in Residence; I was enthralled by his eloquence and erudition, and for a while he took me under his wing. Then my fall 1967 stay in England at the workingman's college of Fircroft, where it seemed as if every interesting person I met was some kind of socialist, provided the final push. Still, I did not want to abandon my early New Left/Beat/existentialist thinking; it had saved me from despair, and was crucial to my identity formation. In that sense I'm a bit conservative—once I become committed to a certain group of ideas, I am rather reluctant to just simply cast them off and move in some totally new direction. But I needed a broader view of history and society in order to develop some vision of the part that I might play, outside and in opposition to the dominant culture and the system it supported. So, while I was hardly alone in making the transition from vague New Left ideas to Marxism in 1968, I did not share the view that the New Left had to be rejected in toto as a middle-class, individualist movement. Nor do I recall undergoing much of the transformative experience of the convert to Marxism. Since I was not exactly leaving the New Left, I felt a lot of skepticism about Marxism in general and the existing political groups in particular. I started off from a position of questioning Marxism, and I am still questioning it. That's why, every now and then, when some old comrade announces, "It's time for us to start questioning Marxism!" I have to sit up and blink. Were there actually other people who moved to Marxism in the sixties and seventies who hadn't been questioning it?

**Hanscom:** It sounds as if you see more continuities between the Old and the New Left. Can you describe your associations with various left-wing organizations and your assessments of these experiences?

**Wald:** In the spring of 1968 I separated from the SDS—the takeover in progress by the Progressive Labor Party and the policies of the other SDS factions had repelled me—and I gradually began working with a group called the Young Socialist Alliance (YSA). This organization doesn't exist anymore, but when I first met members of the Antioch chapter I perceived it as a group that was both classical Marxist, yet culturally sophisticated with a touch of Beat/Bohemianism. I had already encountered a number of its members from inside the SDS chapter, where they seemed to have functioned as hardworking comrades, mainly concerned about the Vietnam War but also promoting a kind of sympathetic but not uncritical view of Cuba, as well as a pro–Malcolm X view of Black Nationalism. They called themselves revolutionaries, and Trotskyists, but the definition of revolution they offered, particularly in a popularized pamphlet called *Socialism on Trial*, seemed utterly democratic and humane. Several members were much involved in the drama department at Antioch, and one had been a sort of inspirer of the SDS community theater in Cleveland in which I had participated. At that moment, they were the people reading Isaac Deutscher, Georg Lukács, Wilhelm Reich, and, so far as I can recall, they sponsored the first talks on women's liberation. Moreover, they boasted of close ties to a French student organization very active in the May 1968 revolt called the JCR (Revolutionary Communist Youth), which had been a kind of Left grouping of crypto-Trotskyists in the French Communist Party Youth who broke off in rebellion against the PCF's temporizing policies. Soon the YSA brought the Belgian Marxist economic theorist Ernest Mandel, and, later, his wife, Gisella Mandel, to Antioch, and after meeting them I started to read essays by Mandel that were appearing in *New Left Review*. This was a publication with which I felt an immediate affinity. From Berkeley, a YSA leader named Peter Camejo visited Antioch to talk about the campus movement there; he, too, seemed sophisticated, creative—and funny.

The YSA was also the youth organization of the historic Trotskyist organization in the U.S., the SWP (Socialist Workers Party, founded in 1938). Soon I met an impressive party intellectual in his sixties, George

Novack, whom I found to have a remarkable breadth of reading. I also hosted, in my apartment, a middle-aged leader of the SWP's anti–Vietnam War activity whom the Party was running for U.S. president as part of a movement-building strategy. This was Fred Halstead, a warm and human guy. So, while there were probably some countervailing elements in the background that I should have seen, my initial belief was the optimistic one that the SWP was an organization through which Old and New Lefts might come together to the benefit of both. So far as I could tell, the Old Guard people like Novack and Halstead were totally friendly to people like me and similar types joining our YSA chapter. The main area where I felt definitely out of sync with the SWP version of Trotskyism at that moment was that I didn't share the kind of virulent hostility toward the Communist Party tradition on which some Trotskyists thrive—a reductive interpretation of everything in the U.S. Communist movement to "Stalinism." I saw much more richness and complexity in the Communist movement, and eventually even a nobility in those who had recognized their movement's mistakes without reverting to anti-Communism. Most importantly, my cultural interests, now shifting toward the achievements of the Left, continued bringing me into more and more contact with former and even a few active Communists, so I felt I was in touch with a growing body of evidence that kept challenging the reductive aspect of the Trotskyist theory.

**Hanscom:** You indicated earlier that Marxism was absent in the university curriculum when you were a student at Antioch, and that it was necessary to seek radical education through other venues and experiences. Within the contemporary setting of the university, can you describe what role Marxism now plays in the curriculum? How does cultural studies, for example, allow for an acceptance of Marxism?

**Wald:** There are many kinds of radical associations in the origins of cultural studies, but, of course, the problem with cultural studies is the problem of appropriation by so many divergent trends. It is clear that Marxism came back into the academy, after having been purged in the Cold War, due to the presence of the generation of the sixties as graduate students and faculty. During the sixties itself, my experience was that Marxism was available only in a somewhat extrainstitutional manner. At Antioch I took an entirely student-run course on Marxism for credit. At Berkeley, I studied the young Marx intensively in a course with Richard Lichtman, but it was taught off campus at a place called the Wright Institute. (Lichtman had not received tenure in the philosophy department.) We also had a student-run course on Marxist literary criticism for a semester out of the Berkeley English department, for which Larzer Ziff was kind enough to front; I recall that Bruce Franklin, still at Stanford, was brought in to lecture on Mao's writings from the Yenan Forum. When I came to Michigan, there was no Marxism taught in the English department; it was suggested that I teach a graduate course called "Social Theory and the Arts," which included Raymond Williams, Lukács, and so forth. But after a while I would be periodically assigned both graduate and undergraduate courses called "Marxist Literary Criticism" and then (at my request) "Marxism and Cultural Studies." Soon other people, influenced by the sixties, were coming into the department and teaching Jameson, Eagleton, and others, and one even referred to herself as a Marxist. I also have a sense that the first wave of Marxist teaching in the late seventies and eighties was more neo-Marxist; that is, not based on the classics, but Althusser and Benjamin. More recently, I have seen signs of people wanting to go back and discuss the ur-writings, especially at the Marxist Literary Group Institute. But early on, the Marxism taught on campus was based on a kind of dogmatic rejection of Engels, Lenin, and Plekhanov, and some of that still exists. One couldn't put in a good word for these guys without being accused of subscribing to a reflection theory, in the same way that people are ritualistically accused of being essentialist today. Still, I have to say that an irony of this new semi-institutionalization of Marxism is that Marxism appears to many students to be just another subject, not an exciting or dangerous topic that one is lucky to have a chance to study.

**Hanscom:** How do you self-identify politically now? Would you describe your own politics specifically in terms of Marxism?

**Wald:** Well, I have no hesitation in describing myself as a revolutionary Marxist, so long as one understands "revolution" in the democratic sense of *Socialism on Trial* and, also, that one can support revolutionary politics but still be a rebel by temperament. I guess what that means in practice is that I am not primarily for electoral strategy, especially of voting for liberals and building the Democratic Party, although I certainly favor using the electoral system to advance socialist causes or the mass movements. And of course I support reforms—not in the sense of reformism, but reforms that empower subaltern groups and increasingly lead to the replacement of systems of exploitation. So far as Marxism goes, I think it is crucial to declare oneself as Marxist in the United States to affirm the Red tradition of uncompromising opposition to racism, imperialism, and so forth, along with an identification with the working-class movement (which extends beyond just trade unions).

But I always say that I am a classical Marxist and not an orthodox Marxist, to make it clear that I am not attracted to class reductionist or economist versions. My understanding of class is similar to that of a scholar like George Lipsitz who fully inflects the category with gender, ethnicity, race, and culture. The more complicated issue, though, probably concerns Trotskyism, Leninism, and Bolshevism, which are generally seen as part of the revolutionary Marxist tradition. The problem is that I see the contemporary socialist movement as much bigger than any of the above, and I am only interested in what these traditions can add to the mix. Certainly I am not a Trotskyist if one's definition of a Trotskyist is one who believes in a Trotskyist program to which one recruits to build a vanguard party. I have written explicitly against that position, and, even in my enthusiastic YSA days of 1968–71, I was still partly wedded to a New Left vision. On the other hand, I find that the overall Trotskyist critique of what happened in the USSR is the most Marxist in broad outlines; I am not here getting into all the little schisms about state capitalism versus bureaucratic collectivism. Moreover, the general Trotskyist understanding of the Soviet experience can also, with appropriate adjustments, be a great help to understanding China, Cuba, and the general dynamic of struggles in economically underdeveloped countries. From 1967 until his death, Ernest Mandel was the leading Trotskyist theoretician with whom I identified.

On the question of Leninism and Bolshevism (which in this context I am treating as synonymous), I think it is important to resist the demonization of Lenin and reject the straight-line thesis that Bolshevism necessarily created Stalinism, or was fulfilled by Stalin's terror. That said, I think there's no question but that Lenin's and Trotsky's actions often contradicted the profoundly democratic claims of their theories. Therefore, it is unhelpful to keep presenting 1917 as a model, since it was a historical experience that went so terribly wrong, and, of course, occurred in a drastically different kind of social formation from the U.S. There is much to be learned from Lenin and the 1917 revolution if we can avoid either of those approaches. So I think it would be fair to say that I am influenced by Trotsky's and Lenin's theories, along with a few dozen others whom I would put at near-equal weight.

**Tritelli:** You edit a series for the University of Illinois Press called The Radical Novel Reconsidered. How do you choose what gets recovered by that series? And, more generally, what are your hopes for the series?

**Wald:** Well, my hopes for the series are to get as many out-of-print left-wing novels—particularly the lesser-known ones from the noncanonical periods by women and writers of color—back into circulation. This will enable us, for the first time, to understand what the history of U.S. literary production has been and begin to theorize it. A central issue in responding to the problem posed by the canon is that we really don't know what is out there—and we haven't yet begun to collectively discuss it. This means that we have no sound basis for making judgments and comparisons. The official instruments of cultural memory, including books about the Left, are very partial in terms of the number of texts and writers discussed in any detail. But to try to rectify even just the radical novel component through the limited resources of one university press, one with a small staff and many other projects, is daunting. The University of Illinois can only bring out two books a year, their research staff is small, and their marketing budget is modest. On my side, I already have a list of two hundred plausible titles, which grows larger every month. My personal priority has been in the area of honoring living writers—that is, struggling to get books out while Myra Page, John Sanford, Ira Wolfert, Alfred Maund, Philip Bonosky, and Abraham Polonsky are still alive. (Unfortunately, Page died just before and Wolfert just after their books appeared.) I also aim for a goal of half the books by women, and of as many by writers of color as possible; but here we have been frustrated by a variety of problems involving copyright, delays in submission of introductions, the inability of the press to reproduce from the extant copies, and so forth. Moreover, it's not a situation where I simply propose a title and the press brings it out. First, I make a case to the director, usually based on my priorities and arguments about the quality of the book; then the director makes a decision based on what can be learned about the previous sales history, the reviews, the copyright and reproduction situations, and potential markets; and finally the Illinois Press board solicits blind readers' reports (usually two, and I have no part in the selection), and then the board comes to a decision. Needless to say, I don't get paid for my work on this, and authors of introductions receive only two hundred dollars per essay. So most of the people involved in this project are offering a kind of service to the Left.

**Tritelli:** How do you see these novels as relevant to socialist activism? This work is obviously useful as an intervention in literary studies, but what is the utility of this kind of project for people outside the academy?

**Wald:** There is a diverse range of uses. One of the most important may be to instill some humility in young activists today. People in the Communist or Trotskyist movements thought they were in the vanguard of humanity and too often acted like it. In the sixties, many people of my generation were pretty ungenerous toward our ancestors. Many of us thought we were a qualitatively "new" New Left and going to do everything differently. Of course, it's true that young people of every new era are going to want to cast up their own new leaders, and that will surely happen again. But one of the things these novels show are commitments similar to those of us in the sixties and to today's young radicals on the eve of the millennium. The Old Left were just as intelligent, just as devoted, and just as cool when they were young. And in many cases they promoted political ideas that later generations thought were part of their own militancy; for example, look at the climax of John Sanford's *The People from Heaven* where the black woman, America Smith, guns down her white rapist, who is a thug and an anti-Semite as well. Sanford is defending armed self-defense for blacks in the face of a white community that is unwilling or not ready to protect one's rights. Sanford's novel appeared during World War II, a time when Communists tended to subordinate national liberation struggles to the antifascist struggle, yet the climax has something of the feel of the armed struggle atmosphere of the sixties—with the addition that the person who picks up the gun is a woman. Another example is Alexander Saxton's *The Great Midland*, which deals with a Communist militant who sublimates the emotional pain of his personal life into class struggle. Equally important is the dilemma of his companion, a working-class woman who has an affair with an aspiring professor while the Communist is in Spain. These are human issues that the Left of all generations needs to confront.

**Hanscom:** Can you comment on the recent movements among graduate students and part-time faculty to gain the right to unionize?

**Wald:** This is a "principled question," as we used to say: graduate students must have the right to organize because they will be victimized and exploited if they do not. Moreover, their self-organization is to everyone's benefit. It clarifies and thereby improves relations between graduate students and faculty. It gives fantastic experiences in collective responsibility to the graduate students. It increases the input, energy, and ideas of graduate students into university and department life. Plus, the graduate student unions invariably raise crucial issues to the health and culture of their university community—such as affirmative action, an end to discrimination, more effective training, smaller class sizes, a living wage, acceptable health benefits, and good relationships with other working people on the campus and in the community.

**Tritelli:** To conclude, as a leftist academic and activist, what do you see as the work that the Left needs to address with academic institutions? What institutional critiques need to be advocated by the Left?

**Wald:** I'm glad that the theme of this interview is activism *and* the academy, rather than *in* the academy. My own experience is that I can be effective in terms of activism on the university campus but I do not base my activism, or my life, in the university. One aspect of this flows from a political perspective; another aspect has to do with background, personal temperament, and so forth. The political aspect is compatible with what you just described: the university is an institution in the larger society, and its problems are connected to that larger society. I identify first of all with the working-class movement, the anticolonialist movement, and the international socialist movement. That is my class and my milieu; it is from where I draw inspiration, and it is with these movements that humanity's long-term interests lie. I'm totally of the mentality that when young people or working people struggle for liberation in some other county, they are fighting for my liberation, too. You might say that I am a scholar and teacher by trade; these are my craft skills, and I work in the university. But I am not first of all a professor or academic; intellectuals are a middle social stratum that is divided in all sorts of ways, and members of this group have diverse loyalties and affinities. So I participate in my profession but from a political perspective based on the outside. This location is what determines my priorities. It is part of the reason why I have primarily been involved, since coming to Michigan, in issues around

Central America, South Africa, Haiti, and in support of various strikes and labor struggles.

In terms of immediate campus issues, affirmative action and support for the graduate students' unionization are top priority. In terms of my own academic units, the main issues have been eliminating the Eurocentric bias of the course offerings and improving the gender/color composition of the faculty and students. By and large I function better in rank-and-file faculty groups, or in student-based groups, or even in community peace groups. Due to my Bohemianism and several decades of activity in Left organizations, I am very uncomfortable in many university settings, including MLA. The often pretentious speech, style of wit, and mode of discourse of the professoriate are irritating. I certainly don't deny the legitimacy of other points of view here. However, to take one example, I myself am not for any attempt to turn MLA or ASA into Left organizations. I already belong to a plethora of these and have many opportunities to promote Marxist and anti-imperialist critiques through their publications and platforms.

What I want is for MLA and ASA to be broad and nonexclusionary, so that those of us with far Left commitments—and of course women and people of color with social commitments—can dialogue with others and function as first-class citizens in a profession that hitherto excluded our views and even our physical presence. At the same time, there are certainly crucial issues—affirmative action, the right of all university personnel to organize unions—which ASA and MLA need to defend in order to maintain their breadth as well as the quality of education. The perspective of the activist Left in the academy is not to capture the leadership or ram through a program but to inspire the rank and file to change their own lives and thereby change the world. Some in the Old Left called that "socialism from below," and it's one of those elements from the past that needs to return in new forms.

# 11

# Politics and Philosophy

## *An Interview with Nancy Fraser*

Nancy Fraser has been a pivotal interlocutor of contemporary theory, adjudicating among Anglo-American and Continental philosophy, feminism and poststructuralism, and Marxism and public sphere theory. She has brought figures such as Habermas, Foucault, and others to analytic-dominated philosophy, and a clearheaded conceptual grounding in philosophy to theory. And she has brought politics to the fore, for instance, examining the U.S. welfare system through the lens of political philosophy, usefully reorienting it in terms not of dependence but of a "politics of needs."

As she discusses here, she has negotiated the dual paths of sixties activism and academic philosophy. In perhaps her most well-known work, she negotiates the current impasse of the Left, after actually-existing socialism and divided between traditional class politics and identity politics, elucidating the stakes and interchange of "the politics of redistribution" and "the politics of recognition." This kind of distinction is characteristic of Fraser's method—instead of Occam's razor, one might call it Fraser's razor, lucidly discriminating key theoretical issues of our day to provide a way out of the confusion of "postsocialism."

Born in 1947, Fraser studied philosophy at Bryn Mawr College (B.A., 1969) but became progressively more involved in radical politics in Philadelphia and New York, as she discusses here. In the aftermath of the sixties, she decided to return to the academy to study at CUNY (M.A., 1979; Ph.D., 1980). She took her first academic position at the University of Georgia in 1980 but in 1982 moved to Northwestern University where she remained until 1995. At that time she moved to the New School in New York, where she is Loeb Professor of Philosophy and Politics.

Fraser first attained her reputation from essays on Foucault, French poststructuralism, Rorty, Habermas, and feminism, many of which are collected in *Unruly Practices: Power, Discourse and Gender in Contemporary Social Theory* (U of Minnesota P, 1989), a book that concludes with her tour de force reconsideration of the U.S. welfare system. *Justice Interruptus: Critical Reflections on the "Postsocialist" Condition* (Routledge, 1997) includes her famous piece "From Redistribution to Recognition? Dilemmas of Justice in a 'Postsocialist' Age" and other essays from 1990–96. A kind of symposium, *Adding Insult to Injury: Social Justice and the Politics of Recognition* (Verso, 1999) features responses from Rorty, Judith Butler, Selya Benhabib, and others to "From Redistribution to Recognition?" along with Fraser's rejoinders. A companion volume, *Redistribution or Recognition? A Political-Philosophical Exchange* (Verso, 2003), is a dialogue between Fraser and the German philosopher Axel Honneth. See also the collection *Feminist Contentions: A Philosophical Exchange*, ed. Linda Nicholson (Routledge, 1994), which stages a debate among Butler, Benhabib, Drucilla Cornell, and Fraser, and Amanda Anderson's response to it, "Debatable Performances: Staging Contentious Feminisms," *Social Text* 54 (1998). Additionally, Fraser has edited *Revaluing French Feminism: Critical Essays on Difference, Agency, and Culture* (Indiana UP, 1992).

This interview took place on 6 April 1999 in the *minnesota review* office at the University of Missouri in Columbia. It was conducted by Jeffrey Williams and transcribed by Annie Pulis, an editorial assistant to the review while a graduate student at Missouri. It originally appeared in an issue of the review on "Activism and the Academy."

**Williams:** I'm curious to know how you came to do philosophy. From what I know about American philosophy departments, you must have had to walk against the current to do what you do, to deal with Continental philosophy, to do feminism, to talk about politics. So, how did you come to do what you do?

**Fraser:** My story is probably not terribly unusual. I was a budding, young intellectual who fell in love with philosophy as an undergraduate. I went to Bryn Mawr College, which did not have any analytic philosophy at all. I studied Plato and Kant and Hegel and so on. And I took every philosophy course that there was to take, and just loved it. But there was a lot going on besides intellectual work—I was in college from 1965 to 1969—and at one point in my senior year, 1968–69, I simply stopped attending the senior seminar because I was caught up in the sit-in demonstrations that were breaking out everywhere.

**Williams:** Where?

**Fraser:** In the Philadelphia area. I was very involved in the Philadelphia SDS. There was a big struggle over the building of a science center in West Philadelphia that involved a consortium of all the area colleges and universities, including Bryn Mawr. Not only was the center slated to do war research, but it would destroy the black working-class neighborhoods around the University of Pennsylvania.

**Williams:** Similar to Columbia's plans to build the gym in Morningside Park that was the occasion for the Columbia takeovers . . .

**Fraser:** Exactly. It was one of the classic struggles of that era. I was intensely involved in all of that and going back and forth between philosophy and radical political activity. And when I graduated I sold all of my books back to the college bookstore, convinced that they were all bourgeois ideology. Five years later, when I decided to go to graduate school, I had to buy all of those goddamn books back and lost a fortune!

When I was a senior in college they brought a visiting professor to Bryn Mawr, a young woman, who taught for the first time a course in analytic philosophy. None of us knew what that was, and I took it and actually found it quite interesting—Wittgenstein, Frege, Russell, and so on. But like a lot of undergraduates interested in philosophy, I didn't really know that analytic philosophy *was* philosophy in the United States. And so I was shocked when I went to graduate school and realized that you couldn't read Sartre, Hegel, and all that stuff. People who were at liberal arts colleges really got a different education, and I fell in love with the more classical tradition. Anyway, I was out of school for five years in the early seventies, from 1969 to 1975, doing political work.

**Williams:** Where?

**Fraser:** Living mostly in New York. By that time the New Left was falling apart. I had been one of those people who really expected a socialist revolution in the seventies. This turned out to be a completely deluded idea, of course, but at the time it seemed to be possible. And when it became clear that it wasn't going to happen and the various Left milieus began to come apart, I looked for a longer-term life plan and . . .

**Williams:** Hence grad school.

**Fraser:** Hence grad school. At first I wasn't at all sure that I would be able to hack it. I didn't know how I would feel about philosophy again. I was determined to stay in New York, so I went to City University, which had opened its new Graduate Center on Forty-second Street. The philosophy department was very analytic and not the sort of place that I should have gone to. But it had one great advantage for me: it was very new and did not yet have a stabilized modus operandi. They were still in the process of establishing a core faculty; various professors throughout the CUNY system in the whole city were jockeying to see who was going to get to teach in the Ph.D. program. People would come and give a course for a semester and then disappear. So it was easy to slip through the cracks and do what you wanted, because no one was minding the store. I was able to take courses in the history department and the sociology department, things that no other graduate program that focused on turning out a certain kind of professionalized product would permit. After I left, it became a normal graduate school.

In terms of graduate school, I was very much self-educated and I have to say I have a love-hate relationship with analytic philosophy. It wasn't all hate, because there is a part of me that really gets into the intellectual game dimension of it—just the sheer technical brilliance and the cleverness of it. I think that, in my work, I've tried to co-opt some of the argumentative clarity and techniques of analytic philosophy and use them for other purposes. There are things about the tradition that I respect.

**Williams:** I was reading your essay in *Feminist Contentions*, "False Antitheses," last night, and was struck by how you lay out issues in a remarkably lucid, straightforward way, reminiscent of the analytic philosophy, of, say, Quine. You discriminate between Butler and Benhabib in a kind of analytic way, making three distinctions, showing that they are sometimes talking about two different categories when they disagree.

**Fraser:** I believe that a lot of what you're referring to is the influence of analytic training. I tried hard to avoid it, and I fought it kicking and screaming at the time, but I actually believe in the end I got a lot out of it.

**Williams:** You fought it because of politics, or rather its total eschewal of politics?

**Fraser:** The problem was that these techniques—the ability to draw distinctions and to develop arguments, to tease out underlying presuppositions that are unspoken, to scrutinize those and to reconstruct arguments, to evaluate arguments and to make arguments—are very valuable for the kind of work that I want to do—and for anybody, in fact. The problem is that in a lot of analytic philosophy, as it was practiced and is still practiced, these very useful techniques are put to work on utterly arid, uninteresting technical problems. I tried to use them in relation to problems that I consider real problems, not artificial, textbook problems.

**Williams:** Like what?

**Fraser:** Well, like the recent work I've done on "redistribution" and "recognition," which concerns the relationship between identity politics and multiculturalism on the one hand and social democratic or socialist politics on the other. That seems to me to be a genuine dilemma and question for our time. One thing I've tried to do in thinking it through is to make use of some of these more analytic styles of thinking.

**Williams:** Where did feminism come in?

**Fraser:** Like everyone else of my generation, I went through the New Left experience noticing belatedly that there was a rather unequal division of labor within the New Left. It's interesting because I went to Bryn Mawr, which is a college with a very long and rather extraordinary feminist tradition. It belonged to a strain of bluestocking, elite feminism, the sort of feminism that said we're going to teach higher mathematics and physics, Latin and Greek, everything serious and difficult, to women. But by the time I got to Bryn Mawr, the specifically feminist rationale had been suppressed. It wasn't until second-wave feminism developed that I understood what my college was all about. I was a Marxist and a radical before I was a feminist, which meant that I had the experience of a mixed-sex Left, which, for all of its problems (and there were many), remained a kind of benchmark for me. I've always been very uncomfortable with the separatist dimensions of second wave feminism, with cultural feminism, with the sort of feminism that is too emphatic about gender difference. It's not my kind of feminism, and I've reluctantly had to accept that a great deal of American feminism is not really Left. At its best it's liberal. To me, liberal is not a dirty word; it's an honorable word, but it's not really Left, and I think of myself as a leftist. I was sympathetic to the kind of socialist feminism that was being developed in the seventies and that is quite forgotten and suppressed today.

**Williams:** In an interview I did with Richard Ohmann, he commented that his book *English in America* arose out of the "critique of everything existing" from that time, from the late sixties and early seventies. That impulse seems almost a forgotten memory now.

**Fraser:** The aspect of the sixties legacy that remains important to me and goes against the grain today is the commitment to a systematic critique of society as a totality. This is not to say that the totality is seamless or that any part of it can be read off automatically from any other. Nevertheless, there is something like what Rawls calls "the basic structure of society" that sets the basic parameters of social life and constrains its possibilities. To do a radical critique means to talk about that level in a systematic way, so I find myself at odds with what I think is the dominant tendency today to reject a systematic critique. Many people now think that to think about the "social totality" in this sense is totalitarian, whereas to me this systematic critique is the essence of radicalism.

**Williams:** I agree entirely. I want to go back to your turn in 1969 from being an ace college student to being a political activist. How did you make that turn?

**Fraser:** It wasn't simply a sudden turn, but rather a stage in a more complicated history. I grew up in Baltimore, Maryland, which was a Jim Crow, segregated city through the early sixties. When I was in junior high and high school, the struggle for desegregation was in full swing. The first and most formative political experience for me was the experience of the sit-ins to desegregate restaurants, amusement parks, swimming pools, and so on. John Waters's *Hairspray*, in a fantasy mode, captures some of that experience; it does strange things with it, but it was based on the desegregation of the Gwynn Oaks amusement park, which I myself was involved in, so I have a real fondness for that movie. So when I went to college, I had already been through a prehistory of political involvement.

But I was also pulled in a different direction. Bryn Mawr was very much an ivory tower sort of place, and I deliberately chose to go there because I wanted to be serious intellectually even though I didn't know what that meant. I didn't come from a particularly intellectual family. When I was in high school, I had an enormous anger and contempt for my teachers, whom I thought were stupid. I thought there was something real and serious elsewhere, and I thought Bryn Mawr was the place where I might find it. I used to cut high school and go to the library at Johns Hopkins and try to pretend that I was a college student, in the hope that other people looking at me would think I was a student!

**Williams:** It's fascinating to me how the university has presented for many of us a vista of a larger world, an entryway into politics and intellectual issues. In some ways, it's the opposite of the stereotypical ivory tower image. Where I grew up, in a working-class neighborhood on Long Island, you either stayed or went to college. For me, when I went to Columbia, I thought it was an escape from provincialism.

**Fraser:** My story is not the same as this, but I think about the New York Intellectuals and what it meant for that generation of guys—they were guys—to be at City College. I think for a stratum of young people that college is a magic signifier of freedom, of exploration, of opening up out of the stifling world of family, whether it's suburbia or the working class. It's the route elsewhere. Sometimes it's connected to class mobility. In my case it was a route out of the banality of middle-class suburbia. What could be more the polar opposite of Jewish middle-class suburbia than Bryn Mawr College?

Anyway, when I got to Bryn Mawr, things were complicated because this activist impulse was strong in me. I was always struggling with it at Bryn Mawr and struggling against Bryn Mawr on behalf of it. So I didn't suddenly become a radical. I went to Israel in the aftermath of the Six Day War, as a volunteer. They called for young people from abroad to come to help with the harvest on the kibbutzim while the population was still mobilized, and I ended up staying for eight months. I only intended to go for a summer, but I had the sense that there was something constructive, socially useful, and committed about the kibbutz life. I was already contrasting it to college life and things like the drug scene. I took a term off from college and didn't go back until February 1968. And then when I came back, I was ready for politics. I knew I didn't want to stay in Israel by then; by the time I left there, I had developed a critique of Israeli nationalism. You had to be there to appreciate it.

When I came back, I spent a lot of time in Philadelphia working for draft resistance and one of my most memorable experiences was calling up the Nation of Islam Mosque in Detroit and asking to speak to Muhammad Ali to invite him to be a speaker at a "Burn Your Draft Card" rally. That was during the time when he had been stripped of his title and was a pariah in the country, so it was not hard to get him on the phone. He just took the phone and said, "Hi." Anyway, it was such an intense time, with the music scene, the drug scene, as well as the political scene. Everything was opening up in all kinds of ways, and it was very exciting, but many people were also very disoriented and destabilized. I went through a period when I was hanging out with a lot of antiwar Quaker clergy in the draft resistance movement. I was deeply confused and actually had thoughts that are frightening now, thoughts to the effect that if I were really committed, really serious about stopping the war, then shouldn't I immolate myself like the Buddhist monks in Vietnam? How could I justify not burning myself alive?

Well, fortunately, I met some Marxists. Then I was really ready. And I had the experience of almost a conversion. I met some members of a Marxist faction of SDS, and I realized then that I didn't have to burn myself. I could figure out other ways to change the world. And then I became very active in the local SDS, which was dominated by a quasi-Trotskyist faction.

**Williams:** Where was this?

**Fraser:** This was still in Philadelphia, and then I moved to New York as part of that group in 1969. I stayed active in this milieu until the mid-seventies when I went to graduate school. That's the story. Feminism was later, in 1975, after a marriage and a divorce, which are also a part of that story.

**Williams:** That's a kind of an allegorical narrative of the feminist movement, no?

**Fraser:** Absolutely. I think a lot of this story is not unusual for the generation of kids who came first to the Civil Rights movement, the antiwar movement, SDS, etcetera. And I went through a familiar progression for my age-group.

**Williams:** So you went back to grad school?

**Fraser:** I experienced a real shriveling of the New Left milieu. A tremendous expansiveness and creativity was turning inward on itself, cannibalizing its own factions in nasty infighting. In my case, it was connected to the breakdown of a marriage, and I was looking around for something else to do and literally thought, "Ah, philosophy, I used to love that. Is it possible that I could still love it?" But not in the sense of wanting to turn my back on or in any way suppress the intervening experience. I didn't want to become an ivory tower, academic philosopher.

**Williams:** An impulse which is unique in philosophy departments . . .

**Fraser:** I don't think that's true. No, I think it's a discipline that always attracts a significant share of radicals. An enormous percentage of the Left radicals began in philosophy. Of course, some of them have made uneasy peaces and repressed a lot of themselves, but a lot of people in philosophy who are as apparently straight as you'd ever find have some suppressed radical history. I don't want to overstate this, but even the seventies and eighties saw a huge flourishing of political philosophy in the American academy. It's a high point in the history of American philosophy; John Rawls is going to be as important in the history of philosophy as John Stuart Mill, I believe. What he and his colleagues did was to revive an absolutely dead area of philosophy. No one was interested in political philosophy, and they resurrected it. They were influenced by the sixties, and they were all social democrats and left-wing liberals, too old themselves to have been student radicals, but they were carried along by this upsurge. The way they work is not the way I work, coming out of the European traditions, but I respect their work a lot and think it really does reflect the influence of radicalism.

**Williams:** So it was when you were in grad school that you learned some of the tradition of political philosophy, and that's the way you got into it? And you mentioned when we were talking over coffee that, in the late seventies you read Rorty, and he opened up a lone counter-voice out of the normal Anglo-American, analytic tradition.

**Fraser:** Well, there I was in the CUNY Graduate Center Ph.D. program, and I was, at that point, a highly self-directed intellectual with my own agenda. My agenda was not analytic, graduate school philosophy. At the time I was trying to read philosophy in a very historical and socially grounded way to understand evolving stages of bourgeois character structure. I wanted to read Hobbes as a kind of emblem of a certain phase of bourgeois character and thought. And I had been very influenced by what I knew of the Frankfurt School, Marcuse especially. Even in my undergraduate days, Marcuse and Sartre were the two important figures that I read, who were trying in philosophy to do Marxism for the present.

**Williams:** Marcuse strikes me as one of those figures who is undergoing a revaluation. He was so enormously influential—one used to see his paperbacks all over—and then he sort of dropped out of the discourse. Lately, it seems as if a lot of people are rediscovering him.

**Fraser:** I think that you're right. I also see the beginnings of a new interest in Marcuse. Who knows how that will develop. One thing about Marcuse that stands out, though, is that, of all of the Frankfurt School refugees, he was the only one who actually embraced the liberatory movements of his time. He was pro-gay, pro-feminist; he was able to ally himself with the radical movements of his time, which most of the other members of the Frankfurt School were not. He's remarkable—both as a thinker and a human being.

Anyway, you asked about Rorty. There I was in the CUNY graduate program, where there was really no one for me to work with. And I liked that because I didn't want anyone paying too much attention to what I was doing. So basically I was struggling with the curriculum, and it was hard for me to find courses that I liked. But there were one or two people there, a guy who taught Hegel and Marx, and a guy who ended up directing my dissertation, Peter Caws, who was working on French structuralism. It was through him that I was exposed to structuralism (there wasn't really anything called poststructuralism then), to Lévi-Strauss, a little bit of Lacan, Barthes, but the person who made a deep impression on me was Foucault. I immediately gravitated to Foucault, whom I recognized as somebody who came out of the New Left. At the same time, I was starting to learn about Habermas. That I had to do on my own because there wasn't anyone there who taught him. Through my interest in Marcuse I knew that Habermas was the leading Frankfurt School person of the coming generation. I knew that I needed to find out more about him, but there was not a lot of his work available in translation. Also studying him—and Foucault—was going against the grain; it was not encouraged, and it was thought of as idiosyncratic. It was not what you should be doing if you wanted to get a job as a philosopher.

That's where Rorty came in. Rorty exploded all of that when he published *Philosophy and the Mirror of Nature* in 1979. I had heard him read from it in manuscript before it was published at a meeting in Dubrovnik (in ex-Yugoslavia). That's where I first met him, and his book blew me away because this was an imminent deconstruction, from the inside, of the whole analytic tradition and its most basic assumptions about mind, about language, and about knowledge. A lot of people like me were having a tough time doing philosophy in American graduate schools. For us, Continental philosophy was oppositional and associated with the Left even though, if you actually looked at it closely, most of it came out of the Catholic school of phenomenology. But I also had this interest in Marxism and the Western Marxist tradition. Rorty, who didn't have that agenda at all, nevertheless had the effect of putting the whole enterprise of analytic philosophy in question and making that a topic of discussion. And he had the credibility and authority to do that in a way that no one I knew possibly did. He had worked in the damn tradition for all those years and knew it inside and out.

**Williams:** I wonder how he came to that turn.

**Fraser:** You'd have to ask him, I guess. If you look at his biography, he's quite complicated. He had his own stories about suffering in analytic philosophy for many years and finally becoming able psychologically to break out of it. And as you know he came from this very interesting family of radicals; a grandfather was a prominent Social Gospel intellectual, his parents . . .

**Williams:** There's a picture of his father, who was a Communist Party journalist, in Alan Wald's *New York Intellectuals* . . .

**Fraser:** Right. What *Philosophy and the Mirror of Nature* did was not to argue for another position within the field of arguments about what was real, but to displace that field and undo its assumptions. So he became a genealogist or deconstructor of the whole problematic. Anyway, he made a very deep impression on me and was one of my major intellectual influences, along with Foucault, Habermas, and Marcuse. I have a great appreciation and admiration for Rorty—for his wit and his writing style, which I think is superb, and for the gift that he gave me and other people in my generation. He made the space for us to do what we went on to do.

**Williams:** It seems like analytic philosophy is quietistic, akin to what happened in literary criticism with the dominance of the New Criticism, which was programmatically ahistorical. There's an argument that the New Criticism enacted a kind of Cold War quietism in literary criticism. It seems like analytical philosophy is a similar kind of response.

**Fraser:** Actually it has a very complicated history. The original analytic philosophers of the Vienna circle were socialists; Bertrand Russell was a great socialist antiwar thinker. Analytic philosophy started out as a radical, heretical philosophical movement that aimed to puncture pseudometaphysics that it associated with superstition, reaction, and mystification. It's part of the Enlightenment tradition, the idea of thinking logically and critically as a mode of enlightenment. But by the time you get to the Oxbridge scene in the fifties and ordinary language philosophy, it had become depoliticized and even antipolitical. But, as I said, analytic philosophy by the late sixties and seventies developed its own left wing, especially within moral and political philosophy.

**Williams:** Just to keep the time line in my head, that brings us up to the early eighties, when there's a pragmatist turn in philosophy. Maybe you could say more about the advent of poststructuralism. I noticed one of your earliest essays is on the French Derrideans, and you've written about the turn to poststructuralism and Lacan in feminism.

**Fraser:** Well, let me pick up the time line. I got my Ph.D. in 1980. I wrote a dissertation on the philosophy of history, which I never published. One day I'd like to go back to it because I had a flash many years later that I had continued to work on that same question without realizing it. The dissertation dealt with the problem of how to adjudicate competing historical interpretations of the same event. This was essentially the Kuhnian problem of scientific paradigms transposed to history. What happens when rival historians operate out of incommensurable paradigms and don't share the same notion of what constitutes evidence? My dissertation worked this out through a case study of the French Revolution of 1848, which meant I got to write about all my favorite books—Marx's *Eighteenth Brumaire*, de Tocqueville's *Recollections*, and I did a chapter on Flaubert's *Sentimental Education*. This was a very unusual philosophy dissertation. But it used a Kuhnian frame and a lot of Gadamer about fusion of horizons. As I said, I only realized much later that a lot of what I've done since, like Habermas versus Foucault about modernity, concerns the same problem. Each of them had a different narrative about modernity and history. How do you adjudicate them?

**Williams:** That's something like what you do in "False Antitheses," adjudicating Butler's and Benhabib's differing frames.

**Fraser:** Right, that would be another case. Anyway, in the early eighties I decided I wanted to write on Foucault. Hubert Dreyfus, a philosopher at Berkeley, inspired me. Soon after finishing my Ph.D., I went to his NEH summer institute, which was about how to bridge the gap between analytic and Continental philosophy. This turned out to be a historic institute; it was the first one that tried to do that. There was talk in the margins about Foucault, and I began to see how Foucault was someone who both shed light on important philosophical problems and who also was close to my political heart. I was so intrigued by *Discipline and Punish* that I decided that this would be a good person to write on. So the first thing I did after graduate school, when I was an assistant professor at the University of Georgia, was write a couple of pieces on Foucault. The first one I presented at the conference in Dubrovnik, the same place where a year or two earlier I had met Rorty. It was an annual thing, an international gathering of critical theory people, before the goddamn nationalists destroyed the whole country. Habermas wasn't there, but he had heard from people who had been there that there had been this paper on Foucault, and he got a copy and was going around giving talks quoting it. So I made contact with him and for a time found myself in the strange position of being Habermas's informant about things French. He was preparing the lectures that later became *The Philosophical Discourse of Modernity*. He had been invited to go to France, and he was very nervous about it. He really didn't understand very much at all about the scene there. He had this idée fixe about Heidegger and was projecting that onto everything he read of Derrida and Foucault, which in Foucault's case especially was completely absurd.

So I found myself in the middle of these two traditions as a mediator. Then I myself went to France—I was desperate to get out of Athens, Georgia—and that's where I met all the people I wrote about in the essay on the French Derrideans. I attended the seminar of Jean-Luc Nancy and Phillippe Lacoue-Labarthe; it was a remarkable moment because the cast of characters in attendance included Derrida, Sarah Kofman, Lyotard, Lefort, and many others. So I had a kind of bird's-eye view of the whole problem of what the political implications of deconstruction were. The rhetoric, especially in the U.S., is that it's Left. Derrida's rhetoric has changed quite a lot, but in those days there was a lot of talk about "shaking up the West."

**Williams:** It strikes me, when I go back to *Of Grammatology*, that it's more of a manifesto than anything else, with cosmic pronouncements about subverting Western metaphysics . . .

**Fraser:** . . . which was supposedly the same as subverting Western society. This rhetoric, which runs through "The End of Man," for example, was both fascinating and disturbing to me. I couldn't immediately grasp its political force. I could see, of course, how Foucault raised an interesting challenge to Marxism, since he was trying to broaden the conception of the political in ways that took in the politics of culture, the politics of sexuality, the politics of micropractices of everyday life and disciplinary institutions, getting outside the traditional Marxist economism. Derrida, in contrast, had this Left rhetoric, but I couldn't really understand what his thought implied for politics, although I knew it was supposed to mean something. I made it my project in Paris to figure this out. I was quite driven; I thought, "I'm going to get to the bottom of this." I was very unsatisfied with Michael Ryan's overly facile *Marxism and Deconstruction*, which was the only thing available, that and Gayatri Spivak's more third-worldist version. Of course she's changed too, but I felt that neither of these was adequate. Having come to deconstruction with skepticism, I found myself in between three camps—German critical theory, French poststructuralism, and American pragmatism. And I would have to add feminism. My whole intellectual career has been about mediating among these and integrating whatever is best in each.

**Williams:** That brings us up to the nineties. I want to ask you about your current work on redistribution and recognition. I'm really struck with the last two chapters of *Unruly Practices*, about the rhetoric of needs and of rights, and their material consequences. Why I'm struck with them is that you take the concepts and moves of theory, which I've been trained in and many of my cohort have been trained in, but apply them to immediate political problems like welfare. You combine discourse critique and gender critique, familiar modes in literary criticism, with practical materialist diagnoses. I guess this relates to the larger question of activism and the academy, and how can we be activists via our intellectual work.

**Fraser:** I'll try to say something about both questions. From my encounter with French thought and with the lit crit world in the United States, I learned an enormous amount about language and meaning. The linguistic turn is incredibly fruitful, and for me the question was to apply it to things that were usually thought of as material, like poverty. So I saw myself as upsetting or destabilizing the standard distinction between the symbolic and the material, or the cultural and the economic. That was something I learned from Foucault; Foucault talked about how meanings were socially constructed in things that you thought of as just brute materiality, like bodies, which have a constructed dimension.

The other thing was that I wanted to do this sort of work in an institutionally grounded way. And this is why I like public sphere theory and the pragmatics tradition in the philosophy of language; they look at the social practices of communication, interpretation, and representation. I've felt that there's a tendency on the part of some people who do literary and cultural studies to study meanings in a way that is too free-floating and ungrounded. I see public sphere theory as a hinge between a critical social theory of the institutional dynamics of society on the one hand, and a cultural studies approach to the cultural and discursive dimension on the other. Public sphere theory connects these by focusing on the social shape of arenas of discursive construction.

Now, in terms of redistribution and recognition, that took a further step by saying it's absolutely true that (a) all of the problems that economic and materially oriented Marxists think of as material have an irreducible symbolic, interpretive dimension, and that cultural studies can articulate that and that is a very useful thing to do. But it is also true that (b) there is a story to be told about the institutional basis and political and economic basis of linguistic and cultural construction that the cultural studies people don't tell. So, in theory, these dimensions need and complement each other.

The next step that I took was to say, however, there is a battle going on today between so-called social politics and cultural politics. It is about whether one should be focusing on demands for redistribution or demands for recognition.

**Williams:** You mean recognition as it's used in identity politics?

**Fraser:** For me, recognition is a generic term for cultural politics; it is broader than identity politics. Or rather identity politics is only one among several alternative politics of recognition. But there's this argument going on between the proponents of redistribution and the proponents of recognition, and I wanted to make an intervention against the dichotomizing idea that this must be an either-or choice. On the other hand, I also wanted to say that this argument is not just a matter of "false consciousness." There are real tensions that need to be dealt with and real political choices that need to be made.

I now think that the current divergence between cultural politics and social democratic politics is rooted in the social formation that we live in. I don't think it's just a mistake. Going beyond what I said in *Justice Interruptus*, I am now trying to understand what it is about the social formation that generates these problems. I have found myself referring back to Max Weber and the problem of the relation between class and status. I am analyzing the harms and injustices associated with misrecognition as status injuries, and the harms and injustices associated with maldistribution as class inequities. Analogously, I am treating demands for recognition as claims to redress status injuries and demands for redistribution as claims to rectify class inequities. And I'm trying to think about the relationship between these two dimensions of injustice, between class harms and status harms. I believe that neither harm is reducible to the other, although they interact constantly. Thus, we live in a social formation in which the status order is not a simple reflection of the class structure, nor vice versa. Understanding the relations between them raises really deep and interesting problems of social theory.

**Williams:** Maybe you could say something about how you see the general connection of activism and academic work.

**Fraser:** For me, anything that I work on intellectually comes out of what I experience in a very immediate way as a real problem, as a social or political problem. These problems become gripping to me and generate a certain passion, and I want to get to the bottom of them. In the case of redistribution and recognition, the current confusion about them demands my attention. For me, that's a way of retrieving my ambitions to think systematically about the social formation. And as I said, that's what it means to me to be radical. I'm now using Weber more than Marx, although I think there's an important Marxist component here.

What I no longer have is the clear sense that I had in the past of an immediate connection between theory and practice. I don't know how to translate what understanding I have into a political program or set of demands, and I'm not sure that would be an appropriate thing to try to do anyway. I feel that we are living through a very confusing time politically; perhaps the best shorthand buzzword for it is globalization. Whatever we call it, there's an important epochal shift under way in the political economy and in the political culture. Aspects include the collapse of Communism, the resurgence of very ugly strains of nationalism, neonationalism, ethnic cleansing, as well as new progressive initiatives around issues such as sexuality. All of this is occurring as the frame that previously undergirded political life—the national Keynesian welfare state—is being seriously called into question. The result is a great disorientation on the Left. It's a time when it's unclear what an activist ought to do. But it's also a time when an intellectual—I prefer that word to theorist—can and should at least try to understand these epochal shifts in a way that could prove relevant at some point to activism. Exactly how, I don't know. But the pressing need is to figure out what's happening, thence to ask questions like:

"Is feminism turning out by some ruse of history to be an ideology in the transition to a new form of capitalism that relies much more heavily on women's labor?"

**Williams:** To close—thanks for sitting here so long—what are you working on now? I know you're finishing a book on redistribution and recognition.

**Fraser:** Actually, three books are in the works that all have to do with these problems. The title of one is *Adding Insult to Injury*, and that is coming out from Verso some time next year. It reprints my original *New Left Review* essay on redistribution and recognition, which is the first chapter of *Justice Interruptus*, followed by seven or eight critiques by Rorty, Benhabib, Butler, Young, Phillips, Elizabeth Anderson, Kevin Olson, and Joe Heath. And it includes my responses to their criticisms. The second book is called *Redistribution or Recognition? A Political and Philosophical Exchange*, coauthored with Axel Honneth, and it's also due out from Verso. It's a dialogue between the two of us. Honneth is to my mind the most important philosopher of recognition writing today. He is a Hegelian who believes that recognition is the fundamental moral category. He sees misrecognition as the fundamental harm or injustice, while assuming that all problems of distribution can be understood in terms of misrecognition. It's a very ambitious theoretical program—but one with which I disagree. Honneth is a kind of latter-day Hegel. My position, in contrast, is that of a latter-day Hegel plus Marx, or perhaps Weber.

The third book I haven't done any work on yet, but I think if I sustain the interest in this problem long enough that I'm going to write a more systematic book that will have chapters on the important historical thinkers who have wrestled with the problem of the economic and the cultural. I would have a chapter on Hegel, a chapter on Marx, a chapter on Weber, and probably a chapter on Bourdieu, whom I consider the most important contemporary theorist of these problems.

**Williams:** It seems, at least by my surmise, that Bourdieu has become the central "master theorist" for literary studies now, whom everyone cites and deals with. Do you have any idea to write a book like Rorty's *Achieving our Country*?

**Fraser:** Not at the moment. I'm glad he did it—it's a complicated book with both strengths and weaknesses—but at the moment I'm more interested in trying to think through what I think of as more technical problems, and I don't want to have to deal with problems of exposition. I have always wanted to have an aspect of my work that is more journalistic—to write for the *Nation* or *Dissent* and the like—but I have very heavy responsibilities with graduate students and dissertations, so I can't do everything I want to do. I hope at some point to make a place for journalism, but so far I haven't been able to and I would rather write an important theoretical book.

# 12

# The Worldly Philosopher

## *An Interview with K. Anthony Appiah*

"In thinking about culture," K. Anthony Appiah remarks in *In My Father's House: Africa in the Philosophy of Culture*, "one is bound to be formed—morally, aesthetically, politically, religiously—by the range of lives one has known." Appiah himself has known a range of lives that cross several worlds, from Africa to England to the United States, from the Ghanaian struggle for independence to the Harvard struggle for African American studes, and from analytic philosophy to postmodern cultural criticism. Drawing on the tools of philosophy, Appiah has turned a clarifying eye on some of the more pressing issues of race and identity of our day.

Appiah's cultural criticism might be considered part of the "posttheory generation." His essay "Is the 'Post' in Postcolonial the 'Post' in Postmodern?" was an influential revision of theory, arguing for a renewed humanism that "can be provisional, historically contingent, antiessentialist (in other words, postmodern), and still be demanding." He has also been a frequent collaborator with Henry Louis Gates Jr., bringing African and African American culture to the mainstream of U.S. literary study. Like many others interviewed in this volume, he foregrounds the importance of cultural politics.

Born in England in 1954, Appiah grew up in Asante, Ghana, on the west coast of Africa. His father, a prominent barrister, was related by marriage to a king of Asante and became a leading figure in the struggle for Pan-Africanism and the establishment of Ghana, at one point serving as its delegate to the United Nations. His mother, from a prominent British family, whose father had been the British Chancellor of the Exchequer, as Appiah tells here. After attending primary school in Kumasi, Appiah traveled to England to attend boarding school and Cambridge University, where he studied analytic philosophy and was the first African to receive a Ph.D. (B.A., 1975; M.A., 1980; Ph.D. 1982). Since then he has taught at Yale (1982–86), Cornell (1986–90), Duke (1990–91), and Harvard (1991–02), where he was one of the "dream team" that Gates recruited to form the African-American Studies department there. In 2002 he moved to Princeton's University Center for Human Values as Rockefeller University Professor of Philosophy.

Appiah's first books, establishing his reputation in philosophy, were *Assertions and Conditionals* (Cambridge UP, 1985); *For Truth in Semantics* (Blackwell, 1986); and the textbook *Necessary Questions: An Introduction to Philosophy* (Prentice-Hall, 1989). Turning more to reflect on cultural politics, he collected many of his influential essays in *In My Father's House: Africa in the Philosophy of Culture* (Oxford UP, 1992) and collaborated with the political scientist Amy Gutmann to write *Color Conscious: The Political Morality of Race* (Princeton UP, 1996). He has also published several mysteries: *Avenging Angel* (St. Martin's, 1991), *Nobody Likes Letitia* (Constable, 1994), and *Another Death in Venice* (Constable, 1995). Recently, he collaborated with his mother, Peggy Appiah, to publish *Bu Me Be: The Proverbs of the Akan* (Center for Intellectual Renewal, 2002), and continued his engagement with philosophy in *Thinking It Through: An Introduction to Contemporary Philosophy* (Oxford UP, 2003).

Additionally, he has edited a shelf of books with Henry Louis Gates Jr., including *Identities* (U of Chicago P, 1995); *A Dictionary of Global Culture* (Knopf, 1999); the Amistad Literary Series of critical anthologies on major African American writers; and the Microsoft Encarta Africana. He also edited the trade paperback *Early African-American Classics* (Bantam, 1990).

This interview took place on 7 January 2003 in K. Anthony Appiah's sun-drenched, antiques-filled Chelsea loft in New York

City. It was conducted and transcribed by Robert S. Boynton, a literary journalist and a professor at NYU's journalism program. It was originally conducted for this volume.

**Boynton:** African American studies played a central intellectual role in the 1980s and 1990s, providing a fertile, multidisciplinary intellectual context in which the most pressing issues of the day (racial discrimination, minority rights, affirmative action) were subject to analysis by scholars drawing on the most dynamic fields of the day (literary theory, critical legal studies, philosophy, cultural studies). As African American studies moves into the twenty-first century, will it play a similar, or completely different, role?

**Appiah:** It is difficult to predict the future, but there are two things happening in the field that are particularly interesting. First, it is internationalizing. People are moving toward a more diasporic conception of the field. That isn't a prediction; it is already happening. African American studies programs are becoming more comparative, more international. It is becoming more open to the idea that one can compare the experience of the African diaspora with other diasporas.

**Boynton:** In your book *In My Father's House*, you suggest moving away from the language of "race" and toward the language of "populations." The move signifies a shift in the way one looks not only at the movements of peoples but also at their classification. Is this shift similar to the one you are describing in African American studies?

**Appiah:** Yes. The notion that identity and race are socially constructed is now so widely accepted that we're looking for other ways of talking about the subject. One option is to talk about the subject as social construction *itself*. And that leads to pursuits like "whiteness studies," etcetera. Another way to look at it is to say, look, there are populations out there who move around the world in various ways, and as they move they get reclassified, and thus give more specificity to the abstract idea of social construction.

**Boynton:** So rather than the study of *a* people—namely, African Americans—the discipline becomes the study of how peoples—with an emphasis on people from Africa—move around the world as a whole?

**Appiah:** Yes, there is a *particular* story, which is the story of the creation of the "Black Atlantic" through the slave trade, but that story is internally very complicated. Where you look determines what you see.

And it is also like other stories about the formation of transnational identity.

Of course, this is not to say that there isn't a part of African American studies that depends on some of its scholars and students thinking of themselves as "black people." The discipline has a very special relation to African Americans, especially those African Americans who are in the middle class. They care a great deal about what happens to African American studies—something that became apparent during the controversy with Cornel West and Larry Summers. It is similar to the relationship between the Jewish identity of the Jewish community and Judaic studies programs, and between Asian Americans and Asian studies.

That has set up a very interesting dynamic in all of these cases between "insiders" and "outsiders." The field is opening up more and more to nonblack people, both as students and as scholars. This is good and has been part of the cosmopolitanizing process that has made it just that much more open. It is an interesting dialectic, and I think it has been healthy for the discipline to have a real relationship to people outside the university. It is one of the ways that American education is socially embedded—in contrast to the way it isn't socially embedded on the opposite side of the Atlantic.

**Boynton:** In addition to thinking about Africa's relationship to the world, you've also thought a great deal about its individual states' relation to each other. At the end of *In My Father's House* you call for a revival of Pan-Africanism, although one not "distracted by a bogus basis for solidarity." You write, "Given the situation in Africa, I think it remains clear that another Pan-Africanism—the project of continental fraternity and sorority, not the project of racialized Negro nationalism—however false or muddled its theoretical roots, can be a progressive force." Twelve years after you wrote these lines, are you still hopeful about the prospects for African unity?

**Appiah:** I do think that the development—feeble and sketchy as it is—of the African Union is an important step. Essentially what they've done is to move beyond the Organization of African Unity toward something that resembles the EU. And in that process, one of the things that has been conceded by the leaders of Africa's various nations is the right of other people on the continent to criticize your internal politics. One of the few resources against state oppression that can work in Africa is the appeal to other African states. Appeals from the Swedes or one of the ex-colonial powers have a different feeling to them. But if it is your people criticizing in the name of African solidarity, that is quite a different thing.

**Boynton:** And what is the basis for this more progressive form of African solidarity?

**Appiah:** A continent, which is ecologically and economically interdependent. And the continent includes all sorts of people who are not obviously black. Now that doesn't mean that there isn't a kind of *shadow* of the racial legacy at work. There is. When the conversation is between a Nigerian and a white South African, it will be phrased differently. That goes the same for a conversation between, say, an Egyptian and an Algerian. But through the AU they all have recourse to various notions of solidarity.

**Boynton:** What concrete forms might that sense of solidarity take?

**Appiah:** Well, at the moment trade between African states is inefficiently run. The enormous number of tariffs and taxes (not to mention frequent bribes) one must pay to move goods from state to state inhibit the growth of the African economy as a whole. There are often even customs stops on roads in the *middle* of countries, which you also have to pay! It is just ridiculous. These are state-created problems which require focused attention of many states to correct. And the situation is similar for problems like disease. For example, river blindness in Niger can't be solved by Niger alone. It is a *West African* problem, which it shares with its neighbors.

**Boynton:** Sounds like an African version of NAFTA.

**Appiah:** Yes, but the difficulty with using the example of NAFTA or the EU is that the growth of European institutions like the EU has also created the opportunity for a new kind of identification, what I call "the new European." One might be a Belgian or Frenchman with very strong *national* loyalties, but who also has a very strong *institutional* loyalty to Europe as a whole. If their country is found guilty in a trade dispute, he won't have any trouble finding against it in the name of the larger interests of the EU. There are similar people like that in Africa, but this form of identity is at an earlier stage.

**Boynton:** You are one of the few scholars of African American thought who has deep roots in *both* terms. How has this influenced your perception of, and work in, the field?

**Appiah:** It is always very difficult to judge how one is influenced by one's background. I suppose what I feel is that it is perfectly possible for someone who is classified as mixed-race to identify with one side rather than the other. I'm not saying that this automatically gives that person any greater insights into the condition of either side. And I'm not saying that it is impossible that such a person could grow to hate one side or the other. But I *do* think that it makes it harder.

**Boynton:** You became a U.S. citizen a few years ago. Why?

**Appiah:** There are very few differences between the things you can do as a resident alien and a citizen, but I wanted to be able to vote and to be on juries. I knew that I wanted to stay here. And I felt that there was a possibility that there would be a backlash against dark-skinned immigrants and it might be difficult to stay here unless one was a citizen.

**Boynton:** Well, your logic was right, but your timing was off by a few years.

**Appiah:** Sadly, it was.

**Boynton:** Your close collaborative friendship with Skip Gates has been enormously productive for the both of you. Outside of the social and hard sciences, collaboration is unusual in American intellectual life, and especially unusual in the humanities. What role has Gates had in your intellectual development?

**Appiah:** Well, for one thing, I wouldn't be in this country if it weren't for Skip. It had never occurred to me to come to the United States before he persuaded me. In fact, I had never been to the United States at that point. As a child growing up in a Pan-Africanist household, I was aware of people like Martin Luther King and Malcolm X, and if you followed those stories it was natural that one's general impression, on the whole, was that the United States wasn't the best place for a non-white person to be.

**Boynton:** How did you and Gates meet?

**Appiah:** He was a Mellon Fellow—the first black one, I think—at Clare College, Cambridge, which was my college as well. There weren't many brown or black people at Clare—I think there were three of us at the time—and Skip says that people kept asking him whether he'd met me, and that when white people keep asking you that question you can usually assume that the other person is black.

We became very close. He was already living with Sharon, his wife, and I would often go over for dinner. Wole Soyinka was at Cambridge, and the three of us would talk about Pan-African issues. He has had an enormous breadth of experience, and was our mentor. It felt very grand to be hanging out with him. He was brilliant and entertaining.

Our collaboration began with a very deep friendship in which we talked about lots of things—quite often Pan-African things. In a way, he revived my interest in the topic, although I had grown up in a household where those issues were discussed all the time, and where figures like Richard Wright and C. L. R. James came to our house. It was a lived experience for me, but I hadn't really thought about it that much. I didn't think of it as something that one needed to theorize.

The main thing about our collaboration is that it has given me the opportunity to have a series of intellectual conversations with someone who isn't a philosopher, but someone who is very good at something else. Someone with my training in analytic philosophy could very easily think that there was nothing very much to a wide range of work in the humanities outside philosophy. Skip saved me from that.

Although I remain temperamentally a philosopher. For example, I find it very difficult to identify the propositional content of much that passes for literary theory. But I do know that it is done by clever people who are thinking very hard about things that I care about. So I take it seriously.

**Boynton:** Your father was a prominent Ghanaian barrister and politician who was deeply involved in the Pan-African movement. Your mother descended from a prominent British family composed of Fabian socialists and landed gentry. How did they meet?

**Appiah:** My father was studying law and was the president of the West African Students Union. My mother knew Colin Turnbull, who had founded an organization called Racial Unity, and as the secretary of Racial Unity, she met the president of West African Students Union.

My mother's father was Sir Stafford Cripps, the Chancellor of the Exchequer in the first postwar government, who helped create the welfare state. Her great-aunt was Beatrice Webb, who, with her husband, Sidney, founded the London School of Economics and were leaders of the Labour Party.

**Boynton:** I assume interracial couples were rare then. How was their marriage perceived?

**Appiah:** People *say* that it was the first British society interracial wedding, although I don't know whether that is true. My maternal grandmother and grandfather knew the leaders of the colonial empire—Indira Ghandi stayed at their house, etcetera—so they were quite familiar with non-English, nonwhite people from various countries. My grandfather had recently died, and my grandmother told my mother, "Well, if you are going to marry him, you've got to go live in his country and find out what it is like."

So my mother showed up on the Gold Coast (as Ghana was called at the time). My father was a very good friend of Nkrumah's at that point, so my mother found herself in an odd position: the daughter of a British cabinet minister traveling around with all these anticolonial types who were trying to get Britain out of the country. And she couldn't tell anyone why she was there. She came back to England and said it was a lovely country.

My father's family were typical aristocrats, so all they cared about was that she came from a "good" family—which she did. Once that was explained, they said the marriage was fine with them.

**Boynton:** Where were you born?

**Appiah:** I was born in England and went to Ghana when I was one. I went to primary school in Ghana, and when I was eight Nkrumah threw my father in prison, for reasons that were never entirely clear. It was a difficult time for the family, and I was sick as well. (I had toxoplasmosis, which wasn't very well understood at the time, and it took a while to figure out what was wrong.) I spent a number of months in the hospital, and at about the time they figured out what I had, the queen of England made her first trip to Ghana.

I was in my hospital bed, and Nkrumah and the queen toured the hospital. Nkrumah didn't speak to me, and as he was leading the queen and the duke of Edinburgh away, the duke turned to me and said, "Do give my regards to your mother," whom he knew. This mightily upset Nkrumah, because the spouse of a visiting head of state was saying nice things about the spouse of someone he had thrown in jail. It was an international incident. My doctor was deported, and the event was on the front page of the British newspapers.

So my mother decided that it was perhaps best for me not to be in Ghana at that point. I was very close to my maternal grandmother in England, so went to stay with her. And from the age of nine I was at an English boarding school.

**Boynton:** In *In My Father's House,* you quote your father as telling you, "Don't disgrace the family" the day before you left for Cambridge. What did he mean by that?

**Appiah:** I wish I knew. I think it was what he thought he ought to say to a son going off into the world. I suppose he wanted me to work hard and not be too dissolute (advice which I can't say that I took any particular notice of, as my university years were in fact quite dissolute). He had grown up in early colonial Ghana, a Cold Coast colony, where relationships between fathers and sons were extremely formal. I don't think my father actually knew his father that well. He lived across the street from us, but it was an extremely decorous, formal relationship.

**Boynton:** How did you decide to attend Cambridge?

**Appiah:** This is moderately embarrassing, but if you were on the track that I was on at school, you went either to Oxford or Cambridge. I also had a lot of relatives who had gone to Oxford, so going to Cambridge was a way of getting away from them. I intended to be a medical student, and Cambridge is better than Oxford for that. I wanted to be a doctor because I was so infatuated with the doctor who took care of me when I was ill as a child.

**Boynton:** So how did you end up studying philosophy?

**Appiah:** It was very difficult to change disciplines. There was a history and philosophy of science option open to medical students, and this was the one philosophy course I took when I got there. Because of the ridiculous way that English education forces one to specialize, I studied only science for the last few years in high school. But I had already read quite a bit of philosophy on my own. I read *Being and Nothingness, The Critique of Pure Reason, Language, Truth and Logic,* although I doubt I understood very much of any of them. And what got me into philosophy was religion: I was an evangelical Christian at the time. We were serious people, so we thought about religion and read theologians like Barth, Bultman, Tillich, etcetera. So it was in the context of thinking about my faith that I got interested in philosophy. A lot of what I read for myself was philosophy of religion.

I told the philosophy tutor that I had made a terrible mistake and wanted to study philosophy rather than medicine. He told me that I had to finish the term, and gave me a stack of philosophy books to read over the summer. If I still wanted to study philosophy after reading them, it was fine with him. I remember reading Rawls's *A Theory of Justice* that summer. It was one of the most exhilarating books I had ever read at the time.

**Boynton:** What was the dominant school of philosophy at Cambridge at the time?

**Appiah:** Philosophy of language was the thing, and the big topic was the debate that Michael Dummet had started about "truth conditions and assertability," which was what I wrote my first monograph on. The debate was whether the essential concept in the theory of meaning was "assertion" or "truth."

There was a group that modeled themselves on Wittgenstein, which I thought was quite phony and pretentious. The Wittgenstein world was a world of disciples. For me, philosophy had been about liberating myself, so I was very put off by this.

My teachers were Phillip Petit, Hugh Mellor, Ian Hacking. There was a sort of Cambridge tradition of thinking about probability. I attended the lectures that became Hacking's wonderful book, *Why Language Matters to Philosophy*.

**Boynton:** The philosopher Jonathan Lear was a philosophy student at Clare College at the same time you were. Both of you moved from logic and the philosophy of language to "softer," more interpretive forms of philosophy, psychoanalysis in his case, and cultural theory in yours. Any similarities?

**Appiah:** I think that what was true about Jonathan and myself was that we were intellectuals who became philosophers. We were people of ideas, not people driven by a particular technical agenda.

**Boynton:** What then drew you to something as technical as analytic philosophy? What satisfaction do you get from it?

**Appiah:** There is a certain pleasure in thinking about how things hang together, or coming up with a solution. Although a large part of what I did was either critical or the working out of some details of thoughts that originated with someone else, I *did* feel that I was making progress; after working through the philosophical problems, I *knew* that certain strategies in the theory of meaning wouldn't work. There is an ocean of possibilities, and knowing that the truth *doesn't* lie in that direction is a kind of knowledge. It may be the only kind of knowledge that is available in this area, although perhaps I shouldn't put it in quite that way.

**Boynton:** Did you go directly from your undergraduate philosophy studies to your graduate studies?

**Appiah:** No. When I finished my undergraduate degree, I had no idea what I was going to do next. It hadn't occurred to me to continue studying philosophy. I thought it was something one did at college, and then one went out into the world and got a job. So I went back to Ghana. I packed all my books into a crate, and my mother had bookshelves made for me at home.

I hadn't yet received my exam results, and one day I got a telegram from Cambridge informing me that I had received a First. So my mother said, "Well, now that you have done so well, why don't you go to the university and see if they'll let you teach." So I taught a course on political philosophy, and some of the introductory philosophy classes. I was teaching Descartes to three hundred people in an enormous lecture room with many fans going. I was younger than most of my students, most of whom looked fairly skeptical about everything I said. I discovered that I enjoyed teaching.

I went back to Cambridge, and in those days there were no courses. You simply hung around and read until someone said, "Why don't you start writing something?" I returned in 1976, and in 1979 Skip persuaded me to teach a course on Pan-Africanism at Yale. That was when I first started investigating the history of Pan-Africanism. While I was there I wrote my dissertation proposal in order to get a research fellowship back at Cambridge. This meant I had room and board and a small stipend, library privileges, and that I could teach.

**Boynton:** I've heard it said that you were the first African to receive a Ph.D. from Cambridge.

**Appiah:** This is what Skip says. It may be true, but I've never really looked into it carefully.

**Boynton:** How did your training in analytic philosophy help or hinder you as you began to retool yourself as a broader cultural critic?

**Appiah:** This is something I've felt from following the philosopher Bernard Williams's career. Bernard's early work was brilliant, but it was largely critical. He was someone who was often held back by his ability to see *a long way* down the road ahead, his ability to anticipate all the problems and the counterarguments. One would start down the philosophical path, happy in the thought that you were making progress. But Bernard had already seen that—five miles away, around the next mountain—there was this huge obstacle. Then, at some point, he liberated himself from this worry and unloosed his philosophical imagination. I hadn't thought of this dilemma in quite this way until Bob Nozick's memorial service this past year. Tom Nagel said the greatest thing about Bob was that he combined enormous analytical rigor with philosophical imagination. And this meant that he would not be held back by his knowledge of all the difficulties ahead.

All of which is to say that I think that training in analytical philosophy *can* have the effect of making you see very quickly what the problems are with any proposal, and therefore not giving it the chance to grow, or to develop the potential insights. Most of my early work was essentially critical. It didn't advocate a substantial position. I showed that you couldn't do this, or you couldn't do that. When I wrote about something like functionalism in the philosophy of mind, I made lots of *little* proposals, but never a large, sweeping one.

So I do think that, on the one hand, it is enormously helpful to have analytic training because you learn to formulate questions clearly and make distinctions well. But it can hobble you because you become too aware of the problems of every argument.

**Boynton:** Are there any particular instances in which you believe your training helped you?

**Appiah:** Yes, when I started to write about race I made quite swift progress, by comparison with much of the recent discussion, because I did what I had been trained to do: cut it up, clarify the question, point out the logical inconsistencies in various proposals, etcetera. I think I made a useful contribution to the field with that work.

I came to be able to do this kind of work through the discovery of a form of writing that I enjoy, which is the philosophical essay. These essays aren't the kinds of things that would be published in philosophy journals because they are too essayistic and anecdotal. This is the way I tend to think about things. Then when I assemble, say, ten of these essays—which is where I am now—I have to stand back and see if there is a book to be made from them.

In his new book, *The Ethics of Memory*, Avishai Margalit makes the distinction between "e.g." and "i.e." philosophers. "E.g." philosophers argue by placing significant examples before us, and the "i.e."

philosophers are explicators. I tend to be on the explicator side, but I value the "e.g." practice of framing certain questions with examples, such as a character in a novel, and from that teasing out an argument.

If I had any criticism of Michael Dummet—whom I admire very much—it is that in his philosophy of language work, a lot of his argument is at this *very* abstract level, without ever coming down and offering concrete examples. All I did in my second book, *For Truth in Semantics*, was delve down and explore cases in order to show why something had gone wrong in his very abstract arguments. I learned a lesson from seeing a very great philosopher have that problem. Even though, by the standards of cultural or literary studies, what I do is quite abstract, I try to be *less* abstract than most philosophers are, and always to have examples in mind when I write.

**Boynton:** You've also written three novels. What influence does philosophy have on your fiction?

**Appiah:** The only philosophy in the novels comes in occasional jokes, and in some of the characters, who are philosophers. I devoured books when I was a child, and for every serious book I would read I would reward myself with a mystery. So I read *War and Peace*, and then *The Murder of Roger Ackyroyd*. I still read a novel or two a week.

**Boynton:** How do you compare writing fiction with writing nonfiction?

**Appiah:** The creation of the fictional world of a novel is the most enjoyable part of the process. They are mystery novels, so tying the story up at the end is particularly satisfying. My novels all have the same protagonist, a retired English barrister whose wife is a novelist. He is a Catholic, and I think you can learn a lot about any nation by looking at people who are fully *of* it, but in some way not fully part of it.

**Boynton:** You've taught in Africa, England, and the U.S. How would you compare the scholarly experiences you've had in each of these?

**Appiah:** I think the English undergraduate education is fundamentally ridiculous because it is too specialized, especially at Oxbridge. I think it is *mad* to have to decide at age fourteen what A-levels and therefore what academic subject one wants to pursue at university.

One of the advantages of philosophy is that students don't really do it before they come to university. The economists spend the first year unteaching their students all the wrong ideas they've learned in high school, while in philosophy you don't have to do that. At Clare College, we'd accept only one or two students a year, and would have these very smart young people. It was fun teaching them one-on-one. My favorite form of teaching has been either teaching tutorials of one or two students at a time, or a seminar where I can actively work through a topic I'm interested in with a group of motivated students.

What I liked about the college system at Cambridge was that I had contact with a wide range of intellectuals. They weren't as spread out as they are at large American universities, so I could sit at dinner and talk to people about what they were studying. Most people didn't do this. They talked about sports or gossip. I broke the rules, as it were, and would talk to everybody.

The greatest pleasure of my last two years at Harvard was being a senior fellow at the Harvard Society of Fellows. Once a week I'd sit around with a bunch of people—none of whom, except Bob Nozick, were philosophers—and discuss the work of young people. One of the nice things about Princeton is that there is an awful lot of intellectually driven socializing. This is not a complaint, just an observation, but I have spent more time talking with my colleagues at the Princeton philosophy department in one semester than I did with my philosophy colleagues at Harvard in eleven years.

**Boynton:** You have famously argued not only that racial rhetoric is the product of bad science but furthermore that "race" itself doesn't exist. Do you still believe this?

**Appiah:** The way I'd formulate that claim now is that while there aren't any "races," there are "racial identities." They don't have any biological significance, but they are important socially. I want to hold on to the first claim as an important part of understanding what is true about the second claim. That is, I believe that racial identities don't make sense unless you understand that *some* of the people who participated in the creation of them have these false biological beliefs. I do not think that racial identities would have the shape they do if they were not tied to biological ideologies.

You need the following distinction: forms of identity that are genealogical, that are based on descent; and forms of identity that are biological. Families, for example, are genealogical: I'm an Appiah and a Cripps. But saying that doesn't commit me to any view about there being any biological properties that the Appiahs share. What the racelike identities have in common—including the ethnic ones—is that they are genealogical. But commitment to genealogy isn't a commitment to there being anything biologically significant about it.

The very *idea* that there was a distinction between what *we* call biological characteristics and other characteristics is itself the *product* of a theoretical development. When you read the eighteenth-century natural historians, they talk about clothing and beards and skin color all in the same paragraph. They don't yet *have* the distinction between those characteristics and biological ones. The distinction in its modern form depends on a genetic theory. Genetic theory was discovered by Mendel in the nineteenth century, but wasn't really noticed by anyone at the time, and is really an early twentieth-century creation. So the very notion that you should have a property that is inherited in the body in the way that genes are is a very modern idea, and the idea that you should have a form of classification in which *those* characteristics are central is extremely modern—well into the twentieth century.

In the case of the West, genealogical identities were theoretically understood as genetic or biological. And this was a mistake.

**Boynton:** These are all abstractions. What concrete differences do these theories make?

**Appiah:** I think that if everybody genuinely gave up the false biological belief, whatever fed our definitions of our racial identities would have to change. You wouldn't even *call* them "racial identities."

**Boynton:** As you well know, there is a vaguely neoconservative position on race, which argues that since it "doesn't exist," we don't need to take account of it when considering a host of issues, ranging from affirmative action to congressional redistricting. How do you distinguish your position from theirs?

**Appiah:** I'm *completely* in favor of getting rid of the bad biology of race. And, to the extent that the neoconservatives believe that it is wrong, I agree with them. What *follows*, though, is that we are left with the question of what we do with the legacy of these sorts of identity, that are *still* written in the shapes of our cities, in the way people dress, perform music, talk, and relate to one another. Now *that* is a different question. And in light of these realities, I think the neoconservative position is almost incoherent. It amounts to saying, "If we pretend all those social realities aren't there, they'll go away." But they won't!

**Boynton:** Do you have any concrete proposals for how race should be dealt with in America?

**Appiah:** If you ask me my thoughts about how to make progress on race in America, I believe that it has very little to do with things we *say*. If you wanted to invest political and financial resources in one thing, I would say that we should mix up the neighborhoods. As long as we have a society in which huge proportions of African Americans grow up in neighborhoods which are 80 percent or more African American, these will remain powerful, salient identities—in *bad* ways, as well as good.

African American identity is like many historically oppressed identities—like Jewishness, gayness, or even being a woman. In the course of their history, things were created, in part, in *response* to oppression that are *valuable*. Just look at the cultural importance of African Americans, for instance. Or the many forms of "care," for example, that have been developed and sustained by women in societies which *obliged* them to be the carers and didn't offer them any other options. But still, they took to it, and they are the keepers of a certain kind of care in our culture. And if you want to extend that care to others, you have to start with what they created.

So the problem with just abandoning these identities is that you would have to abandon both their good *and* bad aspects. I think of it as a project of reform, rather than one of abandonment. And projects of reform are difficult and require more than just thought. They require that you do things.

**Boynton:** You recently told the *Chronicle of Higher Education*, "After you say ten years worth of things about a topic, it's probably time to move along" (5 April 2002). What topics are you "moving along" toward?

**Appiah:** I'm interested in the role and constitution of identity in the making of a life. I'm also interested in what we now call identity in ethical and political life. Once you start thinking about identity, you inevitably start thinking about the organization of social life, and particularly the use of state power in social life. There is a way of understanding a liberal tradition—the tradition of Locke, Mill, Hobhouse, Rawls, and Berlin—which takes very seriously the thought that states have to stand back from what individuals do as they construct their lives, because each of us is ultimately responsible for his or her own lives. Unlike Berlin, I think that it is consistent with that thought to suppose that the state can affirmatively *help* us live our lives.

**Boynton:** In *Color Consciousness* you discuss the process by which the "politics of recognition" requires that a group (whether defined by ethnicity, gender, or orientation) write a new "script" for how it should behave and be perceived. Would you describe your current work as writing a new "script" for identity?

**Appiah:** I've mostly been interested in trying to understand these processes, rather than trying to get people to do things. I somewhat resist being identified as a public intellectual. I'm an intellectual and I care about politics, but I don't think of my responsibility as an intellectual in politics as in any way greater, or different, from that of any citizen. I'm not against people taking those responsibilities, but I haven't done so. There is a kind of fussiness about intellectual distinctions that I think is inappropriate in a struggle where there are two sides, and you know which side you're on. In philosophy there aren't two sides, so scrupulousness is not fussy.

**Boynton:** Another way to proceed might be to analyze different aspects of identity; to do for, say, sexuality what you've done for race. Is that an interest for you?

**Appiah:** People have asked me why, given that I've written so much about race, that I haven't written about sexuality in, say, the mode of queer studies. The answer I've given is that I *did* think philosophically about sexuality when I was starting out, and what struck me is that most of what one has to say was just responding to terribly bad arguments, and this didn't seem very interesting to me.

**Boynton:** But how is this different from the critical philosophical work you've done in the case of race, which also required that you respond to terribly bad arguments?

**Appiah:** Part of it is that I was better equipped to deal with bad arguments concerning the case of race because I had had a rather substantial education in biology. And evolutionary theory was one of the topics I was most interested in, so I actually know a lot about genetics and evolutionary biology.

In the case of race, I mostly concentrated on criticizing the best form of the wrong theory. The bad science in the case of homosexuality has mostly been psychoanalytic and, partly because I came to psychoanalysis through reading critiques of it, I've never had any time for it. Probably to an inappropriate degree, it makes me want to barf. It is just not a sensible way of thinking about sexuality. So disentangling my general skepticism about *all* explanations of homosexuality from my skepticism of these particular explanations would be difficult.

There is a separate problem, which has to do with the nature of ethics. Clearly attitudes toward homosexuals have a lot to do with views about the proper use of sex—the role of sex in pleasure, etcetera. And I must say that it is unclear to me why those are topics on which one ought to have any intrinsic moral thoughts. Sex is important because it produces pleasure, because it produces relationships, because it produces children, and all of *these* are of intrinsic moral importance. But sex itself is like, say, eating—it produces pleasure, it produces sociality, etcetera—but we don't have the sense that we should take eating seriously as a moral topic. I don't feel as if I have anything special to say about sexuality, nor do I feel that it is my obligation to do so.

There is another difference between sex and race as philosophical topics. I am not a radical constructivist about sexual identity. I think there is something biologically there in the sexual sense. I think there is *less* there than most people think, but I don't believe there is *nothing*. Whereas with race, I don't think it is at all interesting from the biological point of view.

**Boynton:** Your most recent book is an introduction to philosophy called *Thinking It Through*. How would you describe your conception of philosophy?

**Appiah:** I think of philosophy as a tradition of arguments about certain topics, and the way a topic becomes a philosophical topic is by connecting itself to that tradition. That means the status of strings in string theory in physics can become a philosophical topic by way of discussions of realism and nominalism. To put it in a slogan form, I think that philosophy has a history, but no essence. It doesn't seem to me appropriate to take a view about whether this is a good or a bad thing. It simply seems inevitable.

The only normative question that one ought to ask of philosophy is, "Is it good for society that the practice exists?" And I'm convinced that the answer to that question is yes. Having an intellectual grasp of how we fit into the world is intrinsically valuable in the sense that a life with it is eo ipso more successful than a life without it. And it is also true that a culture in which people are thinking about the questions of philosophy is better equipped to deal with deciding such questions as whether it OK to lock up dissidents on the say-so of the attorney general. Philosophy isn't the only set of discourses whose presence is helpful for thinking about these questions—I'm glad there are Quakers around as well—but it helps you think it through and make distinctions.

# 13

# Sedgwick Unplugged

## *An Interview with Eve Kosofsky Sedgwick*

By the 1980s, contemporary criticism was demarcated by the major "schools" of theory—structuralism, deconstruction, feminism, Marxism, psychoanalysis, and reader response. Since the mid-eighties, Eve Kosofsky Sedgwick has been a central figure in redrawing the map of theory, forging the fields of gay studies and queer theory. In one sense, Sedgwick's work is an expansion of feminism, as she discusses here. But at the same time, it is a critique of feminism, which focused on the relations between men and women. Instead, in her book *Between Men: English Literature and Male Homosocial Desire*, Sedgwick foregrounded "homosociality" or same-sex relations, and its underside, homophobia.

In *Epistemology of the Closet*, one of the most influential critical books of the nineties, Sedgwick deconstructed the concepts of "heterosexuality" and "homosexuality," arguing that the regime of secrecy they represented—the closet—undergirded modern thought. Drawing on poststructural theory, Sedgwick represents its revisionary tenor through the nineties; working from the concept of gender, Sedgwick has been influential in placing sexuality at the forefront of literary study.

Born in Dayton, Ohio, in 1950, Sedgwick did her undergraduate work at Cornell (B.A., 1971) and graduate work at Yale (Ph.D., 1975) during the heyday of the "Yale School." As she recounts here, she took seminars from Paul de Man, and one can discern the influence of deconstruction through her work. She taught at Boston University, Hamilton College, and Amherst College, but, after the publication of *Between Men*, she was one of those hired on at Duke, where she was Newman Ivey White Professor of

English, during its heyday as a center of contemporary theory under the chairship of Stanley Fish (see also Fish's interview in chapter 1). In 1998 she moved to the CUNY–Graduate Center as a distinguished professor.

Sedgwick's first book, *The Coherence of Gothic Conventions* (Arno, 1980), stems from her dissertation. *Between Men* (Columbia UP, 1985; 2nd ed., 1992), with a series of readings of premodernist English literary works, provided a model for gay studies in literary criticism. *Epistemology of the Closet* (U of California P, 1990), a more directly theoretical investigation, deconstructs the binaries connected to sex, such as public-private. *Tendencies* (Duke UP, 1993) collects many of her well-known essays, such as "Jane Austen and the Masturbating Girl" and "A Poem Is Being Written." The latter essay famously concludes with one of her poems, and she has been a lifelong poet; *Fat Art, Thin Art* (Duke UP, 1994) is a book of her poems. She next edited several collections, including *Shame and Its Sisters: A Silvan Tomkins Reader* (Duke UP, 1995); *Performativity and Performance* (with Andrew Parker; Routledge, 1995); *Gary in Your Pockets: Stories and Notebooks by Gary Fisher* (Duke UP, 1996), which collects the writing of a friend who died of AIDS; and *Novel Gazing: Queer Readings in Fiction* (Duke UP, 1997). Her most recent books are *A Dialogue on Love* (Beacon, 1999), a personal meditation; and *Touching Feeling: Affect, Pedagogy, Performativity* (Duke UP, 2003), which gathers her later essays on Silvan Tomkins and other figures. *Regarding Sedgwick: Essays on Queer Culture and Critical Theory*, edited by Stephen M. Barber and David L. Clark (Routledge, 2002), includes chapters by Lauren Berlant, Nancy K. Miller, Judith Butler, and others assessing the influence of Sedgwick's work.

This interview took place on 4 March 1993 at Jeffrey Williams's apartment in Greenville, North Carolina, on the occasion of Sedgwick's giving a lecture at East Carolina University. It was conducted and transcribed by Williams, and originally appeared in an issue of the *minnesota review* on "The Politics of AIDS."

**Williams:** What do you think is the prospect or horizon of gay studies? Related to that, one notable element of gay studies is its link to activism, to its having an effect in the public sphere. Do you see this as part of the project of gay studies?

**Sedgwick:** I'd compare where lesbian and gay studies is now to where women's studies was fifteen years ago. You have people coming into the field, both students and faculty, whose sense of themselves as having some agency in this inquiry has been very much formed by unmistakable public developments and by things happening in particular urban cultures. I don't think there would be any lesbian or gay studies if there weren't lesbian and gay scholars and students bringing the unanswered questions of their own self-formation into the classroom and study.

**Williams:** Do you see people coming into the field now as slightly different from before?

**Sedgwick:** Well, there wasn't a field twenty years ago. There was a handful of very brave people clinging to the edges of institutions struggling to have the space to ask these questions in their scholarship.

**Williams:** So the institutional space is already cut out?

**Sedgwick:** The institutional space is certainly still not guaranteed. It's most visible in publishing, where there are a lot of new series of lesbian and gay scholarship. That's because people buy the books and read the books, people inside and outside of academia. But most schools will only have one faculty member or maybe two, in one or two departments, often nontenured, teaching courses offered for the first or second time at this moment. Always very embattled, very risky for the untenured faculty. There are very few places where there's anything like a critical mass of faculty.

What seems to be happening, which is intensely interesting to me, is that student demand is raising this curricular issue in a lot of departments. In the consumerist ethos of education right now, schools are more responsive to that than they would have been ten years ago. You have kids who are coming out at fourteen, or who are coming out at twenty. In the last year or two, I've even started to see a lot of kids who are not necessarily dealing with questions about their own sexuality, but they see this as a big public question. They understand that if they're going to be educated, they have to have some chance for finding out about this. That was not the case even three years ago.

**Williams:** To shift specifically to the question of AIDS, I want to ask a theoretical question. In *Epistemology of the Closet*, you make the distinction between "minoritizing" and "universalizing." I think that this is an important distinction, and very much a strength that you note that the two terms are endlessly bound and endlessly undermine each other at the same time. But it seems to me that one pernicious image of AIDS is precisely that it reduces the disease to a gay plague, equated with and scapegoated to gay men. In other words, it minoritizes gay men in a negative and even harmful way, in effect quarantining them, figurally and not so figurally. On the other hand, minoritizing may have some positive benefits. Some people are relieved by this minoritizing function: being gay is similar to being blond—it's according to genetics or the hypothalamus. I guess what I mean is that the move for minority status might have some positive uses, but, as an antiessentialist, I worry that it finally serves a negative ideology in separating those minoritized. Sorry, that's a long question.

**Sedgwick:** To me the important question—the important test for the political underpinnings of a policy or a theory—is, "Does it place a value on the lives of people of varying sexualities, on their experiences, on their survival, on their rights to dignity and expression and thought?" I don't think that there's any way to guarantee that from either minoritizing or universalizing, or either essentialist or antiessentialist points of view. Any of those can offer fuel for homophobic and queer-eradicating forces and energies. Any of them can also be useful for projects that do value the survival of these people and acts and cultures and possibilities. So I'm uncomfortable seeing the question of survival, support, and so forth being collapsed with any version of the essentialist-constructionist question. I see those as basically different questions. It's time that people asked, for instance, politicians, "Do you value the survival and possibilities of these people and these potentials?" Not "Do you believe X or Y about the hypothalamus and what would that lead to?" That can lead to a lot of different things. The question of the value of people's lives and contributions seems to me a different one, and a nonnegotiable one.

**Williams:** To press the point, what would your recommendations for political action be? What should one do?

**Sedgwick:** A scholar does a lot of different things. Being in the classroom in a particular way, writing journalism, writing scholarly books, serving on committees that consider issues of benefits, for instance—those all fall squarely within the definition of academic work, but they involve a wide range of political choices and acts and kinds of impact.

I think different people are going to find that they have very different kinds of political contributions to make, whether in broader or more conventional sites. And none of them can be dispensed with. Call your congressman or congresswoman early and often; support a whole range of lesbian and gay rights issues; do civil disobedience; work with activist and service groups. Do it all, if you can. I do see educators as having a special obligation to support the survival of lesbian and gay young people. Beyond that, I don't have a prescription for one form of activism over another. It seems as though the first question is, "Are those lives to be valued?" And then: "What to do about that?" There are a lot of different right answers.

**Williams:** You'd say that politics are local?

**Sedgwick:** No, politics are local and global. Or local and national. If only they were just one or the other. There certainly aren't enough people doing activist politics that any of us can afford to say, "No, that's the wrong way to do it, don't do it there, don't do it at that level, do it at this level." I think that different people tune in on very different wavelengths to what counts as politics. For some, it's going to be at the school board level; for others, it might be at the level of AIDS treatment data.

**Williams:** I think in theory there's sometimes a view of politics that they take place in a kind of allegorical sphere . . .

**Sedgwick:** Yes, I think that's completely true. Which also means that nobody ever thinks that they're doing politics. Everybody always has a bad conscience about it. Or everyone feels as though if they were to do politics, it would mean completely changing their lives.

**Williams:** Your political commitment seems very personal, very deep-rooted. I can especially see that in "White Glasses" [in *Tendencies*]. Not to pry—on other things I might want to pry—

**Sedgwick:** You can pry.

**Williams:** Can you say something about your personal bearing?

**Sedgwick:** This is one of the areas where you'll feel the difference very strongly between people who are or aren't plugged in to particular cultures. For me specifically, a variety of communities, particularly urban queer communities, have been sites of intimacy. For anybody who's in that situation, the question of whether they have some personal involvement with AIDS is unfortunately a silly question. But the answer is yes, that such a person is going to be talking about her or his history of seeing a lot of people whom they value, some whom they've been very close to and others who have been important to the community, dealing with debilitating illness and death at young ages. Those are lives that you know, lives you know well how to value. That changes the questions you want to ask, and changes your own motives for going on with what you do. It's a very, very widespread and deeply rooted phenomenon at this point in a range of communities. What seems incredible is that that experience is still almost invisible in public culture.

**Williams:** Not to get off track, but with the fiction I get for the *minnesota review*, much of it deals with family—reactions, say, to a brother or son with AIDS. It seems to me very much a literature of witness.

**Sedgwick:** Well, that may tell you something about the demographics of the *minnesota review*, too, because that's not what comes out in *Christopher Street* or in queer anthologies. Not to say that it's not important, but it's a particular slice of the pie.

**Williams:** I see what you mean.

**Sedgwick:** There are moments when it becomes clear that a part of valuing oneself, and of valuing the people that one loves, is to try to think well and forcefully about our lives and values and needs. And the pressure of AIDS ups the ante on that. What's been very formative for me, although it happened pretty late in this process, was to find myself dealing with breast cancer, which both strengthened but also in some ways changed the way I experience the AIDS epidemic. It certainly made my own relation to issues of medicine—and also to mortality—a lot less clear and distant. It made me feel that I *had* been experiencing them as in some ways clear and distant, even though so intimately.

Let me tell you another thing that has really shaped my response to AIDS, or where it seems to me we ought to respond. The first person who ever came out to me as a person with HIV was a student in a class that I was teaching, and it had a big effect on me. First of all, it violated my sense of the way things ought to be in a dramatic way. Not that I think that men in their forties and fifties ought to be dying, but I know in a different way that kids, that my students, shouldn't be. I've had to become conscious over time of how horrifyingly endangered young people are from AIDS, even now, even kids who actually define themselves as gay and who are involved in gay communities. At times when seroconversion rates among older gay men in certain urban settings have dropped radically, young gay men and especially young gay men of color are seroconverting at accelerating rates. There was a recent statistic that 34 percent of gay men under twenty-five and 54 percent of black gay men who are being tested in San Francisco are testing positive, which is staggering. Every single one of these prospective deaths was preventable and isn't anymore. And there are lots more coming along. So for me personally and pedagogically, and as a writer and scholar, that feels like a pretty direct charge. The things that happen in my classroom aren't going to be just about what the most theoretically illuminating way to talk about AIDS and representation is, but also what can I do to make sure that everyone in my class has talked about safer sex, and everyone I teach, to the degree that I have any control over it at all, has at least heard a bunch of language that begins with the premise of the value of queer lives. And the validity of any decisions they can make to take care of their lives and preserve them. We also just talk practically about safer sex, whenever we can do it. I know I should make it happen even more often.

**Williams:** In your undergraduate classes? You don't want them publishing that in the *North Carolina Tarheel.*

**Sedgwick:** I don't give a flying fuck.

**Williams:** I wonder what their parents would say.

**Sedgwick:** I assume that the parents want their children to be alive. I hope they do. One simple thing about teaching is just beginning with the assumption that some significant chunk of your students are gay. They may not think of themselves that way, or they may not think of themselves that way now. Even some who aren't gay now will be in a few years. Just begin with the assumption that you are not speaking to a group of entirely heterosexual students and make sure that they know that they are not speaking to a group of entirely heterosexual fellow students. Think about what you want to have happen in the classroom starting from there. It's really instructive, a really useful heuristic.

**Williams:** Maybe I could ask you a question or two about the Left and its current alliance with gay studies. There's a shaky history to that alliance.

**Sedgwick:** It was interesting to me that at the "Rethinking Marxism" conference this fall there were half a dozen sessions with queer topics, whereas at the last such conference, I was told, people had to struggle to get even half of one session with queer content. Which tells me a few things: it suggests that people perceive, probably rightly, that queer inquiry is a growth area, that something very interesting and powerful is going on there. And also it's in a living relation to a living social movement. Those things might not necessarily be said of Marxist criticism.

**Williams:** Do you take this as a sort of changing of the guard?

**Sedgwick:** It's partly a changing of the guard and partly a sense of where the action is. I don't mean to suggest that's necessarily cynical. I think there are a lot of people now—it's happened with feminism—who see, yes, if I ask this set of questions, I'll come up with some different answers in ways that matter. That's not something that you're born knowing. It's something you need to learn by seeing you can do it.

**Williams:** Can you see a queer Left?

**Sedgwick:** I don't know. I mean, some of those guys, it's hard for me to see them getting queered. If you look at what wearing "the black leather jacket" means to some of the Marxist guys and what wearing "the black leather jacket" means to some of the queer folks, it ain't the same jacket. It doesn't mean the same thing.

**Williams:** To shift gears a bit, how did you come to do what you're doing, in a certain sense to invent the field of gay studies?

**Sedgwick:** I would strongly deprecate a description of me as inventing gay studies. That's just not true, and it eclipses the work of a lot of people who were doing really important work in very, very difficult circumstances for a long time.

**Williams:** I take your point. *Out of the Closets* came out over twenty years ago. Let me phrase it another way: What would be your intellectual autobiography?

**Sedgwick:** A few things I think would probably be important. One would be that I started out assuming that I was going to be a poet, in fact from about age three. It turned out that I wasn't, or that I haven't been recently anyway, but it's always been true that I've thought of myself as a writer before anything else. Problems present themselves to me, it might be fair to say, less as conceptual problems than as writing problems—how to organize a piece of writing, how to make something interesting happen generically. It's never been an option for me to be less than a writerly writer. And it's never seemed conceivable to me that a good kind of writing to do would be writing without texture. I don't think one would have to have taken that particular path to get to something like that set of assumptions, but that's the path that I took.

Then, I think my training was really formative, even though I doubt whether, looking forward from undergraduate or graduate school, anyone would have predicted that I'd be doing what I'm doing. But it's very clearly marked by the conjunction of a strong grounding in New Critical close reading skills and deconstruction; it emerges from that and gives it a different spin.

**Williams:** In *Epistemology of the Closet* you call your readings "deconstructive contestations." And you refer to deconstruction in *Between Men*, although you also mention Marxism.

**Sedgwick:** It's funny—*Between Men* came at a very particular moment, when there were just starting to be Marxist-feminist analyses available to people in literature. I was very excited about that and wanted to see it happen, wanted to see it happen *well*, and felt as though this was a place where I could contribute. I have several ways of describing to myself what happened after that and why the Marxism isn't anything like as central in *Epistemology of the Closet*. Marxism really took off in literary studies, so I didn't feel as though just seeing that that was a good thing to have happened necessarily meant that it remained my responsibility to make it happen. Also, once you get past writing about the nineteenth century in England, the terms aren't as crisp anymore. You have to do new conceptual work to make the class stories intelligible, as far as I can tell. And there was other conceptual work that that book was more about, that seemed to me more in need of getting done.

**Williams:** Your writing seems to me distinctly different from previous theory—from, say, de Man or the people at Yale. In general, the current moment seems much more assimilative, a remove from the polemics of High Theory in the late seventies and early eighties, when you could hardly combine Marxism and feminism, or Marxism and deconstruction. Your work seems indicative of the current moment, in that theory serves a different purpose or functions in a different way.

**Sedgwick:** I'm not quite young enough to feel as though somebody just handed me a toolbox: you take the theory course and you learn to use the wrench and the screwdriver and so forth.

**Williams:** Which I sometimes find annoying, or incoherent, as if theory is just a menu of choices. I think particular theories assume certain commitments.

**Sedgwick:** Well, sometimes annoying, but it's kind of fabulous because people don't have to sign their soul away or invent wholly new identities for themselves in order to use some tools that are wonderfully useful tools to know how to use.

I'm not sure that I would describe the commitments that motivate me most as theoretical commitments, although it's certainly true that my sense or intuition about how one would go about something is very much fused with a theoretical history. The real assumptions behind my work may even be theoretically untenable, but anyway they are not particularly couched as theory. I mean, I try to write things that are powerful and intensely interesting and make it possible to think other things. That doesn't seem to me of the essence of Theory with a capital "T" necessarily.

**Williams:** How would you articulate your relation to feminism or the relation of gay studies to feminism? In some ways, your work is enabled and influenced by feminism, but in another way it disrupts the assumption of the difference between masculine and feminine, usually defined on a heterosexual basis, on a mommy-daddy-me model. As you say in "Tales of the Avunculate" [in *Tendencies*], those are floating categories, and there are uncles too. Is there an implicit critique of feminism in this deconstruction of heterosexuality? Does it go against the grain of feminism in a certain way?

**Sedgwick:** *Between Men* was very much meant to be an intervention in feminist thought. I think it was probably less successful as that than as a way of offering some new conceptual possibilities for gay and lesbian thought. But yes, it went and was meant to go against the grain of the assumption that, first of all, feminism could be adequate if it were by, for, and about women exclusively. It seemed important to say at that time that conceptually such an assumption wasn't going to work. But also men appeared in feminist thought of that time almost exclusively in terms of their heterosexual relation to women. Which also meant that a lot of exchanges about "men in feminism" came out sounding like marital quarrels. Marital quarrels are boring to listen to because people can go on fighting forever, and yet you know that the same people are still going to have the same fights in fifty years. It seemed to me that the radical potential of a lot of lesbian thought was being completely marginalized by that framework, as was the radical potential of a lot of gay male thought. Also, it marginalized the ways in which women and gay men have mutually formed each other, and men and lesbians have mutually formed each other. So the bickering-heterosexual-couples model of feminist contestation I just thought had to go.

**Williams:** I wanted to ask you about Yale and Duke, obviously central places for the way in which theory has been formed.

**Sedgwick:** Well, I never felt that I got that much out of Yale, partly because it was such a hideously hostile and frigid environment for graduate students in general and for me in particular. But also because, unlike many people in the early seventies, I'd already had a pretty good exposure to deconstruction in my undergraduate training at Cornell. I had learned what I think were in some ways maybe even more interesting ways to do it. It was a great privilege to get to take courses from de Man, but aside from that, I don't feel as though I got anything substantive from the instruction at Yale. Maybe I would be a better person if I had been someone who was equipped to do so, but, as it happened, I wasn't and didn't. Even though I was there at the "Yale moment," I didn't feel at all part of the Yale moment or even particularly formed by it.

As for the Duke moment, well, maybe I'm just not somebody who is ever going to identify all that strongly with an institutional nexus. I'm in my cottage; I'm in my house, which I share with a colleague, Michael Moon, who does queer work that's very much on a lot of the wavelengths that mine is. A lot of our pedagogical activities are conducted in relation to each other, and so is a lot of our reading and talking and thinking. But so far neither of us has acquired the institutional jockey skills that would turn our collaboration into a part of a building, or a squad of secretaries, or a bunch of graduate assistantships, or a program bearing our mark.

**Williams:** It must be extraordinary to have someone to have an ongoing conversation with.

**Sedgwick:** It's heavenly. I can't imagine anything luckier.

**Williams:** How do you feel about your institutional position? If I were to write a history of criticism, I would have to mention Eve Sedgwick to define the current scene, or if somebody were to put together an anthology, they might put your name in block capitals, EVE KOSOFSKY SEDGWICK, GAY AND LESBIAN CRITICISM. How does it feel to be monumentalized or reified, in one's own lifetime?

**Sedgwick:** Well, it's weird. I feel as though I have to work very, very hard to try to make sure that my name won't appear in isolation in any of these contexts, because I don't think it's a good thing for any one name to be so isolated, particularly my name. On the other hand, realistically, this is a cultural scene where ideas or narratives are circulated through the unit of the persona. Inescapably, one is formed by that; one can't unilaterally withdraw from that economy. In fact, it is a powerful heuristic among other things. You learn a lot from the experiment of having a public-private persona, edging its way through ideas and issues. That would be hard to give up, but it would be completely counterproductive for all of that to result chiefly in the magnification of that particular person. It's only a meaningful project to the extent that it invites and incites and empowers and makes new kinds of space for other people who have some important uses to make of it.

**Williams:** As a closing question, what are you working on now? And, more generally, what do you see as the direction of the field? Who do you read and think is interesting now?

**Sedgwick:** Interesting work in this field is going in some different directions. I'd say that the most exciting thought is coming from graduate students and is focused on intersections between issues of race and nationality and issues of sexuality. It's hard to think of anything more urgent than that or with more potential for opening up categories that couldn't be formulated before now. There's also an interesting current of scholars trying in a variety of different ways to think about queer issues in relation to something like a public sphere: Lauren Berlant, Michael Warner, or someone like Cindy Patton, who are trying to think about what queer space means and to use some self-consciously postmodern conceptual tools to describe unconventional relations to the public sphere and the state.

My own work I am less able to describe at this moment. I seem to be somewhat hung up on two hunches. One is that the notion of performativity, specifically at the intersection between speech act theory and performance, is going to pay off in some pretty unexpected ways. This partly comes from a reading of Judith Butler's work, which I admire immensely, and from some exchanges with her. Timothy Gould's work is perhaps even more formative for me here. At the same time—and I think these are related—there's a hunch that thinking about politics—and in particular identity politics, politics around issues of identity—without thinking about shame is a dead end. I'm trying to understand the dynamics of what I keep finding myself calling the transformational grammar of shame: how shame motivates politics, how shame turns into dignity, pride, assertion, exhibitionism, solidarity, identification, a whole raft of things that are easier to identify as politically useful terms. That, at the moment, is involving me in thinking about *affect* in general.

Specifically, I'm interested in the work of Silvan Tomkins. He tried to develop a theory of affect, somewhere in between drive theory from psychoanalysis and the space of cognition, mediating back and forth between those, and amplifying, but also assigning new meaning to those. It's not at all something I expected to find myself fascinated by, and it's embarrassing. There are a lot of people talking about shame, but I don't think there are very many people doing anything interesting with what does however seem to be quite a central issue. The work on affect I've been reading is from the late fifties, early sixties, and very much marked by that moment, so I'm finding myself having to think about the history of cybernetics and systems theory, just to make enough sense of this work historically to figure out what is actually going to be usable in it. It's a bit more to the side of explicitly gay intellectual agendas than I'm comfortable with. On the other hand, I feel if I don't trust my hunches, what am I going to trust?

**Williams:** People will be surprised if you start writing on cybernetics.

**Sedgwick:** It doesn't mean I'm less responsive to the imperative to keep powerfully occupying, and keep helping other people to powerfully occupy, the space of queer thought. But I do have the sense that we *need* these extra tools, and I'm trying to dig them out and make them usable.

# 14

# Citizen Berlant

## *An Interview with Lauren Berlant*

Looking at classic and colloquial American texts from Hawthorne to *Forrest Gump*, Lauren Berlant has charted our "national fantasy." In *The Queen of America Goes to Washington City: Essays on Sex and Citizenship*, one of the most influential critical books of the past decade, Berlant critiques the turn since the Reagan years to a shrinking and privatized public sphere in the United States. In analyses ranging from *The Simpsons* to the Lewinsky scandal, she traces the diminished ideal of citizenship, which is now projected not as a public practice but as an issue of intimate life and personal behavior.

Like Andrew Ross (interviewed in chapter 15), Berlant focuses on cultural politics, seeing culture not as ornamental or a separate realm from real-world politics but as fundamental in the construction of national identity and citizenship. Though versed in theory, Berlant might be said to be a member of "the posttheory generation"; her work does not adumbrate a singular, overarching paradigm but performs the hybrid criticism of cultural studies, feminism, and queer theory, mobilizing theories of subjectivity, sexuality, and the public sphere to analyze the social effects of both high literature and popular culture.

Berlant was born in 1957 and grew up near Philadelphia, but a formative moment for her, as she discusses here, was living in the Twin Oaks commune in Virginia in her teens. From there, she attended Oberlin College, receiving her B.A. in 1979, and Cornell University, receiving her Ph.D. in 1985. She has taught at the University of Chicago since 1984, where she is a professor of English, directs the Center for Gender Studies, and serves as one of the editors of *Critical Inquiry* and of *Public Culture*.

Trained as an Americanist, Berlant wrote a dissertation called "Executing the Love Plot: Hawthorne and the Romance of Power" (1985) and in 1991 published her first book, *The Anatomy of National Fantasy: Hawthorne, Utopia, and Everyday Life* (U of Chicago P). *The Queen of America* (Duke UP, 1997) continues her analysis of national construction in contemporary culture. Her more recent work focuses especially on the intersection of sexuality and national identity, in two edited collections, *Intimacy* (U of Chicago P, 2000; from a special issue of *Critical Inquiry*) and *Our Monica, Ourselves: The Clinton Affair and the National Interest* (NYU P, 2001); and in two books in progress, *The Female Complaint: The Unfinished Business of Sentimentality in American Culture* and *Cruel Optimism: Trauma, Impersonality, and Ordinariness in the Contemporary U.S.* Related essays include "The Female Complaint," *Social Text* (1988); "National Brands/National Body: *Imitation of Life*," in *The Phantom Public Sphere*, ed. Bruce Robbins (U of Minnesota P, 1993); "'68, or Something," in *Mapping Multiculturalism*, ed. Chris Newfield and Avery F. Gordon (U of Minnesota P, 1996); "Collegiality, Crisis, and Cultural Studies," *Profession* (1998); and, with Michael Warner, "Sex in Public," *Critical Inquiry* (1998). Additionally, Berlant introduces a collection of photographs by Laura Letinsky in *Venus Inferred* (U of Chicago P, 2000).

This interview took place on 18 February 2000 at the University of Missouri–Columbia. It was conducted by Andrew Hoberek, an assistant professor of English at Missouri specializing in modern American literature, and transcribed by Jacqueline Chambers, an editorial assistant for the *minnesota review* while a Ph.D. student at Missouri. It originally appeared in an issue of the review on "Academostars."

**Hoberek:** Let's start with a counterintuitive question. Everybody automatically disses the star system. Do you have anything good to say about it?

**Berlant:** I don't know whether I think the star system exists right now. What is a star, anyway? People whose theoretical work resonates across disciplines and historical divisions within the disciplines; people popular with graduate students; people who, tautologically, get the kind of reputation that makes their appearance in print or at conferences an event? This language comes from a particular historical moment in the early eighties, no? I'm not certain whether that kind of metatheory has the same status now.

**Hoberek:** Perhaps this is a product of disciplinary fragmentation: subdisciplines now throw up stars for themselves and not for the profession as a whole, as they did in the seventies and eighties. What would you say to this?

**Berlant:** That's interesting. You might say that European high theory and the traditional literary-critical production of high cultural value attracted people to "stars." Now, in addition to that—because I don't think that's entirely archaic—you have people who are politically engaged in their work or engaged in the creation of a different kind of critical value. This is related to the rise of feminist, antiracist, GLBTQ, and postcolonial etcetera work that emerges from what you're calling "subdisciplines" but which I might call "transdisciplines." Some might say that this work also aspires to star value and that group X is no longer "marginalized" once it demands transdisciplinary attention. Others, like myself, see that kind of statement as *ressentiment*, as a symptom of what happens in the face of change in the normative parameters of critical value.

**Hoberek:** Do you think that the critique of the star system in some ways postdates the actual existence of the star system that's being critiqued? So the critique we now have addresses something that no longer has the institutional power it once did?

**Berlant:** That's certainly part of it. People tend to be stuck reading the profession in terms of where it was when they entered or left graduate school. If the star system is what dominated their relation to theory and to doing disciplinary work in graduate school, it's going to factor in to the way they continue to read the profession. For many people who are around now, looking at themselves over the last twenty years, it would be hard not to think about their career in terms of how it circulated as a "position" within the star system.

But to return to the question of whether the star system is a good thing, do you think anybody ever thought of it in this way? Isn't it just a cynical, resentful phrase that has to do with people's fear of what is seen as undue influence over graduate students, or an undue, unfair boundary drawn between what's cool and what isn't cool?

**Hoberek:** In a recent essay, Bruce Robbins says that there's a way in which the star system was a good thing for female academics or academics of color, for whom it provided a circuit of institutionalization and cultural capital outside of the old boys' network.

To move to a different point, in the introduction to your book *The Queen of America*, you stress the ways in which your work differs from that of the high theorists who trained you. In particular, you don't feel that you have to rely on European high theory to authorize how you talk about "low" cultural material. Could you talk about that a bit?

**Berlant:** It's never occurred to me to distinguish between high and low objects, because the questions that I was asking required a different organization of knowledge than that distinction or the related one between the canonical and the noncanonical. My dissertation was called "Executing the Love Plot." It was about Hawthorne and history, and about how plots of desire and domesticity and sentiment operate in texts that are supposed to be fundamentally "historical" in their concerns. So it never really occurred to me to think that I couldn't learn a lot from anything or from everything. I just read whatever I could find. That had to do partly with having a conservative intellectual training as an Americanist, because when I was working on Hawthorne, I had to read everything that Hawthorne had read in order to be deemed an appropriate Hawthornist. This meant reading philosophy and newspaper articles, it meant reading popular fiction and Milton, it meant knowing a lot of different kinds of things. In addition, I was interested in women's popular culture, and in the ways that a certain index of intelligible femininity ran through the production of U.S. literary texts at all degrees of value. I had to train myself in this field, because there wasn't anybody at Cornell who was really in it, or much to go on at all, except for the work of Nina Baym.

So the way I got through graduate school (1979–84)—and this is probably the way I dealt with theory anxiety—was by reading everything I could that would help me answer the questions I was asking. That included a lot of theoretical work and it included a lot of primary texts, and that's how my work got to be called cultural studies. Before I was called a cultural studies person, I was called a New Historicist, and before I got called a New Historicist, people just couldn't really recognize what I was doing at the time as a kind of thing. As a result, I now find myself defending cultural studies when it's being attacked, though I never thought of what I did as officially in that mold.

**Hoberek:** Do you think that in order to be fully certified as a member of the academic star system one needs to be identified with some school or method? And, as a corollary, does the shift in the star system have to do with the fact that fewer people are being branded in that way?

**Berlant:** I don't know. Judith Butler and Teresa DeLauretis, for example, came from feminism but helped to make from it queer theory, yet from very different disciplinary backgrounds. There are great differences between the versions of queer theory they helped to bring forth. This doesn't weaken the project—it strengthens it—but it's more about a commitment to a project of thought than it is to a school or method. And I suppose in the introduction to Cary Nelson and Dilip Gaonkar's *Disciplinarity and Dissent in Cultural Studies*, Andrew Ross and I are made the chief examples of people who were in English and who became something else, what they're calling cultural studies. So it's possible that, in order to be marketed or translated as transdisciplinary, one needs to be both.

**Hoberek:** Do you think that the star system distorts people's work?

**Berlant:** The people I have talked to about this tell me that when you become a "name," you become dehumanized to people who feel licensed to simplify your work so that they can then try to destroy their simplification as though it were you. You become responsible for a lot of views that you personally didn't generate but that your work generated. You become vulnerable to lots of personalizing attacks for distorted and often incoherent reasons. For example, you have Martha Nussbaum critiquing Butler's work in ways that seem partly thoughtful, partly paranoid, and largely un-worked-through, in order to destroy a fantasy of Judith Butler's effect and effectiveness in the academy. It's a mirage of a mirage of a mirage.

**Hoberek:** Does this relate to recent calls from both inside and outside the academy for more clarity in academic writing?

**Berlant:** Skip Gates said recently in the *Chicago Tribune* that he just did all that theory stuff to get tenure, and now he's liberated from it. It makes me so angry that he won't fight for having been able to ask his questions in different kinds of registers and to speak and organize knowledge in those registers. He's now saying that that was just something he had to do for the one-dimensional academy. My view about this is that it's not really jargon or difficulty that distinguishes what academic people do from what nonacademic people do. It's much more about the way we frame our objects. The ways that Judith Butler or Gayatri Spivak frame their objects would be obscure to most people who are thinking about themes of power and inequality, whether or not their sentences were journalistic.

**Hoberek:** So the call for academics to be intelligible in the public sphere or spheres blurs the more fundamental issue of theory's function of thinking outside the normal routes of thought or discourse?

**Berlant:** Or, as they used to say in the eighties, against common sense. Which raises the whole question of whether the academy has the right to produce counter–common sense. The only reason that I can live within a university context intellectually and politically is that I think the university's central function is to support the kinds of ideas that aren't supported by the marketplace—thought that you can't find in normal culture. That's what makes teaching important: students are not going to be able to learn these modes of thought later. They'll learn other ways of explaining things that serve normativity, but we have the opportunity to show them different narratives and ways of explaining things now. That is a radical task. So not all academic work should be intelligible in a putative public sphere.

**Hoberek:** Jerry Graff has noted that while much of the discourse about public intellectuals foregrounds a journalistic model, most academics still reach a far greater audience in the classroom than they will ever reach through *Harper's* or the *Nation*. So what gets lost in the journalistic model is the idea of the classroom itself as a public, a public that's available not only to crossover academic stars but to anybody who's teaching four sections of composition.

**Berlant:** I think people usually see their classroom as their own little private thing, as though it were a kind of familial zone or private property. That's why they don't like outsiders sitting in on their classes or interfering with their pedagogy: it interferes with a fantasy of intellectual mastery that frequently depends on the seductive magic of virtuoso teaching. Seeing your classroom as a public requires an entirely different understanding of your pedagogy, your opinion, and your relation to students. This includes realizing that what you say in a classroom is not just between you and your class but actually participates in a larger social environment and has resonances that one cannot circumscribe by one's "good intentions."

**Hoberek:** While some of us don't think of the classroom as a public, many of our enemies in state legislatures and elsewhere do. I'd argue that this is what's behind recent calls for academics to do more teaching, and less research and publishing.

**Berlant:** Why should we be surprised at this, since everything else has been privatized in the U.S.? Why shouldn't public education go next? It's not surprising, in a way, that people would be less interested in funding public education now because they're less interested in funding anything public. Such academic downsizing goes hand in hand with numerous other attempts to shrink the machinery of redistribution and to minimize what would constitute full citizenship in the state. What's ironic is that this is happening at a moment when the rhetoric around children and education is intensifying. People are actually quite happy to increase elementary school education funding relative to what we might call adult education funding. They want more school choice so parents can get *exactly* what they want for their children. But the farther away children get from parents—like in college—the less people feel obligated toward education as such. And to the degree that they still pay attention to what goes on in universities, they want the same kind of intensively disciplined and disciplinary training that they now want for their kids in elementary school.

The second thing I think is that teaching and research in the nontechnological domains of the academy are being diminished in value now, and that's why people can advocate distance education, because it no longer seems like humanist education requires actual humans to be in the room. And so the idea of the classroom as a space where people learn how to sustain a thought or learn how to think and analyze because humans are actually helping each other do it is getting lost. It's no longer deemed the skill that literate members of a democracy should have. It's deemed less necessary for capitalist success. Instead, it is said that students should just get the information that they need in order to be good members of a technocracy. Again, this process has something to do with the privatization of citizenship and the atrophying of a notion of critical public culture as a good. Instead we want good workers and a reduction of the scene of citizenship to the machinery of family and work in which productivity can be measured and assured. The pressure many state legislatures are placing on universities to regulate on an hourly or daily basis professorial labor is one symptom of this general trend.

**Hoberek:** So the obvious and probably unanswerable question is, What can academics do about this?

**Berlant:** People have different views about how they can respond to the redefinition of academic labor. Some people are interested in union organization, others in movements that will have proactive plans for protecting academic freedom, but which won't address so much the economic and political factors emerging from the particularity of academic labor. Another kind of solution to the problem has to do with advocating a really serious moral and economic discussion about the use of adjuncts and the place of nontenured faculty in the university system. This becomes particularly important if tenure does get phased out because it's less profitable than other modes of employment. It's also important not to give up on theory and noncommon sense.

**Hoberek:** Maybe we can shift a little bit here. One of the things I also wanted to talk about was your own intellectual formation.

**Berlant:** My deformation . . .

**Hoberek:** Or your deformation, yes. So maybe you could explain why you prefer to call it your deformation, and then talk about the specific forms this deformation took. I know that you grew up in an East Coast suburb near Philadelphia. Could you talk a little about your path from there to the University of Chicago?

**Berlant:** I went to a mixed-class public high school with people who are now working in department stores, auto shops, and pizza joints as well as being lawyers, writing television shows, and running think tanks. It was a very hierarchical place, one that trapped you: each class was homogenized according to some pretested level of intelligence. Because of my family's own weird class formation I had friends that cut across class divides, but I experienced myself mainly as unfit, a monster, uncomfortable everywhere. I did very well in school, but I also cut classes like crazy. Now I'm going to sound incoherent for a minute. School was always a space of incredible freedom for me. It was always first a refuge from home. It was a place where people thought my mind was interesting, where my teachers were always incredibly encouraging. But I was also a very unformed, inarticulate, and isolated person and very shy and angry, so by the time I got to high school, I was ready to drop out.

Then I visited a commune called Twin Oaks, which is a Skinnerian community outside of Richmond, Virginia, in between Charlottesville and Richmond. I had read about it in *Psychology Today* and in the *New York Times*. (What a nerd!) I was always very interested in utopias; I'd read everything, historical and fictional, old and new. So I went to this commune often and learned a lot of things there that made it possible for me to exist. One thing was that I really got along with people, which was kind of shocking because in my own home and school I was anomalous in a lot of ways. But I found out at Twin Oaks that environmental factors had a lot to do with my happiness. I also discovered how much I love to work: it's where I learned to be a colleague. I worked really hard there, and I found out that working attaches you to other people; it doesn't necessarily isolate you. Of course, that was true on the commune and isn't always true anywhere else, but it became an ideal for me to think about working as something that made worlds with others rather than as something that isolated people.

I came back from that, and my life was really changed—I had optimism. Then, college. I chose Oberlin because I thought it seemed like a place that would respect people's different creativities, and it really did. Nonetheless, I was very ill while I was there with anorexia, which stemmed from a lot of things, including poverty and rape, and I returned to the game of *fort-da* with my own existence. I was supporting myself—I put myself through college—and it was all very insecure. At the same time, my teachers went out of their way to encourage my mind and helped me take control of my education. I had three concentrations there: creative writing, social psychology, and English. The other great thing about Oberlin was that it had an institution called the

Experimental College where students could take and teach their own courses for credit. I taught women in popular culture courses at least two of the years I was there, and I found that I loved teaching. So that was Oberlin.

People thought I was going to go to Iowa for writing school, and instead I decided to go to graduate school to do a Ph.D. I was still quite ill and didn't think I was quite ready to do more creative writing. I went to Cornell and almost dropped out right away because it was just too overwhelming for me. (You see the pattern!) I don't mean the work was too hard, but I was so contingent and uncomfortable, and it just takes a lot of courage to go to graduate school. I think people forget how destabilizing it is to enter a professionalizing context after having honed a more personal image of what they love and what they're good at. I didn't know whether I had any potential to translate my intelligence to the world, such as it was.

Everything was extremely poststructural at Cornell, and besides not having a Continental philosophical background—which I quickly had to cultivate—I was also a Marxist and a feminist. I didn't think that these should be deemed vulgar compared to what was deemed high theory. So I did a lot of autodidactic browsing around the library and sitting in the stacks and finding books that nobody could tell me were good or bad. I had to cultivate myself at my own pace and at the same time worked in study groups with my own generation, along with taking classes. Eventually a group of people came to Cornell who were more on my planet, like Chris Newfield, Ann Cvetkovich, and Jeff Nunokowa, but I had been in graduate school for over four years before that happened. So I had all these years of being quite blundery and martianlike from the point of view of my colleagues as well as myself, which is the story that continues at my university, though for different reasons and less agonistically, perhaps.

I meant to write my dissertation on why historical novels use love plots, since everybody who ever read a historical novel critically thought that the love plot was an accident of bad writing, whereas the history was deemed the really important thing. I thought, well, if it's a mistake that people keep making, maybe it isn't an accident and we should find out some things about it. So that's how I became who I am professionally. I wrote my Hawthorne chapter first and became an Americanist by accident, when I got a job as an Americanist at Chicago. I taught the American survey (which we had then) and I discovered that the students took it as a citizenship training course. They would disagree with Emerson, and I would be like, "You're disagreeing with Emerson?! What does it mean to say he's wrong about what an American is?" And then I realized that if you are teaching a national literature in its own context, you have a political responsibility not to presume the context, but to generate that context in the classroom. And that's how I developed my interests in nationality and in the analysis of citizenship as a category that is simultaneously juridical and also a normative in national culture. My work would be entirely different if I hadn't had that particular experience.

**Hoberek:** So to return to our question of branding, you were hired as an Americanist?

**Berlant:** An Americanist and a feminist. At my job interview, they asked me, "Are you more of an Americanist or a feminist?" and I just laughed, it was such an absurd question. I said, "Well, I'm trained to be an Americanist, I'm trained to do feminist theory, and I'm feminist—but those are different things," and they nodded. I have no idea what they thought.

**Hoberek:** Can you talk a bit about what you imagine your constituencies to be now?

**Berlant:** I get invited to queer theory conferences. I am less frequently asked to go to feminist and Americanist conferences, and I'm as likely to be talking to law and political theory people as I am to people in literature, so this either means that I'm transdisciplinary or I'm nowhere and I'm just lucky that anyone reads me. I basically think I'm just lucky.

**Hoberek:** It's interesting that when you describe your intellectual trajectory you locate yourself on the margins of the profession, and yet in conversations with your colleagues now you emerge as a proponent of professionalization. Do you think that your experience on the margins has in some way made you more favorable toward professionalization?

**Berlant:** I don't generally think of myself as professionally marginal—more martian than margin. But at one point Elizabeth Freeman said in a feminist theory reading group at Chicago that she thought that the relations between feminist faculty and feminist students or queer faculty and queer students or lesbian faculty and lesbian students were always difficult because there was no metadiscourse about what exactly it was that they were doing with each other. Were they involved in the same political project? What was the relation between the political, professional, and personal projects? And I thought that was totally true, and it changed my relation to professionalism positively, and in a profound way.

I've written an essay, "Feminism and the Institutions of Intimacy," that addresses these issues. I've become dedicated to thinking about ways of dedramatizing relations with graduate students, to be a resource while still enabling—well, forcing—them to have some degree of professional self-consciousness. I've tried to think about what's useful about the impersonality of the professional relationship, so when I begin to work with someone I'll say: "Here are the things that I require. One, I want to minimize infantilization, so don't hide from me in the hall, because, believe me, whatever it is you're ashamed of (like an unfinished chapter), couldn't be that bad. Two, if you feel like you're not getting the kind of attention from me that you think you need, talk to me. I might not be able to give it to you, but you're never going to know if you don't ask. Instead of getting resigned and bitter about it, you might as well try to have the relationship in which you can get the education that you want. Likewise, I need to be able to say to you if I think you're not being serious or dedicated enough for the project of work you've set forth." I've never actually had to say that to a student, although occasionally I have had to say, "I really need to not be reading chapters that you haven't finished yet." There's a certain amount of "Here's a mess, can you fix it for me?" that I just can't bear to do anymore. Usually I do what I can, though.

I think being able to have these relations of impersonality with graduate students is really important to their capacity to be responsible to their own thought rather than to the views of a committee. That's where my style of professionalism comes from. It's very personal but it's also very explicit about its institutional context. It comes from seeing how disabling it has been for so many graduate students not to be able to make claims or demands on their education once they start working with a dissertation committee. I've seen students take on the psychodramas of the faculty; I've seen students have imaginary relationships with faculty members because they can't talk to them or because they talk with them too much; I've seen people's work get really deformed because students feel that they have to do what the faculty member says, or otherwise they won't get a job. I've seen students really believe that faculty have magic, or be angry and furious that faculty don't have magic. We need a metalanguage of professional relations, a language that enables things to get spoken about and distinguished and clarified, so that people can have the education that they need, and so that teachers don't pass on to their students their own professional structures of betrayal, disappointment, desire, anxiety, and neglect.

**Hoberek:** You were talking earlier about your discovery at Twin Oaks that work could attach you to other people. Clearly hanging in the air is the fact that work frequently *doesn't* attach one to other people in the academy. In your essay "Crisis, Collegiality, and Cultural Studies," you talk about the ways that collegiality becomes a problem in academic departments because there are no explicit languages for how one relates to one's colleagues. We go into this career imagining ourselves as loners who don't have to work with others, and as a result the ways we do relate to our colleagues become totally fucked up.

**Berlant:** In *The Academic Revolution* Christopher Jencks and David Riesman describe the emergence of the notion that faculty members are autonomous or relatively autonomous from their institutions. This is a relatively new formation, as they note, but we really experience ourselves very much that way now. "This is *my* work. I'm doing *my* work, and nobody should interfere with *my* work." And that's why so many departments and people become dysfunctional. But I'd say, "Hey, we work for this institution and we have to work together for X." So my investment in having languages of negotiation is partly on behalf of trying to build a sustainable world in the academy and elsewhere. As in my relations to graduate students, it's also partly on behalf of reducing the intensity of mistrust and paranoia that comes from faculty defensiveness about whether other people recognize the value of their labor.

**Hoberek:** I've been working on Ayn Rand, and on the parallel between Rand's outlook and what academics mean when they use that phrase "my work"—as in, "I can't wait until I get done teaching this semester so I can do *my* work." What's fascinating to me about a novel like *The Fountainhead*, which is about an architect who doesn't want anybody to tell him what to build, including his clients, is that he's really an academic, because he imagines that his work can be absolutely autonomous, absolutely free from other people.

**Berlant:** And he also thinks he's expressing his true self. In that way, he's doing sexuality in the Foucauldian sense: he's expressing the truth about himself. That's what so many academics (humanists and humanist social scientists, anyway) think that they're doing. It's no accident that questions of intellectual property are so hot in the academy these days. Suddenly the virtuoistic presumptions of intellectual value are encountering the productivity fetish of universities, which are now veering toward claiming as their own the intellectual work (especially of teaching) that their faculty does. This threatens all sorts of norms about intellectual autonomy but also norms of what it means that person X with an excellent brain can write such excellent things. Meanwhile, it is stunning to see how often our anxieties about the value of intellectual virtuosity produce terrible collegiality. Anyone who writes knows the difference between all the things that they've conceived and what comes out on the page. And yet people have very little patience for each other's unfinishedness.

**Hoberek:** So then is professionalism one of the "institutions of intimacy" that you've been exploring in your recent work?

**Berlant:** I have an anxiety about the word "professionalism," and so instead would say that I'm talking about collegiality. This is because I want to think about the relations of reciprocity, and the language of professionalism is much more a language of code. Or maybe I'm working between them. I'm interested in the relations between the desire for collegiality and the desire for reciprocity. That's the way that knowledge builds worlds and institutions, which are always going to disappoint the fantasy that produces them in the first place. But it's still an important thing to try to do. This is why I took on the directorship of the Center for Gender Studies at Chicago. It's about the possibility of making a space responsive to the urgency of having ideas. People's biographies and their baggage and their demons always enter into those spaces, but I think because school for me has been a place where it was possible to have one's history and to produce thought that hasn't existed yet, I'm on the side of trying to make resources for people institutionally. And that is what collegiality is about for me.

**Hoberek:** By way of concluding, could you talk about the other projects that you're working on now, about the "Intimacy" issue of *Critical Inquiry* and about *The Female Complaint*?

**Berlant:** I'm always working on more than one project at a time, not because I think it's a good thing to do but just because that's what my unconscious has me do. When I started to work on the Hawthorne book, I started to work on the female complaint book. And when I finished the Hawthorne book, I thought the female complaint book would be the second thing, but then I started working on *The Queen of America*, and because of my "constituency" *The Queen* got finished first. *The Anatomy of National Fantasy, The Female Complaint*, and *The Queen of America* are part of a national sentimentality trilogy that looks at how questions of intimacy and sexuality and desire are deployed in political contexts to produce images of the law and the nation that become normative. The Hawthorne book is about the relation between ordinary affect and the law. The female complaint book is about women's culture as the first subaltern commodity culture in America, a culture that simultaneously promotes a normative way of being feminine and a space of critique. I read it as a place in which liberal notions of freedom are acted out in their contradictory ways—for example, in the freedom white people take to appropriate as the form of their interiority the pain of people of color and the working classes and immigrants and so on. Sentimentality authorizes empathy as a way of humanizing the structurally dehumanized, which places the hermeticism of privilege at risk but can also confirm it as a site where people with good intentions can have good emotions that absolve them from risking the material conditions that privilege them. So the book tells a lot of different stories, about migrations to cities, entertainment, health, and why pain gets turned into entertainment and gets placed at the center of liberal culture as the site of white ethics—how, therefore, the traffic in pain and the traffic in entertainment and the traffic in femininity become a part of the same consciousness. *The Queen of America* tracks how the intimate public sphere became the norm and not just a subaltern discourse in the contemporary United States.

During the production of this thought about sentimentality and national intimacy, I developed my work in queer theory, which is about trying to proliferate the kinds of narratives, practices, and institutions in which people can imagine sustaining life over time, and that's where "Intimacy" came from. I thought of it while driving around one day, and then I started beating myself up about it because intimacy is such a marginal topic in the face of so much social violence—the systematic incarceration of African Americans, transnational exploitation, virulent erotophobias impacting women and queers, etcetera. Intimacy as a concept enabled me, though, to talk about the thing I'm really interested in, which is, how do people sustain their optimism about living in the face of so much violence and negation? Is it possible to separate out the forms we have invested in from the desire for a better good life? That's what the intimacy book is trying to do: people from different disciplines get together and try to figure out how the story of attachment has been told and might be told better.

Then, when I finish *The Female Complaint*, I'm going to write a book whose tentative title is *What I've Learned about Love*. The second half of that book is going to be a bunch of keyword essays I've written over the last few years, including an essay on desire, an essay on queer love or love of queer feeling. Then there's an essay I'm going to write on femininity whose title I believe is going to be "Soft." The first half is going to be a personal essay where I try to talk about pedagogy, sexuality, and femininity and their relation to what one does for a living, to thought and freedom. It has something to do with trying to write without getting incredibly depressed by the compulsion to repeat femininity, and by the fact that so many of my students remain paralyzed by a certain defensive obligation to normalcy, and by the fact that the political world has become less and less a place for mass criticism and more and more a site of pain, mourning, and disinvestment. So I hope it interferes with the reproduction of pain culture as a form of therapy, for women but also for liberals.

I also have a collection of essays on trauma that seems to be getting big enough to put together. The argument is from my essay called "The Subject of True Feeling," which was a section of the fat-fetus essay I couldn't bear to write before. It's really a refinement of the national sentimentality argument about how the traffic in pain has produced transformations of the law and reproduction in contemporary culture, and also why everybody needs to recognize their suffering and trauma now. It deals with the notion that trauma has to do with events, that its temporality is very significant, whereas a lot of the things that are getting called trauma now really have to do with people's relation to ongoing subordination that has become banalized and ordinary in their lives. I'm trying to challenge that rhetoric and to change it. So that's what I'm doing right now: small topics like love, pain, and intimacy.

# 15

# Undisciplined

## *An Interview with Andrew Ross*

To many, Andrew Ross personifies cultural studies in the United States. He has written on topics ranging from intellectuals to Disney, from modernist poetry to global warming, and from Madonna to sweatshops, and has gained high visibility doing it. His work has appeared in many prominent academic venues, such as *Critical Inquiry*, *Cultural Critique*, *Screen*, and *Social Text* (which he coedited for many years), but he also regularly writes for journalistic venues such as the *Nation*, the *Village Voice*, and *Artforum* (for which he wrote a regular column), and he has received media coverage that few academics get, the subject of write-ups in *New York* magazine, *GQ*, and *Lingua franca* and occasionally appearing on television. However, his profile has cut both ways: while heralded as an innovator of several new fields of inquiry, such as ecocriticism and technocriticism, he has also been attacked as fostering the decline of literary studies, as a postmodern relativist, and as an unqualified interlocutor of science. Ross discusses some of the vagaries of visibility, as well as the prospects for cultural politics, in the interview that follows.

Though trained in literature, like many other critics of his generation, in one sense Ross represents the "posttheory generation" and efforts to broaden the traditional borders of literary studies. Yet, in another sense one could see Ross as a latter-day literary intellectual, updating the role of the New York Intellectuals, whose work covered a wide range of culture and ideas of their day for a literate audience. Perhaps the key difference is the relation to popular culture; as Ross discusses in one of his most well-known books, *No Respect: Intellectuals and Popular Culture*, the New York Intellectuals disdained popular culture, whereas Ross's work has consistently brought to the fore its cultural politics.

Born in Scotland in 1956, Ross was educated at Aberdeen University (M.A., 1978) and the University of Kent (Ph.D., 1984). Ross first came to the United States in 1980, teaching at Illinois State University and elsewhere until 1985, when he took an appointment at Princeton. While at Princeton, Ross first drew media coverage, at one point famously appearing in a mustard-color Commes des Garcon jacket in a *New York Times Magazine* feature on the MLA convention. In 1993, he moved to NYU to become director of the graduate program in American Studies, a project that he discusses here.

A tireless writer, Ross is the author of almost two hundred articles and a growing shelf of books, including *The Failure of Modernism: Symptoms of American Poetry* (Columbia UP, 1986); *No Respect* (Routledge, 1989); *Strange Weather: Culture, Science, and Technology in the Age of Limits* (Verso, 1991); *The Chicago Gangster Theory of Life: Nature's Debt to Society* (Verso, 1994); *Real Love: In Pursuit of Cultural Justice* (NYU P, 1998); *The Celebration Chronicles: Life, Liberty, and the Pursuit of Property Value in Disney's New Town* (Ballantine, 1999), an account of a year spent living in the new urbanist town of Celebration, Florida; and *No-Collar: The Humane Workplace and Its Hidden Costs* (Basic Books, 2003). Alongside his own writing, Ross has also been a tireless editor, sponsoring special issues of *Social Text* and a symposium in the *minnesota review* 32 (1989) on Language poetry; his edited collections include *Universal Abandon? The Politics of Postmodernism* (U of Minnesota P, 1988); *Technoculture* (with Constance Penley; U of Minnesota P, 1991); *Microphone Fiends: Youth Music and Youth Culture* (with Tricia Rose; Routledge, 1994); *Science Wars* (Duke UP, 1996), stemming from the controversial *Social Text* issue; and *No Sweat: Fashion, Free Trade, and the Rights of Garment Workers* (Verso, 1997).

For some of Ross's essays relevant to this interview, see "Earth to Gore, Earth to Gore," *Social Text* 41 (1994); "'Culture Wars' Spill Over: Science Backlash on Technoskeptics," *Nation* (2 Oct. 1995); and "A Few Good Species," *Social Text* 46–47 (1996). For some of the coverage of Ross, see Lawrence R. Stains, "Lunch with Andrew Ross," *GQ* (July 1993); Rebecca Mead, "Yo, Professor," *New York* (14 Nov. 1994); Mark McGurl, "Green Ideas Sleep Furiously: Andrew Ross on Ecocriticism," *Lingua franca* (Dec. 1994); and Tony Hendra, "Hackedemia," *GQ* (July 1995).

This interview took place on 6 July 1995 at Andrew Ross's office in the American Studies Program suite at NYU. It was conducted by Jeffrey Williams and Mike Hill, associate editor of the *minnesota review* then teaching at Marymount Manhattan College and now at SUNY-Albany, and transcribed by Williams. It originally appeared in an issue of the review on "Institutional Questions," and some questions here bear on the subsequent "White Issue."

**Williams:** How would you define yourself? Your work has been associated primarily, I guess, with pop culture.

**Ross:** Well, actually, this is a misconception; in fact, it's something of an unearned reputation. Especially since my last two books, and the next one, are about science and technology studies, and environmentalism, and *No Respect*, which certainly deals with popular culture, is more a work of intellectual history than anything else. And I had an earlier career as a poetry critic and as a psychoanalytic critic of sorts . . .

**Williams:** I was going to ask you about that, your relationship vis-à-vis literature, as evidenced by your first book. There's even a piece in an old *minnesota review* about the Language poets.

**Ross:** Yes, I spent some time hanging out with the Language poetry community in the Bay Area. In essence, that actually was what brought me to the U.S., quote-unquote "the love of poetry," and contemporary poetry in particular.

**Williams:** Oh really? So it was the love of literature after all?

**Hill:** That's one for the record. It wasn't glossy magazines?

**Ross:** Well, it was the love of living literature.

**Williams:** I had wanted to ask you about your intellectual formation. Where did you do your graduate work?

**Ross:** Primarily at the University of Kent, which at the time, in the late seventies, was a center for film theory. Many of the *Screen* group were teaching there. That was after a training in the legacy of the Scottish Enlightenment as an undergraduate—high moral seriousness—philosophy, Leavisite literary criticism, and social anthropology. When I went to graduate school in England, I was very much committed to the avant-garde idea, both politically and culturally, and in retrospect this tradition, to which the *Screen* school adhered, was very much at loggerheads with the more populist cultural studies tradition that had been active in Birmingham for some time. My chief focus turned out to be in poetry, however, and since the contemporary poetry scene in

Britain was somewhat moribund in comparison to North America, I started coming over here to teach and to study, completing my graduate years at Indiana University and at Berkeley. After that, I was based in Champaign-Urbana for a couple of years, where folks were pioneering the U.S. interest in cultural studies in the early to mid-eighties. And that's the point at which, really, my work began to be associated with cultural studies. Not because of some academic change of habit, but because it was at that time that I realized I was going to stay in the U.S., and cultural studies for me meant learning what it would be like to behave like a citizen—researching the traditions of cultural citizenship and the like.

**Hill:** How did that mesh with the love of poetry? Was it an easy transition?

**Ross:** I really can't remember. But I suspect that it's always been easier for Americanists, from the point of view of disciplinarity, to broaden their scope as cultural critics. Because of the interdisciplinary nature of American Studies, the literary critical tradition has been a little less formalistic than in the case of British literature. The more difficult transition was in the area of theories of popular culture. Among the folks who were versed in critical theory at that time, when it came to thinking about commercial culture, they would simply reach for their Frankfurt School readers, which struck me as not at all the best way of looking at the issue from an American angle. So that's why I began to research the history of the relationship between American intellectuals and popular culture, and that led to *No Respect*. It was written to try to fill an existing gap in cultural history and theory, and to bring some of the European work to bear upon the American history without doing the local too many injustices. Subsequently, the questions raised in the book about institutional authority and expertise and populism spilled over into the work on science and technology that has governed some of my work since then.

**Hill:** Has it become respectable to study popular culture in a way that it had been to study literature in the past? With the disciplinary shifts and the restructuring of institutions and the retraining of graduate students, to what extent is there a correspondence between that kind of training and the kind of work that's being done now in the academy with popular culture, cultural studies, that kind of thing?

**Ross:** Well, I think there are two issues here. Popular culture has been taught, researched, and studied within the academy for quite some time. To read neocon accounts demonizing this turn to cultural studies, you wouldn't believe that was the case, but of course it has been there, in various versions: in sociology departments, in history departments, in communications departments, and, of course, in places like the Bowling Green Center [of Popular Culture]. Each of these locations has a particular history and disciplinary angle. And of course leftists of whatever stripe have always had an interest in the popular. There's a long history of talking about those issues in an academic context.

**Hill:** But not attached to literary studies?

**Ross:** To varying degrees, literary historians and critics have always been interested in popular literature, theater, and film. And in the sixties, there was that strange moment when English professors were teaching Bob Dylan lyrics in response to student demands for relevance. It's true, however, that the more decisive breaks came with the wholesale erosion of disciplinarity in the eighties. Literary studies, because of its weak disciplinary formation, collapsed more quickly than others, and, for better or worse, has become a relatively safe haven in some places for work that is called cultural studies. It was by default, rather than by design, that literary studies became an institutional refuge for that kind of work. I don't think it was viewed then or now as anything more than a temporary location, however, and it certainly was temporary for me. This flightiness has registered in the field and in the methodology. What was produced was a generation of scholars who trained themselves to do something like post-Fordist scholarship, by which I mean that their careers would not be distinguished by assembly line production in a particular field—literary modernism, let's say—but rather that they undertook flexible, specialized production-on-demand, mounting analyses that drew upon knowledge in different fields or disciplines, and then moved on to wherever they thought they could do useful, political work.

**Williams:** Sort of free-floating intellectuals?

**Ross:** Well, that's the romantic model for this kind of intellectual. The way I've described it, however tongue-in-cheek, suggests that it resonates to some extent with the dominant mode of production. On the other hand, it has proven an efficient way of avoiding the kind of professional career that was so opposed to our sense of useful political work—whereby you accumulate cultural capital in a particular field or area, and become a disciplinary fetishist. Of course, that whole process has become compromised by the job crisis.

**Williams:** Maybe you could say something about what you think about "postdisciplinarity." That's one phrase that seems associated with your work.

**Hill:** You made me think of something that relates to Jeff's question about postdisciplinarity when you were speaking a second ago. Is cultural studies something that is just a loose set of practices that moves between disciplines and therefore is in some sense dependent on those disciplines for that act of displacement, or can it itself become postdisciplinary to the extent that disciplines no longer exist?

**Ross:** Some part of the answer to that question is tied to the declining job market. When graduate students can no longer be trained as career academics with any degree of confidence, then the whole model of coherent disciplines will fall apart in practice. The other part relates, I suppose, to the influence of movements like cultural studies. And I must say that I am not terribly comfortable talking about cultural studies, because I prefer doing it, and I think in general there's been a lot more talk about cultural studies than there has been doing it, in terms of practical studies.

**Hill:** So maybe cultural studies is what you're doing when you're not answering the question, "What is cultural studies?"

**Ross:** Perhaps, and in addition, there's a certain pathology of being in denial about doing cultural studies, which is a symptom of a field, as has often been noted, that has no master mold. Unlike other critical movements, there isn't really a master thinker who produced magisterial readings, which are then copied and built upon by acolytes. If there were a figure who would have occupied that position, it would have been Stuart Hall, and Stuart—by design, as much as by anything else—submerged his own identity in collective work in the formative period of the Birmingham school, so that he himself has not really come to be associated with a set of definitive readings. Michael Denning recently described cultural studies as little more than a slogan at this point in time—a term that is loosely employed to describe the implosion of the field of knowledge covered by the humanities and non-quantitative sectors of the social sciences. It's a term that's entered academic and to some extent public currency in ways that are now impossible to track, let alone police.

As for myself, I have chosen to work in the field of American Studies, for all sorts of reasons. I think American Studies is a very vibrant field at the moment, and not just because it is a sort of granddaddy of interdisciplinary fields. It has undergone a boom period in the last ten years or so. Membership in the ASA has tripled . . .

**Williams:** It has a sort of suspect lineage, though.

**Ross:** Oh, you mean the chauvinism? Well, of course, there was an absurd degree of nationalist celebration, continuing even through the period of what's often referred to as critical nationalism, from the sixties through, I guess, the mid-eighties.

**Williams:** Wasn't the American Studies Program inaugurated at Yale by James Jesus Angleton, under the auspices of the OSS, the forerunner of the CIA?

**Ross:** Well, there is always a relationship to national security that needs to be interrogated.

**Hill:** That's why we're taping this.

**Ross:** To go back to origins, it's fair to say that the first courses in Western civ, for example, were offered by the Department of War for officers who were going out to fight on the European fronts in the First World War. It had to be established for the officers what it actually was they were defending, in terms of ideas and values and so on. Thirty years later, the whole idea of studies in American civilization was formed around a particular group of academics who worked fairly closely together and coherently—some of them in intelligence operations—during the Second World War. A similar origin then applies to the field; there was a sense of an exclusive set of values that were to be defended and protected in some way. This was all solidified by the celebratory period of liberal consensus and Cold War culture, driven by security concerns both here and abroad, where American Studies programs were set up all over the U.S. clientist world. During the period of critical nationalism, American Studies was also in direct competition with emerging ethnic studies programs and women's studies programs, and, in a sense, it survived very well largely because of its receptive response to issues raised in these other fields. Its receptivity to new intellectual movements and cultural politics has ushered in what Don Pease and others refer to as its postnationalist phase, where tracking the role of the U.S. in the age of global integration takes American Studies well beyond national borders. As a transdisciplinary field, American Studies is a relatively comfortable place to be for my kind of work.

**Williams:** When did you start directing the American Studies Program at NYU?

**Ross:** I started here a couple years ago, in the summer of 1993, with the task of renovating a fairly large graduate program that had been based, in the traditional sense, in literature and in history. Student applications have risen accordingly, and what we've found is we get applications not only from students who are ordinarily aiming themselves at American Studies programs but also from students who are looking for a progressive interdisciplinary program. And there are very few of them on the ground. There are virtually no cultural studies programs, as we know; for all sorts of reasons the departmentalization of cultural studies just has not occurred. So American Studies has been a natural place to turn to.

**Williams:** You were saying at breakfast that you're gearing the program toward not only producing yet more academics but giving people different kinds of skills that they can use.

**Ross:** This has been our way of trying to confront the job crisis honestly. First of all, American Studies has always had a tradition of people going into journalism, museums . . .

**Hill:** The State Department . . .

**Ross:** No doubt, yes, the State Department.

**Williams:** In a way, isn't it accommodationist? Wouldn't it funnel directly into a corporate or postcorporate role?

**Ross:** Look, the Left's basic interest in graduate education is that it presents an opportunity to train a political class, quite frankly. Where those "cadres" work is less important than the fact that there continue to be institutional sites for training radical intellectuals. We should not be solely in the business of producing a job bourgeoisie, which is the traditional career academic model. And so it is imperative not to accept the shrinkage injunction that has been presented as a response, in some Left circles, to the job crunch. Graduate education must continue to be an expansionary project, if only because it is one of few places where the work of training a generation of radical intellectuals can occur. Now let's suppose a goodly number of these students move into nonacademic institutions, even in the commercial sector. Is that accommodationist? To some degree, their day job will be compromised, but they will presumably carry their Left politics along with them. There should be nowhere that the Left cannot be. The alternative is marginalization and self-exclusion. It's an injunction, almost, to seed all kinds of institutions with progressive intellectuals. The challenge is to rethink graduate education with this aim in mind. And so we confront students in the program from the very outset with the idea that they'll be marshaling their ideas and their scholarship in ways that will make them functional in different kinds of locations, and we won't presume that they're bound for an academic career. Many of them will be academics, but others will choose not to. The idea is to be multilingual, to learn different languages, different tongues, since they'll need all of these skills.

**Williams:** In other words, to reconceive how to be an intellectual beyond just being an academic?

**Ross:** Probably. And in this respect, to go back to the earlier question, I don't know where postdisciplinary begins and interdisciplinary ends. In the traditional American Studies sense of interdisciplinarity, you have an historian and a literary analyst, and perhaps a sociologist and an anthropologist, who come together, and they share their individual expertise on some topic symposium, and presumably the cumulative result is something that is interdisciplinary.

**Hill:** Cliff Siskin uses the term "de-disciplinary," and I think by that he means disciplines don't ever fully go away—they're sort of rearranged, as you were talking about before, or sampled. You never get away from that moment of disciplinarity per se, you just have different structures or combinations of disciplinarity to produce something else those disciplines wouldn't have been able to produce by themselves.

**Ross:** I think it's fine to talk in the abstract. On the other hand, what is practical varies from university to university, because some departments are so different from other departments in other universities, especially as you move over into the social sciences. In fact, in this university, we are based in the social sciences—we're not in the humanities—for administrative reasons, primarily. To me this represents a relevant challenge, since the most pressing need, in American Studies as a whole, is to try to involve more of the social sciences. There are certain departments, like anthropology, that are intellectually secure and progressive, and other departments in the social sciences which have been more or less given over to models of rational choice or mathematical model worship. Because of this essentially uneven development, what you can actually achieve in any one place often depends upon what's available in terms of the resources on the ground.

**Williams:** I'd like to go back to a question I asked at the beginning, about how you define yourself, and get a capsule definition of what you think one should do. Should we be cultural critics, and what does that entail?

**Ross:** The term we present to students here is "intellectual activist." Some of them seem to like the sound of it.

**Williams:** What I want to ask you about next is the way that intellectuals are now constituted as celebrities. In a way, you've been constituted as a celebrity intellectual, but one can also see this in the recent apotheosis of the "public intellectual"—Cornel West, Gates, one could go down the list. What do you think about that constitution of an intellectual's role, and what do you think of your position?

**Ross:** The tendency that you're talking about isn't something that's specific to intellectuals or intellectual work. Celebrity culture is something that we've seen evolving and developing in all social sectors, and it seems to me one of the more astonishing things—especially when it comes to academics and the academy—is the extent to which academics actually still believe that the world they inhabit is immune to socioeconomic developments in other sectors of society. I think the job crisis has brought home that astonishing degree of denial among academics. The low-wage revolution has affected every other sector of society; how could the academy have been different? But there remains this sense of immunity.

**Williams:** Nostalgia for being monks or something like that?

**Ross:** Perhaps. Maybe nostalgia for the Inquisition too. And of course it's stronger in the more solid core humanistic disciplines than in others. But now to get back to the phenomenon of academic celebrity, in some respects it's an extension of the genre of academic gossip, which is a culture unto itself—this extraordinary phenomenon whereby high-powered intellectuals spend a lot of their downtime trading scurrilous and detailed rumors about faraway colleagues.

**Hill:** Even not so famous or high-powered intellectuals do that.

**Ross:** Exactly. But in other respects, the celebrity thing has to be seen in the context of the Red-baiting that exploded during the course of the culture wars. The right-wing backlash to the academic Left, and the cultural studies Left especially, has fed into a particular kind of attack-dog journalism. The attack-dog op-ed piece became a tried-and-true tactic of the anti-PC scare. And we all know of instances where particular individuals and comments and so forth became favorite targets to demonize. For certain reasons, I was selected as one of those "easy" targets.

**Williams:** So you have Rush Limbaugh and the "Hackademia" article in *GQ*?

**Ross:** Oh yeah. That was a particularly appalling article. I mean, it was so bad, I wonder how it ever got past the editors. It really doesn't matter what you say in an interview with such writers. They will quite simply invent the comments they want to print and attribute them to you. It's not worth suing of course, they know that. But this hankering after scandalous sound bites is not confined to the realm of glossy journalism; you find it to varying degrees in organs of academic opinion or journals that seek to cover academic opinion. *Lingua franca*, obviously, and in the *Chronicle of Higher Education* there are similar tendencies, most of them quite harmless. Some not so harmless. The "Hot Type" column in the *Chronicle*, for example, recently reported for the third time in less than eight months the peculiar fact that Andrew Ross doesn't read books anymore, which was a highly doctored version of comments that were simply invented by a journalist at *New York* magazine.

**Hill:** How do you deal with that kind of sloppiness? I think of activist intellectuals as folks who, when they are engaged in activism, are also being acted upon, and acted upon in ways that they don't have a lot of control over. Instead of the Enlightenment notion of speaking benevolence to the masses, being a public intellectual means you're appropriated and turned out *as* popular culture. How do you deal with that?

**Ross:** It's a good question, because of course you are right about being acted upon and used in ways that none of us has much control over. On the other hand, our fantasy, as potentially useless intellectuals, is precisely to be of use to people we do not know and have never met—to write something, anything, no matter how fleeting, that readers will be able to use to get themselves a little farther down the road. That's why I don't put a very high premium on smartness. There's no shortage of highly educated and supersmart critics, who write to be admired rather than used. I know that sounds like good old pragmatism, but there you are. I take responsibility for my version of the fantasy, at least.

As far as the media goes, academics think of themselves as sophisticated interpreters of texts, but when it comes to reading journalism, they can be quite naive. They have little sense of the mechanics of journalism, and what happens when a journalist puts a story together. And they can often read it, especially when it's a story about academic life, as a transparent commentary that reveals some truth. That seems to me astonishing. On the other hand, speaking to the media is an obligation in my view. We all know that journalists working on a story need some comment from an accredited specialist, and they usually know what they want before they call you. We know that 98 percent of what we say will be neglected, and whatever we think we said will appear in some form that is quite alien to us. That's something that's just part of the standard practice in sensationalist journalism, and to a lesser extent, even quality journalism. The techniques of speaking to the press one has to learn. Sometimes I do okay, at other times not so well.

**Hill:** You've even been turned into a verb or I guess noun, "rossification," as I think I read in *Lingua franca*. It's a strange kind of activism when you're in the medium of the action.

**Ross:** The alternative is to select silence. The alternative is self-censorship. And to me that's always been a no-no. If you choose not to speak, then someone else, with worse politics, will do so. In addition, I believe that university intellectuals should be a source of opinion for journalists to access. Keeping those channels open is part of our job. And being in New York, and especially at NYU, we field a lot of calls from the media. Every other day, we get some media request, someone who's working a tight deadline, needs an opinion, needs an interview, whatever. That is what's fairly specific, I think, about working as an academic in New York. Academics here are very, very small fish in a big pond of ideas and opinions, unlike in university towns, where they're big fish in small ponds. So you have the media behemoth of midtown, and then Wall Street to the south, and in between you have the political economy of the art world, which vampirizes people as well. A good deal of my activities are actually in the art world. I write a regular column for *ArtForum*, and I do a lot of talks and symposiums within the art world, because that in many ways is the intellectual community on my doorstep. And then you have other worlds: the literati, the world of clublife, the fashion world, local activism, and so on. So it's a little different working in New York than it is in the university towns I have lived in. Your time and your availability are circumscribed in ways that you often don't have too many choices over. What that metropolitanism also means is that you lose sight of, if not contact with, much of the national academic scene.

**Williams:** How does it affect you personally, the celebrity thing? I guess this is the Connie Chung question.

**Hill:** Just whisper it to us. We won't tell anyone.

**Ross:** Not very much. When I'm not working hard at school, at *Social Text*, or at my own writing, then I'm being a very private person, usually too private, as my friends can attest. For a while there were some stories in magazines and the press that were quite hurtful, personally. But it's because I'm a fairly easy target, I think. At Princeton I stood out like a sore thumb, and there's a genre of story about the "untweedy Ivy League professor" that virtually required me to be called in from central casting. At a nouveau riche place like NYU there is a different, but no less conventional, role that is cast for me, and for my other freshly hired colleagues here.

**Williams:** How would you define your politics? In some ways, you're very much Left-affiliated—Socialist Scholars, MLG [Marxist Literary Group], the various journals you're affiliated with, like *Social Text*. However, there are some who have registered the complaint that you're not politically engaged enough. How would you answer that?

**Ross:** They must be tripping. When I think about it, my worldview is probably more Marxist than it's ever been, not just in regard to economism but even in terms of how I look at cultural and social questions. On the other hand, it's not the only tradition to draw upon. I think that's true for a lot of folks in the intellectual circles I grew up within, who were weaned on the essentially transgressive politics of the cultural Left—i.e., destroy all bourgeois institutions—and who also owe allegiance to the constructive Left that wants to build a better world. There's also an anarchist tradition, and anarchist ideas (Left-Libertarian) that one draws upon, there is a populist tradition, there's a radical democracy tradition that one draws upon as well, in addition to the very urgent injunctions of the new social movements. And I also grew up as an anticolonial nationalist—as a socialist and a nationalist—in Scotland in a very particular time. In a country that's still grappling with its peculiarly self-colonized history and self-colonizing traditions in relation to Westminster. So there are a number of different political traditions which are relevant to me, which might annoy those who hew to a more pure Marxist line. The emotional roots of my politics are quite simple: I am allergic to despair.

**Williams:** Your work is sometimes classified as "cultural politics." Is that a kind of localized politics, and how does that work out?

**Ross:** Cultural politics is usually slotted in with the cultural justice rather than the social justice wing of the Left. That great gulf that's been created, artificially or not, between these two wings in the last twenty years is something that really needs to be resolved. It seems to me completely absurd to think of political economy as simply the realm of unreconstructed Marxist thought, and to think of cultural politics as a sideshow or as a deflection or displacement of energy, if only as a result of the culture wars. Cultural issues and cultural values have been adopted as a vehicle for political campaigns by the Right; it's astonishing to think that anyone on the Left could think that cultural politics is still a diversionary issue. I mean, if anything, the culture wars have established cultural politics as a legitimate aspect of political thinking and political activism. If anything good has come of them, it's been that. If these issues are not political, then I'm Carmen Miranda.

**Williams:** Related to the issue of cultural politics, what's the relation of cultural studies to multiculturalism, with which it's sometimes confused?

**Ross:** Well, cultural studies communities exist in Britain, Australia, Canada, and the U.S., and each of these nation-states has different policy attitudes toward multiculturalism. In Australia and Canada, multiculturalism is sort of official state policy; it's a top-down policy. In Britain it has only ceased to exist as merely an immigration policy issue. In the U.S., it's very much been a bottom-up movement. So there are really three different placements, in terms of cultural policy issues. I think that's why, in the cultural studies community in Australia, there's been a lot of debate about cultural policy issues. That's partly a reflection of the fact that you've had a relatively benign social democratic administration in power for the last ten years or longer. In Australia, where intellectuals have fairly easy access to decisions about policy making, the whole idea of cultural policy making has become a big issue. It's not without its downside, since it's been in conflict with the much lionized, sort of nomadic tradition of the freethinking, freestanding intellectual. In the U.S., it seems to me the debates about cultural policy have been taking place in a de facto way, as a result of the culture wars. Intellectuals have been involved in it not under conditions of their own choosing, but nonetheless have been involved. And the difference between the U.S. and places like Australia is that you now have this vast right-wing intellectual pseudobureaucracy of "experts" that was created through the free-enterprise think tanks and the Heritage Institutes and so forth, specifically for the purpose of swaying cultural and social policy.

**Hill:** To segue from multiculturalism to a topic that an upcoming issue of the *minnesota review* will take up, it seems that now there is a kind of movement within critical race studies to forefront whiteness. One of the things that I've been thinking about in particular has to do with the crossover of hip-hop culture. You think of pop culture as something majority-oriented, popular, and yet hip-hop is, at least in certain aspects, minority discourse. You've talked about how pop culture remediates majority identity. Maybe that's too dense a question, but what kind of problems do white folks bring, say, to ghetto politics?

**Ross:** As far as hip-hop goes, too much has been made of the fact or the statistical citation that an enormous number of suburban white kids listen to hip-hop or buy hip-hop records. And perhaps it seems like a large number of white people are very familiar with hip-hop. Now, that's not unusual in the history of black music in this country. We do have a white majority, and it tends to have more spending power, and there are always going to be more white people buying any product basically than people of color. Added to which, a lot of musical product that has been purchased in minority communities circulates more freely from person to person. There isn't so much of a single individual ownership or consumption, in terms of buying and purchasing. So the fact that you're going to have large numbers of white people consuming black music has never, demographically, been incongruous. In the case of hip-hop itself and the audience for youth, the kind of black, brown, and white coalition or alliance that the audience consists of is, again, perhaps not completely unusual in terms of the history of black music, but because of economic conditions or patterns over the last twenty years or so, there's less of a difference between the white kids and the kids of color, in terms of their economic opportunities and their futures than there was, say, in the days of the "white negro." And the industry, in particular, depends on millions of white negroes, these days, to shift its product. In other words, there are aspects that are historically consistent, it seems, and then there are differences in the last fifteen years or so that one can point to.

**Williams:** Is there a kind of race poaching, particularly in fashion—I'm thinking about pictures of you sitting on a fire escape in *GQ* about a year ago, where they asked you questions about fashion?

**Ross:** Oh yeah. Another interview that didn't actually take place. It was something that they made up, largely. But there are just as many appropriations on the other side of the so-called color line, where hip-hop kids choose to wear clothing that is associated with suburban, white lifestyles.

**Williams:** You mean Hilfiger . . .

**Hill:** Timberlands . . .

**Ross:** Even Timberlands is still a live issue because Timberlands have tried overtly to dissociate themselves—their name—from inner-city clothing in a series of very racist ads. And the response on the part of a lot of hip-hop kids is to make an issue out of continuing to wear

Timberlands and embarrassing the hell out of them. Not to boycott, which would have been an older form of consumer politics, but quite the opposite, predicated upon the political principle that there's nowhere we cannot be, nothing that we can be denied access to. And the Hilfiger craze, for the time being, is a similar form of appropriation, luckily for Mr. Tommy, of course, who doesn't quite know what he did right. So it works both ways, and there's always been that kind of two-way dialogue. It's never been an equal conversation, but it's always been a two-way exchange between South Central and Beverly Hills.

**Hill:** Has identity politics run out of gas as a politically efficacious thing to do? Do you think that there's still a role for identity politics?

**Ross:** Well, in the kind of austerity society that we're forced to live in—I think we are increasingly living in a society governed by pro-scarcity politics—in that coercive fiscal climate, where everything is sacrificed at the budgetary altar, there's a limited good that's made available, in terms of resources and employment opportunities, and a competitive environment that is set up in the realm of state distribution of resources. That means all sorts of minorities and identity groups have to compete with each another for those resources. Identity politics becomes very important in that process. In this city, for example, Caribbean identity has emerged as a role in the fiscal politics of block grants where such an identity makes no sense at all in the Caribbean itself. Ditto for Asian American, Latino, and others, which are quite loose pan-ethnic identities. Of course, in this kind of resource environment that is highly competitive, appeals to hybridity don't get you very far at all. And so the politics of ethnoracial tradition are such that appeals to blood purity, appeals to unified cultural heritage and so on and so forth—the kinds of ideas commonly associated with minority identity politics—are reinforced by the fiscal climate. Therefore, what a lot of people who dream about postidentity political culture would like to see—an acknowledgment of racial and cultural mixing—is not allowed to come into being in this current fiscal climate because it's suicidal for minority leaders to appeal to those ideas under those conditions.

**Hill:** Would class be a better category?

**Ross:** I don't know. I'm kind of suspicious of that response, especially in the context of the affirmative action debates. I thought initially that here was a test case for the analysis of the behavior of North American elites. I mean, North American elites have always been willing to grant forms of symbolic justice when pushed to the wall. Never economic justice. So, affirmative action—this statistical machinery that was put in place after the Civil Rights Act (notwithstanding its administrative introduction by Nixon as part of a racially divisive "southern strategy")—was an inexpensive way for North American elites to provide symbolic justice. In historically similar instances—and I think that Reconstruction is a case in point—there's always a rollback at a certain point, even of symbolic justice. Reconstruction was enforced by Northern soldiers who were garrisoned in the South for long enough to ensure the penetration of Northern capital, and then all the racial gains were rolled back. We are witnessing a similar movement today. What seems quite different, however, in terms of looking over North American history, is the growth of the state and the functions of the state. That makes all the difference between, say, the early Republic and now. In the early Republic, debates went on about states' rights and federalism, where it was the Left, the radical Democrats, who were for states' rights and against central authority in government. Today it's almost exactly the opposite, where you have the Gingrichites arguing for the same sort of things, even though they've appropriated, as it's often been pointed out, New Left critiques of welfare state clientism, the push for more direct forms of democracy and popular sovereignty, and so on and so forth. What intervenes is the growth of the state as a major organ of redistributing wealth and ensuring that the principle of proportional representation is abided by at the level of federal government. In the last fifteen or twenty years or so, I think what we've seen—and the Clinton administration has been no exception in this regard—has been the dismantling of the redistributive component of the state, and a reinforcement of that part of the state which capital requires to legislate, support, and socialize the transition from one industrial regime to another.

**Williams:** Would you see the current attention to whiteness as an evacuation of a certain kind of identity politics or a reappropriation of identity politics?

**Ross:** I think to some extent, on the part of the right wing, that happened long ago, with white supremacist groups. I'm much less clear about where the Left is going on this issue. The discussions I've witnessed, as opposed to the texts I have read, have been occasions for white folks to talk about themselves, and to forget entirely folks of color. I'm afraid that this will happen more and more. It reminds me a little of the "male feminist" debate of the early eighties. On the other hand, it might help folks to use "white" more as an adjective to differentiate people and qualities in the daily world. That would be a good start. But really, there are still so many of us white intellectuals who have never gotten beyond Racism 101 that I can't help being skeptical.

**Williams:** To ask a final question, what are you working on now? What's down the road?

**Ross:** Most recently, as a result of *Strange Weather* and *The Chicago Gangster Theory of Life*, I've been dragged into the so-called science wars, successor to the culture wars. Conservatives in science opened up a new front in the culture wars, and to some extent, it's been coordinated by the same folks—the National Association of Scholars—who coordinated the culture wars. It's been moving up the media food chain from the weeklies toward the op-ed pages. The issues are not the issues that can be easily sensationalized, although the rhetoric has been very similar—"Here comes Afrocentric molecular biology," and "Here comes queer quantum mechanics," and so on and so forth. But because there is no hermeneutic tradition in the training or education of scientists—there's no tradition of self-critique, or even swapping critiques of each other's work, in the way that is endemic to the training of humanists and, to some extent, social scientists—there's a completely different dimension to the debate. But currently—and I hesitate to try to give a succinct characterization of the state of the wars . . .

**Williams:** Especially of your place in the war . . .

**Ross:** Well, I have edited a double issue of *Social Text* that's an attempt to coordinate some of the responses from the Left.

**Williams:** What's it called?

**Ross:** *Science Wars*, what else? Although it's an unfortunate term, because, like the culture wars, it suggests that in peacetime, as it were, culture and science are not politicized. But the vehicle of demonization is the idea of the flight from reason, and there's an attempt to link up the Aryan science of Nazis and Lysenkoism in the Soviet Union with the flood of irrationalism that sweeps along New Age movements, scientific creationism, postmodernism, and social constructionism—all riding the same flood. The defense of this last bastion of objectivity in the Western tradition, which is the kind of rearguard rhetoric that is used, attempts to equate all of these different movements as part of a holy war of purification of the scientific method against all these antagonists, not just barbarians at the gates, but folks—and there are many in science studies—who love science. Even though there's been maybe fifty years now of social critique of science, from the science and society movements of the thirties onward, it's only in the last few years or so, with the "science as culture" school, that this brouhaha has emerged. And in that fifty years, there's really no evidence that any of the critiques of science have had any effect upon funding, which, of course, is a major concern of those science professionals who sell their work to the highest bidder. The large stake is, of course, the democratization of technoscience at a time when corporate and military science have racked up a level of nuclear, biogenic, and chemical overdevelopment that cannot be insured against its own annihilation, let alone guarantee its own sustainability.

**Williams:** So your work is mostly focused on science and technology?

**Ross:** A good deal of it currently, and it has meant going off to give lectures at the New York Academy of Science and at university departments of biology and the like. In addition, I've been working on a book about "cultural justice" which will be my own account of the climate of the culture wars. The other project I'd like to do properly, if I ever get another sabbatical, is a study of Pentagon "culture." I've been able to do some work on the growth of environmental security programs at the Pentagon, and discovered what a very complex institution it is. There are ultraleftists who consider that the military has been one of the most progressive institutions in this country's history, if only because it is not strictly beholden to the logic of corporate capitalism. On the contrary, since it occupies the commanding heights of the economy, in a sense, the military establishment is in a peculiar position to be progressive in a way that corporate capitalism doesn't ordinarily allow. Added to which, there are a lot of people who think the Pentagon is riddled with pacifists. Look at the differences of opinion among military intellectuals in publications like the *Army Times* and the *Air Force Journal*, and there's a goodly amount of debate among folks who are employed as military intellectuals to write in these publications. I'd like to get to know more about them.

16

# History and Hope

## *An Interview with Robin D. G. Kelley*

In *Freedom Dreams: The Black Radical Imagination*, Robin D. G. Kelley recounts attending a conference on the future of socialism at which "an older generation of white leftists . . . proposed replacing retrograde 'pop' music with the revolutionary 'working-class' music of Phil Ochs, Woody Guthrie," and so on. Kelley responded, with some humor but also with a point, "No way! After the revolution, we STILL want Bootsy! That's right, we want Bootsy! We need the funk!" The point, as he puts it elsewhere, is not to look backward but to seek "new sources for political imagination and new prospects for freedom."

Kelley has been hailed as a leading African American historian of the modern era, investigating black working-class history, notably in his precocious *Hammer and Hoe: Alabama Communists during the Great Depression*, and the history of black radicalism from Aimé Césaire to Cedric Robinson. More recently, he has also turned to comment on contemporary black culture and politics in extra-academic venues such as the *New York Times*.

Barely forty, Kelley represents a new generation investigating culture and politics. Like many of the other critics interviewed in this volume, he is committed to social equality, but, having come of age after the sixties, he imagines the prospects of radicalism after communism. Though persistently foregrounding class, he has assimilated the poststructural critique of essentialism and calls attention to the intersection of class and race. And, though still working from an academic base in history, he has turned progressively to public intellectual work.

Born in 1962, Kelley grew up in Harlem until an abrupt move west, as he tells here, to Seattle. When he was fifteen he moved to

Pasadena, remaining in southern California to attend Cal State–Long Beach, from which he received a B.A. in three years (1983), and where he explored the All-African People's Revolutionary Party and the Communist Workers' Party. He continued his fast march through the university at UCLA, where he received an M.A. in African history in 1985 and a Ph.D. in U.S. history in 1987. After brief sojourns at Southeastern Massachusetts and Emory universities, he taught at the University of Michigan (1990–94) and NYU (1994-2003). In fall 2003, he moved uptown to Columbia University, where he is professor of African American studies and anthropology.

Stemming from his dissertation, *Hammer and Hoe* (U of North Carolina P, 1990) uncovered the largely invisible history of the Communist Party in Alabama and the work of African Americans in the Party during the 1930s. *Race Rebels: Culture, Politics, and the Black Working Class* (Free Press, 1994) extends the span of his historical research, ranging from African Americans in the Spanish civil war to contemporary hip-hop culture, and marks a turn to crossover writing. *Into the Fire: African Americans since 1970* (Oxford UP, 1996) is an entrant in the Young Oxford History of African Americans. *Yo' Mama's Disfunktional! Fighting the Culture Wars in Urban America* (Beacon, 1997) disabuses the construction of "ghetto culture" in academic and political discourse and foregrounds the hope of working-class social movements to redeem urban America. *Freedom Dreams* (Beacon, 2002), drawing on black, feminist, and socialist radical traditions, stakes out the terms of hope for future politics. Kelley is currently finishing a biography, *Misteriosos: The Art of Thelonius Monk*. He also publishes journalism in places like the *Nation*, the *Village Voice*, and the *New York Times*, where he occasionally writes music pieces for the Sunday Arts and Leisure section.

Alongside his own books, Kelley has written introductions to new editions of Césaire's *Discourse on Colonialism* (Monthly Review P, 2000) and Robinson's *Black Marxism: The Making of the Black Radical Tradition* (U of North Carolina P, 2000); edited (with Sidney Lemelle) *Imagining Home: Class, Culture, and Nationalism in the African Diaspora* (Verso, 1994), (with Vincent Harding and Earl Lewis) *We Changed the World: African Americans, 1945–1970* (Oxford UP, 1997), and (with Earl Lewis) *To Make Our World*

*Anew: A History of African Americans* (Oxford UP, 2000); and written the foreword to Deborah Willis's *Reflections in Black: A History of Black Photographers* (Norton, 2000).

This interview took place on 7 February 2003 in Robin Kelley's office at NYU. It was conducted by Jeffrey Williams and transcribed by Laura Rotunno, managing editor of the *minnesota review* while a Ph.D. student at University of Missouri. It originally appeared in an issue of the journal focused on "The Legacies of Michael Sprinker," an influential leftist theorist, teacher, and editor (who was a onetime editor of the *minnesota review* and the commissioning editor of Kelley's *Imagining Home* at Verso).

**Williams:** Your discipline is history, but people who come upon your work now would probably know you through *Freedom Dreams* or *Yo' Mama's Disfunktional!*, and stuff in the *Village Voice* and the *New York Times*. Your first book, of course, is *Hammer and Hoe*, which looks at the fact, unexpectedly, that there were a good many Communists in Alabama in the 1920s or 1930s, and many of them were African Americans. How did you come to do this project? How did you start out?

**Kelley:** It's funny because I didn't study history to be a historian. I studied history to attempt to solve a series of political problems. When I was an undergraduate, I chose history as a discipline that would allow me to look at social movements in the most holistic way. I studied political science and was a political science major, I was a philosophy major, but I was interested in social movements.

So I went to graduate school to study history not to be a history professor but to be a professional Communist. That was my thing, and I was a member of the Communist Workers' Party. I chose to go back to the period of Stalinism to figure out what happens when you build a movement around the notion of the self-determination of African Americans. What happens when you say that African Americans in the Black Belt counties of the South constitute a nation, and your politics are built around that? Did they actually try to achieve self-determination? Were they struggling for land?

The original conception of the project was not just to look at the South but to look at South Africa. I went to graduate school to study African history. Actually my M.A. is in African history and my Ph.D. would have been, but I had to switch fields. The only reason that South Africa didn't come into the equation was strictly political—with the state of emergency in 1986, I couldn't get into the country. So Alabama became the focal point . . .

**Williams:** Why couldn't you get into the country?

**Kelley:** Because with the state of emergency in '86, no one was getting in, and I was foolish enough (I say foolish in quotes) to have protested, along with my comrades, at the South African consulate the day before I turned in my paperwork for my visa.

**Williams:** They knew who you were?

**Kelley:** Oh yeah, they remembered me. I was hassled by a police officer up there—the South African consulate was in Beverly Hills, in an unmarked building, but we knew where it was.

Anyway, the study on Alabama became a way to test the thesis about self-determination. But once I got to the archives and once I began to interview people, I realized I was asking the wrong questions.

**Williams:** What were the questions that you asked?

**Kelley:** Well, the questions that I started out with were: Were these black people in the South fighting for self-determination? What did they do to implement what was called the Black Nation thesis—the idea of self-determination of the Black Belt? In fact, the question I should have been asking and that I ended up asking was: What happened when these homegrown, rural and urban African American workers and sharecroppers confronted an international movement? How did they transform that movement? What are the kinds of cultural baggage they brought to the movement? Suddenly I had something much more exciting.

It was a critical lesson in terms of the importance of archival research, in terms of being open to new sources and reading sources in new ways. I'm not saying that my politics weren't fundamentally driving me to study the Communist Party in Alabama. They were fundamental in raising the questions, but I realized that sometimes when you get inside of a movement the questions arise from the movement. That was exciting to me, and *Hammer and Hoe* is still my favorite book.

It was a kind of detective project because it meant methodologically trying to write a history of a movement which purposefully left no traces. It was too dangerous to keep records and minutes. This was a movement that did everything they could to erase every evidence of their existence because they were constantly being chased by the police, and to try to reconstruct that history required an enormous amount of work but also creativity and imagination in terms of how to find sources.

**Williams:** So you interviewed a lot of people? It's kind of poignant when you talk about the people that you talked to, like Lemon Johnson.

**Kelley:** Yeah, I interviewed quite a few people, like Lemon Johnson and Charles Smith and Hosea Hudson. These are people who luckily survived long enough for me to write the book. Had I tried to write it ten years later, they would have all been gone. But then a lot of it was archival work. Besides the party newspapers, the police were very good about keeping tabs on people. You go through the governor's files, and they have all these little mimeographed leaflets and handbills that they passed out. There are a lot of gaps, but I got enough to be able to tell the story.

Another thing about *Hammer and Hoe* is that in some ways it is not really African American history. Some of the key figures were white, many of whom were second-, third-generation Jews who migrated to the South and who ended up as central figures in the Communist movement in Montgomery, Alabama. It forced me to learn a lot about twentieth-century American history. It was a very exciting project.

**Williams:** You went to grad school in California, and you mention in one of your books that you worked at McDonald's in Pasadena when you were a teenager. I also read that you lived in Seattle, but it seems clear you're a New Yorker, and you've written about growing up in Harlem in the sixties. Could you tell me about your background?

**Kelley:** Sure. The first nine years of my life I spent in Harlem, in Washington Heights. My mom, for the most part, was single. We lived in a low-income community, as they say. Growing up in Harlem in that period—we're talking about roughly the mid-sixties to 1971—was an exciting time for our generation, because the streets were very politicized. There was a very strong presence of Black Nationalism. Third world liberation movements were present. There was a certain language of the street, where everyone talked about freedom—"Freedom now," "Free the land." So I grew up in a generation that really believed that freedom was at hand, and that freedom was not a national project but an international one.

As a little kid, I remember being at a Black Panther Party breakfast program once or twice. It was just being involved in demonstrations or walking down the street and watching exchanges between people or going to the store. All of us grew up knowing that black people were part of a world majority. We were not minorities; every person of color was claimed as part of this world majority. We identified with the Chinese, with people from Latin America. All those struggles became part of the discourse, and living in Harlem, which was predominantly black and, at that time, Puerto Rican, also gave us a sense of a world majority. Then I ended up moving to Seattle . . .

**Williams:** Why did you move to Seattle?

**Kelley:** Basically I was kidnapped by my father. He remarried, and they convinced my sister and me to visit and kept us pretty much in captivity for five years. My mother, who was very poor, couldn't afford a lawyer. She had legal custody. I'll never forget the day when she actually raised enough money to take a bus from New York to Seattle. She arrived on Christmas Day, after we had been there for about three months, to get her children. And my father pulls out a gun and sticks it to her head and says, "You're not getting these kids. You might as well go back." My mom ended up moving to California in order to be closer to us, and she had relatives in California. The way that we ended up leaving my father and his wife was by running away from home.

**Williams:** My god . . . you were about twelve or thirteen?

**Kelley:** We were older than that. Let's see, I left New York when I was nine to live in Seattle. Fifteen. Two weeks after my fifteenth birthday, I got out.

Moving from New York to Seattle threw me into a black community but a predominantly white world. We were part of the busing program, so suddenly I was bused out to a predominantly white school in the suburbs. There were like twenty-three of us, and we all rode the bus together. There wasn't a single person of color, whether they were Asian, Latino, or black, who went to this school in a city that had a very large Asian population. So that was a shock. I suddenly had to deal with a majority white world in a way that I was insulated from. Politically it had a huge impact on me just in terms of dealing with racism in a direct way.

So we left for California, and we were thrown into a somewhat similar situation. Pasadena, at least the community I lived in, was predominantly Chicano and black. We lived on this small street called Penn Street, and there was a lot of drug dealing and gang activity. We ended up moving to Altadena right afterward. It was still predominantly black. You could walk from my old house to the new place in twenty-five minutes, going uphill.

**Williams:** So from there you went to Cal State–Long Beach?

**Kelley:** Yeah. Cal State–Long Beach was basically a third-tier state university, and in those days, in the 1980s when I entered college, the tuition was like ninety dollars a semester. And I had financial aid; it was a great deal!

**Williams:** When I went to Stony Brook in the early eighties, I got TAP [Tuition Assistance Program] and had to pay something like a hundred dollars a semester for fees. That was when there was still a liberal welfare state, and college, especially at state universities, was actually affordable.

**Kelley:** Absolutely. Cal State-Long Beach turned out to be a very important decision because it had a significant group of activists, many of whom were in the Black Student Union. I was immediately drawn to that group. I went from major to major until I settled on history and black studies. I came to love black studies because of politics, not because, like a lot of students, I took a class here and there that I liked. My first response, like a lot of African American students, was "I've been robbed! All this information I should know. I should know about the African slave trade. I should know about the great pyramids of Gaza. I should know about the great accomplishments that the history books omitted!" So these courses radicalized my generation. They introduced us to texts as disparate as George E. M. James's *Stolen Legacy*, which is about the way that the Egyptians stole ideas from the Greeks. We read Cheikh Anta Diop's *The African Origins of Civilization*. We read C. L. R. James. We read W. E. B. Du Bois. These things blew our minds!

From there I became involved in study groups, because in those days, in the eighties, if you were involved in politics, you had a study group too. Politics wasn't just leaflets or having a program or being a speaker. It was study, study, study, and I spent so much time in the library. I spent time in the study groups debating these texts and became an intellectual, really, outside the classroom more so than inside. It was a milieu you would not expect because these were working-class students. We all met in remedial classes. I was in remedial English because anyone who got Cal grant money was automatically put in remedial English. It didn't matter if you were a star in high school; if you got Cal grant money, which is minority money for the most part, they assumed that you had to take remedial English.

I never ever took a course in English literature in college. They felt remedial writing, technical writing, was the curriculum that was appropriate for poor, underprivileged minority students. And yet there was this intellectual core, with a vibrant intellectual culture centered around reading texts about struggle, from Du Bois and James to Walter Rodney's *How Europe Underdeveloped Africa*. We began to follow the footnotes, and it was through the footnotes that we began to read Marx, Engels, Lenin, Rosa Luxemburg, Karl Kautsky. We were reading everything.

You know, I tell this story because there's this presumption that there's multiple political worlds that just don't meet. There's the Black Nationalists, unreconstructed nationalists, cultural essentialist group of folk, which was my entrée. And then there's the serious Marxists-Leninists. It was through that circle that I came to Marxism—not through being recruited by the Spartacus Youth League, and not from a class I took—and that training I brought into the classroom. My cohort, my friends and I, would go into the classroom and wage war on the professor.

**Williams:** How did that work?

**Kelley:** It was hilarious. We would strategize before class. It didn't matter who it was. We had no sympathy for African American or African professors who we thought were just reactionary running dogs. None. We had one professor, a West African scholar, and we thought her course was horrible. It was about African nationalism, so for every book she'd assign, we'd go to the library and read five or six more books, and we'd come in armed with information. We'd stand up in the back of the class and say, "Well, you know, professor, what about the fact that 50 percent of the gross national product of such and such a country is going to pay for the bureaucratic bourgeoisie? The state is not doing anything but oppressing people." These are the kinds of issues we'd raise, and it was fun, it was great to treat your professors as adversaries as opposed to all-knowing.

And we weren't always right. But it was in the engagement and struggle and debate that we actually learned something.

**Williams:** Did they ever prove you wrong?

**Kelley:** Sure. A couple times I remember being embarrassed and being wrong about information because we just didn't know enough, but every time you can't respond to a query or critique, you run back to the library. And that's what we did. We ran back to the library and got some more information and more books.

As a result of some of those classes, I had a couple of professors who took me under their wing. Not black professors. Two old lefties, Jack Stuart, who was an old Trotskyite from the early sixties, and Leo Rifkin, who since passed, who was a Young Communist Leaguer back in the thirties and became a kind of Rockefeller Republican, but still had left-wing leanings. He said, "You should go to graduate school. You should get a Ph.D." I didn't know what graduate school was. I thought you just go to college, get a degree, and go get a job. But he was saying that you should be an intellectual, you should go get a Ph.D. I said, "What, be a teacher?" It took a long time for me to figure out that to be a scholar is so much more than standing in front of a classroom and lecturing. You are part of what you do, and that was the most amazing, eye-opening thing to me. They really supported me, allowed me to write additional papers . . .

**Williams:** So that was in—let's see, you were born in 1962–83 or '84? Then you went to UCLA.

**Kelley:** In '83. I finished my B.A. in three years because I was anxious to get out. Once I became an activist, I was anxious to get on with the work of making revolution. I felt that I can't just be in school all the time because there is a revolution to make.

And then I also wanted to get married. My fiancée at the time, who is my wife now, told me when I finished my degree, then we could go forward, so I ended up taking courses in summer school in order to finish in three years.

**Williams:** How did you end up at UCLA? Was it a natural progression from Long Beach?

**Kelley:** It's a good question. I wanted to go to a place with a strong African history program, and I did not want to leave southern California. And UCLA had the best program. I kind of hustled my way in because the word on the streets was the UC system does not admit Cal State students. That's not universal, but Cal State was considered a notch above a community college, especially Cal State–Long Beach and Cal State–LA. So I knew that I had a disadvantage, and in last year of college I went up to UCLA almost every week to attend various open lectures and seminars—anything having to do with African history or African studies. And I'd always ask a question. I'd introduce myself, "I'm Robin Kelley. I'm an undergrad at Cal State–Long Beach, and I'd like to know blah-blah-blah," and ask my question. Sometimes I'd have really good questions, sometimes they weren't so good, but I made them know me.

After doing this for about three months, then I started making appointments with the faculty. I remember meeting the person who became my graduate adviser: I'd show up and bring papers I was writing, 150-page papers on the Mozambican revolution or the revolution in the Congo, huge things. There was no honors thesis at Long Beach, so I'd write these papers, based on primary research, teaching myself French to read the documents. Then I handed these big papers to big-time faculty, saying, "I really want to come to UCLA, but, you know, I'm being recruited by Boston University and the University of Wisconsin." I was lying! I didn't even apply to those places! I only applied to UCLA, but I wanted to make sure that they knew that I was worthy. And it worked; they remembered me when my name came up in the admissions committee. That's how I got into graduate school.

**Williams:** That's a great story, but I don't know if you'd want to tell it to your students.

**Kelley:** Well, my sister and I are both first-generation college students. We knew nothing about the culture. It was so important for me to get in that I just used what I would call my hustling instinct. Yet the work had to prove itself. I did a lot of work to demonstrate how serious I was about it, and I had great mentors.

**Williams:** What was UCLA like?

**Kelley:** Again, as soon as I got to UCLA, I got involved in politics. I got involved in the African Activists Association, and a lot of the work we did was around anti-imperialism, which drove my scholarship. I was less interested in social movements and more interested in the history of capitalism in Africa. I thought I was going to be an economic historian and write books about cashews and ground nuts and railroads, and I was loving that.

**Williams:** Just to keep the time line straight, that was around 1985.

**Kelley:** I went in '83, so I was in graduate school from '83 to '87. I completed my Ph.D. in 1987.

**Williams:** And you got your master's in African history, and then you switched to American history?

**Kelley:** Yeah, basically what happened was that I took my qualifying exams in African history and then, when I realized I couldn't get into South Africa, I petitioned to switch fields. So I took the U.S. history exams having taken only one U.S. history course. I'm a U.S. historian with a Ph.D. in U.S. history and only took one American history course at UCLA! And that was with John Laslett. I'm proud of the fact that, when I petitioned to take the exams in U.S. history, they said, "Well, you're going to fail it anyway," but of the five people who took it, only three passed, and I was one.

I'm basically an autodidact, which means that the various strategies that got me through elementary school, junior high and high school, and through college required individual initiative and self-training. When I decided that U.S. history would be my field, I got everyone's syllabus in the whole department. I read *Reviews in American History*, made a massive list of about four hundred books, and decided I'm going to master this field on my own.

**Williams:** How long did it take you?

**Kelley:** Oh, about a year. I was a reading fool. I was reading everything. I remember so vividly how I was concerned that my advisers, at least in the U.S. field, would treat me as someone who only did African American history. I'd already been reading African American history, so I said, "I need to be prepared, I need to read the mainstream stuff." I was reading Richard Hofstadter, Vernon Parrington, the major works in American history.

I'll never forget the day when I took my exams, and they had a question about a major U.S. historian; I remember asking the proctor, who was my adviser, "Would W. E. B. Du Bois count?" And he said no! Of course this was 1985. So I wrote about U. B. Phillips, who was an unreconstructed racist but a great scholar of slavery and plantation life. They were impressed with the essay because I had read everything by Phillips, not only the major stuff but also *The History of Transportation in the Southeast in the Eastern Cotton Belt to 1860*, which I think was published in 1907. I was reading just mad, crazy stuff and wrote this essay about whether or not U. B. Phillips could fall within the framework of a Progressive historian. They assumed I was going to fail the exam and were so pissed off that I passed, the next year they changed the whole structure.

**Williams:** That's when you started working on the South and the stuff that became *Hammer and Hoe*?

**Kelley:** Yeah, *Hammer and Hoe* was my dissertation, but before I switched fields, I'd already conceived of a project that was comparative. My original idea was to study Johannesburg, South Africa and

Birmingham, Alabama—which was a bad project, a bad idea. I'm glad I didn't do it; the best thing that ever happened to me was being denied access to South Africa.

I ended up publishing some stuff on South Africa anyway, but I was able to focus on Alabama and write this dissertation with very little guidance. John Laslett was somewhat interested in my project, but he wasn't overly enthusiastic about it. The only person who really gave me guidance was not a historian, and he wasn't at UCLA. It was Cedric Robinson at Santa Barbara. He had just published *Black Marxism*, and I'd reviewed it. No, actually I didn't review it; I tried to review it, but it was too difficult. It was such a challenge for me, that book, that I sought him out and begged him to be on my dissertation committee, and I've been working with him ever since. I ended up getting it reprinted through North Carolina, and I wrote the foreword.

After I finished the dissertation, I reached out to other people in the academy who didn't know me from Adam, Nell Painter and Mark Naison. I'd never met them, but I knew their work; their work was liberally cited in my own work. I sent them my dissertation, which was almost seven hundred pages, and they both read it. They both cursed me out, but they gave me wonderful feedback and were mentors to me in a kind of postgraduate situation. Whereas most people have a very clear division between their graduate education and after, for me finishing the degree wasn't the end. After the degree I was still a graduate of these people—Naison, Nell Painter, and George Lipsitz, who mentored me after I finished. I needed it because I was twenty-five years old.

**Williams:** Most of the literature on professionalism is about the formation in graduate school and the formal protocols you have to go through. But I think that your first job, or whatever else you do after you graduate, is just as formative.

**Kelley:** That's true for me. And my first job wasn't even tenure-track. It was a one-year non-tenure-track visiting position at Southeastern Massachusetts University, and then I got a post-doc at UNC and a job at Emory . . .

**Williams:** Then you went to Michigan . . .

**Kelley:** Which was great. In fact, in terms of the development of my thinking, Michigan became like a second graduate school. Books like *Race Rebels* and all the articles I published around that time were significantly influenced by my colleagues at Michigan, not just in history but across the board—anthropology, Afro-American studies, American culture. It was a very vibrant intellectual environment where people talked to each other. There were a lot of study groups; I was part of a group called MSG, which was the Marxist Study Group. Every once in a while it did give you the sense that you had MSG, you got kind of sleepy and had a headache, but I learned a lot in that group, and it really shaped my work.

**Williams:** You were at Michigan until '94, and you've been at NYU for nine years?

**Kelley:** That's right. I was at Emory from '88 to '90, but I was on leave in '88 , and I arrived at Michigan in '91 because I was off my first year. Michigan institutionally was and still is my best academic experience. I learned a lot from other people reading my work and being introduced to other scholarship there—subaltern studies was introduced to me through colleagues at Michigan; a lot of critical theory that became sublimated but is still present in some of my work was there. So in some ways my work became more interdisciplinary as a result of being at Michigan.

The New York transition had more to do with my work becoming more accessible and writing for a general public. That's what the move to New York was about.

**Williams:** That's a convenient marker for me. Around the mid-nineties, the time of *Race Rebels*, you made a shift. I think I started seeing some of your pieces in the *Nation* and the *Voice* around then. Even though you have plenty of scholarly footnotes in your recent trade books, it seems to me that you deliberately turned to do more accessible, public, political writing. In another way, it's almost a kind of Horatio Alger story: with hustle, hard work, gumption, or pluck, you've actually built a successful American career.

**Kelley:** There's a few things to say about that. One is when I wrote *Hammer and Hoe*, accessibility was very important to me. That's why much of the theory was actually hidden in the footnotes, or just not mentioned.

**Williams:** I did notice there are serious footnotes in that book—something like 150 pages worth.

**Kelley:** Yeah, George Lipsitz is always making fun of me for that. He says I could write a book that's all endnotes. It was important to me, for political reasons, that *Hammer and Hoe* was accessible because I wanted the people I interviewed to be able to read it. Actually I sent them the manuscript, the dissertation, and got feedback. Some people I interviewed couldn't read or write or lost their vision, but those who could read and write were able to give me feedback, and it was wonderful. Things they didn't understand I had to change to make them understand it. So it was always a goal for me to be able to write for other venues. I've always wanted to do that.

When I got to Michigan, I began reading as much as possible outside of my field, but also I began to submit things to publications like the *Nation*. The *Nation* was really the first turning point.

**Williams:** What did you write on for them?

**Kelley:** In '92, the first thing I did was on the LA Rebellion. It was about hip-hop and what it could teach us about the construction of LA.

It's like a snowball effect; if you get one or two pieces in the public, then you start to get invitations to write more, and it just started to open up for me. Moving to New York had an even greater impact because I could actually talk to people and be a part of forums that ended up being translated into public pieces. For me, writing those pieces was never about publicity; it really was about trying to make some sharp critical interventions, and it's always been about that. The whole issue about the success story . . .

**Williams:** Now is a lot different from McDonald's at sixteen. I don't say that cynically, but it's a difference.

**Kelley:** You know, I'm so lucky. I'm always thankful and I'm always encouraging the young people I talk to—I have a lot of conversations with urban working-class youth—to consider intellectual work as work, and I tell them what kind of money I make and how I'm living. I think it's a great thing, because, for them, a lot of times the only option is sports or entertainment. When I leave them, there's always a handful that's like, "Wow, I could do that."

**Williams:** What kind of places do you speak?

**Kelley:** Oh, youth centers, churches. In Michigan, I was going to a place called Boys Town, which is a youth detention center, in Saline, outside of Ann Arbor. I'd go there twice a year and talk to these kids about Malcolm X, and I still do that. Sometimes I talk about hip-hop; I talk about whatever it is that they want to talk about, and they love it, in part because they just can't imagine that there could be like a fairly young-looking black person who makes money as a professor, and who is not boring or crazy.

Some of these kids write me, and I correspond with some of them. Some end up in prison, and I still correspond with them, and it gives them a sense of hope and possibility. That's why I'd never shirk from my position of privilege and treat it as if it's an embarrassment. As a first-generation college graduate who went from working at McDonald's to being a professor at a major university and an author—my family's so proud of me. I know a lot of young black people who also feel the same way, and a lot of older people who feel the same way—that this is an amazing achievement. And it really does give these young people hope that, "if that boy can do it, and he's not so smart, I know I can do it."

**Williams:** I want to go back to *Race Rebels* to trace the path of your work. You started as a historian; *Race Rebels* is a transitional book, still centered on working-class history, but it also takes up current politics, with the closing chapter on hip-hop, and the middle on Malcolm X and the fifties. Your more recent *Yo' Mama's Disfunktional!* is more directly focused on contemporary cultural politics or cultural commentary, and obviously *Freedom Dreams* is too. Maybe you could say something about your path to cultural politics.

**Kelley:** With *Race Rebels*, I put a lot of emphasis on reading texts and representations of cultural reality, as opposed to paying attention to aesthetic questions. The gangsta rap chapter really is about "this is what they're saying about the police, this is what they're saying about the state and state oppression, this is what they're saying about women and gender." By the end, I felt really uncomfortable with how much I ignored the politics of pleasure and style, so I ended up doing a remix version, which became *Yo' Mama's Disfunktional!* If anything, *Yo' Mama's Disfunktional!* is in some ways a critique of things in *Race Rebels*. It's reflecting back. In the first chapter I'm saying, look, social scientists have often made the mistake of making very literal readings of expressive culture . . .

**Williams:** And social scientists have gone to a lot of trouble producing an image of a degraded culture . . .

**Kelley:** Exactly, but the way they succeed in producing it is by reading the culture literally as a text that speaks to the immediate social reality. So if someone's talking about someone's mama, the social psychologist or sociologist says, "Well, this is clearly an issue of matriarchy dominating family culture, it's about the breakup of the family, it's all about sex."

So in *Yo' Mama's Disfunktional!* I try to distance myself from my own heavy-handed reading of hip-hop. But *Yo' Mama's Disfunktional!*, just to go back to what we began with, was not written solely as a public policy intervention. It was not on any agenda of mine; it was a product of a series of talks and lectures and essays I'd been publishing as a kind of immediate intervention in debates about what the culture is, debates around the black neoconservatives. All of these debates centered on: how does culture matter? why is culture so fundamental to the explanations of urban poverty? and how can we enter this debate without having to accept an explanation of urban poverty and deprivation as either structure or culture? how can we develop analyses that challenge this bifurcation, which I think is a real problem?

**Williams:** Your most recent book, *Freedom Dreams*, seems a little different. *Yo' Mama's Disfunktional!* is more on policy, whereas *Freedom Dreams* is more hopeful, more visionary. There's a passage on Aimé Césaire where you quote him: "It is not a dead society that we want to revive. We leave that to those who go in for exoticism. . . . It is a new society that we must create." It seems to me that is your credo, on African American cultural politics as well as on American politics overall. On the other hand, I could see how some people might say that *Freedom Dreams* is almost New Agey. You've abandoned wanting to be a professional Communist.

**Kelley:** Yeah, I've definitely abandoned being a professional Communist, but I haven't abandoned social movements and on-the-ground material struggle as the way to make change or some kind of socialist solution. That's one of the things about *Freedom Dreams*. It's probably the most transitional book of all: in some ways, it's a return to history, recovering historical narratives of social movements, even though it's based largely (but not entirely) on secondary sources. Still, I'm trying to create a kind of popular history of the black radical imagination for readers, for nonacademics. The idea of constructing this popular history is to say in the past there have been movements that may not have succeeded in terms of our definition of success, but have left us a very powerful legacy of possibility.

Let me back up. I was saying it's transitional. It's somewhat autobiographical, and that's because I want to convey to readers exactly what brings people to social movements in the first place. It's not oppression, it's not failure or deprivation; it's the sense of hope and possibility, and in some ways that makes me an old-school Communist. This is what the Communists said, you know. Think about the "Internationale": that song is about throwing off the shackles and creating new people. I wanted to convey that to people.

I think the chapter that's most controversial is the chapter on surrealism, and that's where people say it seems New Agey. I don't think it is. My understanding of New Age ideology is that it is another version of corporate ideology that suggests a withdrawal into individualism. I'm talking about the collective, how to deal with the community, how to change people's relationships to one another. I do invoke the term "love," not because it's a new thing and not in a New Age way but because it's an old thing that is rooted, I think, in a long tradition of black Christian, communitarian, radical movements. In other words, the love I talk about is the love that Dr. King invoked.

**Williams:** But it seems to me it's also different from, say, Cornel West or Michael Eric Dyson, insofar as it's a redemptive politics without Christianity.

**Kelley:** In some ways that's true. My interest in surrealism was an avenue to try to talk about redemptive politics, but specifically to think about freedom in new ways that are nonreligious. That might get me into some trouble, but I don't think that's necessarily an antithesis of what Dr. King was saying. I don't really have an answer for this. I love reading the surrealists like Suzanne Césaire and Aimé Césaire, even Richard Wright's surrealism, because it seems to me to break with the old language. As you were saying before, we need new songs. I think I'd go even further and say that we need a new language of struggle, a new language of hope and possibility. I don't think we even have the language to talk about what kind of world we want to create. In some ways, poetry is the quest to explode language as we know it, to open it up.

**Williams:** A couple more questions. How would you place yourself in current African American cultural politics? There are a few lines, for instance, the more conservative line, of people like William Julius Wilson, whom you parody in the section at the end of *Yo' Mama's Disfunktional!* that updates *Looking Backward*. And there's a more centrist line, for lack of a better word, of people like Gates at Harvard, who does not espouse a radical politics but who has obviously been pivotal in putting African American studies in the academic mainstream. And then there's a more radical line that you're more affiliated with, of people like Michael Eric Dyson (to an extent), Cedric Robinson, Manning Marable (who's a leading figure in Committees of Correspondence), and Angela Davis (whom you thank in your acknowledgments).

**Kelley:** Social Democrats. Well, I'm very catholic when it comes to the Left, which has been my downfall in some ways, because I've always been willing to support movements at war with each other. I can't say I agree with every single thing that these Social Democratic movements support, but the general consensus is that capitalism is not serving us well. I still don't think it's serving us well. And so I feel an imperative to support movements that are trying to claim a radical path. Even if it's not really clear what that path will be, it's still important just to defend them.

Now that I'm an older person with a twelve-year-old daughter, I'm much more critical of black popular culture—I'm especially concerned about the dominance of consumerism, the misogyny, the deep materialism. Still, the black middle-class critique of popular culture centers around the uncouth, unrepresentative Negro desiring these things, rather than the mere fact of this desire. What I find disturbing is an identity centered around the possession of things like diamonds and expensive cars. Yet, the same black middle class shares some of the same consumerist impulses.

**Williams:** You mean the kind of things they show on MTV's *House of Style*?

**Kelley:** Exactly. The culture's really becoming bankrupt in some ways, and I feel like I'm caught between a lot of different movements. I feel like I'm still somewhat of a Marxist, but that Marxism is too little. I feel like my roots are in Black Nationalism, as critical as I am of nationalism and of nations. The core of that movement, that attracted me in the first place, was the idea of building a sense of humanity. Black Nationalism allowed ordinary black people to stake a claim to history, to say that we're contributing to the world. That sense of pride is something that I'm still very much connected to, as much as I'm antinationalist.

And then there's the sense of emergency. I too get caught up in the immediate moment and the need to solve immediate problems, whether it's to keep the U.S. out of the war or to save battered children. Whatever it is, I will continue and many people will continue to fight those battles on a day-to-day basis. I'm simply saying that, as we fight these battles, they should be opportunities to produce new visions of the future.

I honestly, to this day, cannot map out that new vision. One of the main points of *Freedom Dreams* is to say that one doesn't map out a new future simply by "dreaming." I don't know what the future of politics will look like. I think that we are in a tremendous ideological transformation, but, if I believe my own argument, I can't know what that is because part of knowing is learning in the process of struggle, in a collective movement. In other words, no one can see it. That's New Age, where you meditate, or you're in a steam room, and all of a sudden you're able to see and envision it. No, it's on picket lines; it's in the streets; it's participation in social movements; it's in study groups. Even the failures are very, very important, for they provide very important lessons for thinking about the future. But it requires work, it requires organizing, it requires study, to read, to think, to debate.

**Williams:** In a *New York Times* piece you did on Miles Davis and his hustler or "pimp aesthetic" (13 May 2001), you mention his unlikable traits and say, "By dividing Miles up like this we miss how the things we don't like about the man are fundamental to what we love about his music." So what are the things—I fear this is my Barbara Walters question—that people don't like about you that are fundamental to your writing?

**Kelley:** The main thing, I think, would be my optimism. It's the thing people love to hate. I get so much static about it—"Kelley's got such a sanguine view, he's not paying attention to reality, the hard work and political reality that confronts us all, and he's talking about dreams." The sense of the future and what's possible is in all the books. It's in *Hammer and Hoe*, it's in my other books, that you can win, that the next generation will take us there.

If you think of something like the end of slavery as one of the most revolutionary moments in U.S. history, in 1854—a decade before the end of slavery—none of those people thought slavery would end. It wasn't even in the cards. Imagine if we write history not from the perspective of the victors or even in hindsight—by that I mean standing in the present, turning back, and trying to explain how we got here. But, if you stand in 1854, what you see ahead is not the end of slavery. You don't see any of that.

Too often we're told that if you're a real radical, you're not supposed to be optimistic. That's the culture we grew up in. But, the radicals I wrote about, they're all optimistic. Just imagine what it meant in the middle of the Depression in 1934 to join a movement where they were going to inherit the earth, "a better world's in birth." The future was theirs, and they knew it. That's why they fought every day.

That was in starvation times, and here we are in the year 2003, and it's still starvation times for a lot of people, and if you stand up and say, "Yeah, well, we know we're going to win. Capitalism is going to be dead, we're going to kill it, we're going to replace it with something much better," people are like, "You're crazy. You're out of your mind."

**Williams:** There does seem to be a tenor of inevitability about the all-ruling market.

**Kelley:** Absolutely, and I think that the inevitability of the success and strength of capitalism is as dangerous the idea that its death is inevitable. That's the other thing that some people say, "You're suggesting that this is just going to happen at a certain time," when, in fact, I'm saying that it's going to happen if we do the work to make it happen. It's always the work of struggle, the thing that transforms the conditions in which we operate, that makes things possible. You cannot dream your way out of your situation. You dream to imagine where you're going to go next, but without social movement, without struggle, you're stuck.

**Williams:** One last question. I read somewhere that you're writing a book on Thelonious Monk. I know you wrote a piece in the *Times* on Monk and his wife, Nellie Monk [21 July 2002]. Does this mean you're not going to be a historian anymore but are going to be a music critic?

**Kelley:** Not exactly. I'll always be a historian, but I've kind of remade myself as a jazz scholar. I've gone back to being a historian because of this book on Monk, because it's all based on primary sources. It's based on the kind of archival research I love to do. It's detective work to a certain degree, and the story that I'm writing is not just a typical jazz book—the story of the rise and fall of a great artist, and drugs and all that stuff. It's a narrative about postwar culture, American culture and beyond the United States. Monk is a template for that.

It's a book that draws on art history, on literature, on all kinds of visual culture, as well as music and musicology and history. Part of what I end up talking about is why it is, in 1964 for example, that Monk became the darling of the Right. *National Review* loved him. And he was the darling of the black Left. The *Liberator* and other publications claimed him as one of the greatest. And he was the darling of the center—on the cover of *Time* magazine. All at the same time! How could they write political meaning on his body and on his music in that way? I explain that. It's the most fun, the most interesting thing I've done in years!

# About the Editor

**Jeffrey J. Williams** is Professor of English at the University of Missouri, Columbia. His books include *Theory and the Novel: Narrative Reflexivity in the British Tradition* (1998) and, as editor, *PC Wars: Politics and Theory in the Academy* (1995) and *The Institution of Literature* (2002). He is also an editor of the *Norton Anthology of Theory and Criticism* (2001) and, since 1992, editor of the literary and critical journal the *minnesota review*.